P9-BHX-123

226.8
B153p

Bailey, Kenneth E.

Poet and peasant

DATE			
5/9/80			
MAY 27 1986			
OCT 27 1986			
NOV 17 1986			
OCT 15 1980			
MAR 18 2002			

© THE BAKER & TAYLOR CO.

Poet and Peasant

Poet and Peasant

A LITERARY CULTURAL APPROACH
TO THE PARABLES IN LUKE

by
Kenneth Ewing Bailey

William B. Eerdmans Publishing Company

Copyright © 1976 by William B. Eerdmans Publishing Company
255 Jefferson Ave. S.E., Grand Rapids, Michigan 49502
All rights reserved

Printed in the United States of America

Library of Congress Cataloging in Publication Data

Bailey, Kenneth E
 Poet and peasant.

 Bibliography: p. 217.
 Includes index.
 1. Jesus Christ—Parables. 2. Bible. N.T.
Luke—Criticism, interpretation, etc. I. Title.
BT375.2.B23   226'.8   75-41405
ISBN 0-8028-3476-0

.26.8
3153p

LIFE Pacific College
Alumni Library
1100 West Covina Blvd.
San Dimas, CA 91773

DEDICATION

To my parents, Dr. Ewing and Annette Bailey, who spent their lives humbly in the service of God in Kentucky, Egypt, and Ethiopia. They lived and labored among the very Middle Eastern peasants whose insights were a starting point for this study. Without my parents' life of dedication as a constant example and inspiration I would never have gone to the Middle East and this study would never have been written. To them this work is gratefully and affectionately dedicated.

017927

ACKNOWLEDGMENTS

The poet and peasant may be able to labor without a library, but not the exegete. The present writer wishes to pay special tribute to Miss Lucille Hager and Mrs. William Danker, formerly of Concordia Seminary library, St. Louis, Missouri, for their many extra efforts in acquiring relatively rare resources; to Father L. J. Daly and Dr. C. J. Ermatinger of the Knights of Columbus Vatican Film Library at the Pope Pius XII Library of the St. Louis University, for making available the inestimable treasures of the Vatican Library; and to the directors of the British Museum, London, for allowing access to the Arabic manuscript holdings.

Beyond the written resources, this study relies heavily on twenty years of discussion of the culture that informs the text of the parables, with countless friends all across the Middle East from farmer, mayor, and pastor to professor, merchant, and doctor. To these countless hundreds no words of thanks are adequate to express the debt owed.

To my students and colleagues at the Near East School of Theology, Beirut, Lebanon, a special word of thanks must be expressed for their constant stimulation and encouragement. Most of all I wish to express my appreciation to Rev. Hovannes Aharonian, President, who was kind enough to release me from teaching duties that this study might be written; to Dr. Paul Löffler, whose counsel and encouragement convinced me to make the study; and to Dr. William Holladay, whose work in Old Testament poetry first opened my eyes to new possibilities in the New Testament.

No word of thanks is adequate to express the debt owed to the faculty of Concordia Seminary, St. Louis, Missouri, among whom and for whom this study was originally written in 1972. Whatever merit the work may have is due to a significant degree to the tireless efforts of Dr. Martin Scharlemann, my advisor.

Above all, I must express formally my gratitude to my dear wife Ethel, who has sustained me through to the dawn, and to my children Sara and David, who have been "fatherless" for too long.

CONTENTS

ABBREVIATIONS

Arndt *St. Luke*	William F. Arndt, *The Gospel According to St. Luke* (St. Louis: Concordia, 1956).
ATR	*Anglican Theological Review*
Bauer-A., G. *Lexicon*	W. Bauer, *A Greek-English Lexicon of the New Testament and Other Early Christian Literature,* trans. and adapted by W. F. Arndt and F. W. Gingrich (Chicago: University of Chicago Press, 1957).
Bengel *Gnomon*	Johann A. Bengel, *Gnomon of the New Testament,* trans. C. T. Lewis and M. R. Vincent; 2 vols. (New York: Sheldon, 1963 [1742]).
Bishop *Jesus*	E. F. F. Bishop, *Jesus of Palestine* (London: Lutterworth, 1955).
BJRL	*Bulletin of the John Rylands Library*
Black *Aramaic Approach*	Matthew Black, *An Aramaic Approach to the Gospels and Acts,* 3rd ed. (Oxford: Clarendon, 1967).
Bornkamm *Jesus*	G. Bornkamm, *Jesus of Nazareth,* trans. Irene and Fraser McLuskey from the 3rd German ed. (New York: Harper, 1960).
Bruce *Synoptic Gospels*	A. B. Bruce, *The Synoptic Gospels. The Expositor's Greek Testament,* Vol. I (New York: Doran; Grand Rapids: Eerdmans, n.d.).
Bruce *Parabolic*	A. B. Bruce, *The Parabolic Teaching of Christ,* 3rd rev. ed. (New York: A. C. Armstrong, 1890).
Bultmann *Tradition*	Rudolf Bultmann, *The History of the Synoptic Tradition,* trans. from the 2nd German ed. by John Marsh (New York: Harper, 1968).
Burney *Poetry*	C. F. Burney, *The Poetry of Our Lord* (Oxford: Clarendon, 1925).

Cadoux *Parables*   A. T. Cadoux, *The Parables of Jesus* (London: James Clarke, n.d.).

Caird *Luke*   G. B. Caird, *The Gospel of St. Luke* (Baltimore: Penguin, 1963).

CBQ   *The Catholic Biblical Quarterly*

Creed *St. Luke*   J. M. Creed, *The Gospel According to St. Luke* (London: St. Martin, 1930; New York: Macmillan, 1965).

Crossan, *In Parables*   J. D. Crossan, *In Parables* (New York: Harper, 1973).

Daube "Inheritance"   David Daube, "Inheritance in Two Lukan Pericopes," *Zeitschrift der Savigny-Stiftung für Rechtsgeschichte, Romanistische Abteilung* 72 (1955), 326–344.

Derrett "Prodigal Son"   J. D. M. Derrett, "Law in the New Testament: The Parable of the Prodigal Son," *NTS* 14 (1967), 56–74.

Derrett "Steward"   J. D. M. Derrett, "Fresh Light on St. Luke XVI. 1. The Parable of the Unjust Steward," *NTS* 7 (1961), 198–219.

Dodd *Parables*   C. H. Dodd, *The Parables of the Kingdom*, rev. ed. (London: Nisbet, 1961).

ExpT   *The Expository Times*

Feldman *Similes*   A. Feldman, *The Parables and Similes of the Rabbis*, 2nd ed. (Cambridge: University Press, 1927).

Fitzmyer "Manager"   J. A. Fitzmyer, "The Story of the Dishonest Manager (Lk. 16: 1–13)," *Theological Studies* 25 (1964), 23–42.

Fletcher "Riddle"   D. R. Fletcher, "The Riddle of the Unjust Steward. Is Irony the Key?" *JBL* 82 (1963), 15–30.

Gächter "Oriental"   P. Gächter, "The Parable of the Dishonest Steward after Oriental Conceptions," *CBQ* 12 (1950), 121–131.

Giblin "Luke 15"   Charles H. Giblin, "Structural and Theological Considerations on Luke 15," *CBQ* 24 (1962), 15–31.

Godet *St. Luke*   F. Godet, *A Commentary on the Gospel of St. Luke*, trans. from the 2nd French ed. by E. W. Shalders and M. D. Cusin (New York: Funk & Wagnalls, 1887).

Goebel *Parables*   Siegfried Goebel, *The Parables of Jesus*, trans. Professor Banks (Edinburgh: T. & T. Clark, 1883).

Horowitz *Jewish Law*   George Horowitz, *The Spirit of Jewish Law* (New York: Central Book, 1953).

HUCA   *Hebrew Union College Annual*

JBL	*The Journal of Biblical Literature*
Jeremias *Jerusalem*	Joachim Jeremias, *Jerusalem in the Time of Jesus,* trans. F. H. and C. H. Cave; 3rd ed. (Philadelphia: Fortress, 1969).
Jeremias *Parables*	Joachim Jeremias, *The Parables of Jesus,* rev. ed.; trans. from the 6th German ed. by S. H. Hooke (London: SCM, 1963).
Jeremias *Theology*	Joachim Jeremias, *Theology of the New Testament* (New York: Scribner, 1971).
Jones *Art*	G. V. Jones, *The Art and Truth of the Parables: A Study in Their Literary Form and Modern Interpretation* (London: SPCK, 1964).
JSS	*Journal of Semitic Studies*
JTS	*Journal of Theological Studies*
Jülicher *Gleichnisreden*	Adolf Jülicher, *Die Gleichnisreden Jesu,* 2 vols. (Tübingen: J. C. B. Mohr, 1910).
Kelley *Significance*	Robert Kelley, "The Significance of the Parable of the Prodigal Son for Three Major Issues in Current Synoptic Study" (unpublished Ph.D. thesis, Princeton University, 1971).
Leaney *St. Luke*	A. R. C. Leaney, *A Commentary on the Gospel according to St. Luke. Black's New Testament Commentaries;* 2nd ed. (London: A. & C. Black, 1966).
Levison *Local Setting*	N. Levison, *The Parables: Their Background and Local Setting* (Edinburgh: T. & T. Clark, 1926).
Linnemann *Parables*	E. Linnemann, *Jesus of the Parables,* trans. John Sturdy (New York: Harper, 1966).
Lund *Chiasmus*	N. W. Lund, *Chiasmus in the New Testament* (Chapel Hill: University of North Carolina Press, 1942).
Manson *Sayings*	T. W. Manson, *The Sayings of Jesus* (London: SCM, 1937).
Manson *Teaching*	T. W. Manson, *The Teaching of Jesus,* 2nd ed. (Cambridge: University Press, 1935).
Miesner *Chiasm and Paul*	D. R. Miesner, "Chiasm and the Composition and Message of Paul's Missionary Sermons" (unpublished Th.D. Thesis, Concordia Seminary in Exile, 306 North Grand, St. Louis, Missouri, 1974).
Miller *Luke*	Donald G. Miller, *The Gospel According to Luke* (Richmond: John Knox, 1959).
Montefiore *Rabbinic*	C. J. G. Montefiore, *Rabbinic Literature and Gospel Teaching* (London: Macmillan, 1930).

NTS	*New Testament Studies*
Oesterley *Jewish Background*	William O. E. Oesterley, *The Gospel Parables in the Light of Their Jewish Background* (London: SPCK, 1936).
Plummer *St. Luke*	A. Plummer, *The Gospel According to St. Luke. International Critical Commentary,* ed. C. A. Briggs *et al.,* Vol. XXVII (New York: Scribner, 1906).
Rengstorf *Re-Investitur*	K. H. Rengstorf, *Die Re-Investitur des Verlorenen Sohnes in der Gleichniserzählung Jesu Luke 15:11–32* (Cologne: Westdeutscher Verlag, 1957).
Rihbany *Syrian*	A. M. Rihbany, *The Syrian Christ* (Boston: Houghton Mifflin, 1916).
Sa'īd *Lūqā*	Ibrāhīm Sa'īd, *Sharḥ Bishārat Lūqā* (Beirut: Near East Council of Churches, 1935, 1970).
Scharlemann *Parables*	Martin H. Scharlemann, *Proclaiming the Parables* (St. Louis: Concordia, 1963).
B. T. D. Smith *Parables*	B. T. D. Smith, *The Parables of the Synoptic Gospels* (Cambridge: University Press, 1937).
C. W. F. Smith *Parables*	C. W. F. Smith, *The Jesus of the Parables* (Philadelphia: Westminster, 1948).
Str.-B.	P. Billerbeck and H. Strack, *Kommentar zum Neuen Testament aus Talmud und Midrasch,* 6 vols.; 2nd ed. (Munich: C. H. Beck, 1924, 1956).
Stuhlmueller *Luke*	Carroll Stuhlmueller, "The Gospel According to Luke," *The Jerome Biblical Commentary,* ed. Raymond E. Brown, Joseph A. Fitzmyer, and Roland E. Murphy (Englewood Cliffs: Prentice-Hall, 1971), Vol. II, pp. 115–164.
TDNT	*Theological Dictionary of the New Testament,* ed. G. Kittel and G. Friedrich; trans. and ed. G. W. Bromiley; 9 vols. (Grand Rapids: Eerdmans, 1964–1974).
Thomson *The Land*	W. M. Thomson, *The Land and the Book,* 2 vols. (New York: Harper, 1871).
Trench *Notes*	R. C. Trench, *Notes on the Parables of Our Lord* (New York: Harper/Revell, n.d.).
Via *Parables*	D. O. Via, *The Parables: Their Literary and Existential Dimension* (Philadelphia: Fortress, 1967).
ZNW	*Zeitschrift für die neutestamentliche Wissenschaft und die Kunde der älteren Kirche*

Part One
INTRODUCTION

Chapter 1

THE PROBLEM AND THE TASK

THE UNFINISHED WORK

William Thomson, famous nineteenth-century missionary, traveler, and author, described twenty-five years of surface study of Palestine as it relates to the Bible in his two-volume work, *The Land and the Book*. When he comes to describe Jerusalem he makes this remarkable statement:

> Do not set out . . . resolved to make *discoveries*. There is not a foot of ground that has not been already scrutinized by a thousand eyes as keen as yours, and the old adage, "If *true* not *new*, if *new* not *true*," may be applied to Jerusalem and her monuments with more propriety than to any other place on earth.[1]

Many in our day doubtless feel the same way about the parables of Jesus. Surely after centuries of study and reflection there is nothing fundamentally new in these stories. But even as there was far more to be discovered about the city of Jerusalem than Thomson ever dreamed, even so there is a great deal yet to be precisely understood in the deceptively simple parables of Jesus.

In spite of the wide attention given to the parables in past and in recent scholarship, two aspects of parabolic interpretation still need serious attention. These aspects are the cultural milieu and the literary structure of the parables. The culture reflected in the Dominical parables is that of first-century Palestine.[2] While the externals of the Palestinian scene relevant to the parables have been analyzed with precision, the internal aspects of personal relationship and attitude have been imprecisely discerned. A more precise delineation of the Oriental culture that informs the text of four major Lucan parables is the first task of this study. The second aspect is that of literary structure, a facet of the parables that has probably had less attention than any other. The theology of the four

---

[1]Thomson, *The Land,* II, 468 (emphasis his). The author gathered his material during a trip through Palestine in 1857.
[2]Bultmann, *Tradition,* 166.

parables selected will then be set forth in the light of this reappraisal of the underlying culture and our analysis of their structure.

These two tools, an understanding of the cultural setting and an analysis of literary form, are here applied to four major Lucan parables against the background of contemporary critical discussions of the material. Before proceeding to a discussion of these two tools, we shall examine briefly three contemporary approaches to the parables.

MAJOR TRENDS IN RECENT PARABOLIC INTERPRETATION

The major interpretive method followed by the Church throughout the centuries was the allegorical method. A full review of this method and its history has been set forth elsewhere and need not detain us.[3] The modern period was initiated by Adolf Jülicher, who demonstrated conclusively the inadequacies of the allegorical method but offered no satisfactory alternative.[4] Bugge and Fiebig along with Strack and Billerbeck opened to scholarship the Jewish background of the parables.[5] This brings us to an examination of the three major approaches of the current scene. The first of these is that of C. H. Dodd and Joachim Jeremias.

(1) The Historical-Eschatological: Dodd and Jeremias

With Dodd another of the presuppositions of Jülicher was seriously challenged. His famous expression "realized eschatology" became the starting point for a reappraisal of the parables in his influential book, *The Parables of the Kingdom* (1935, rev. 1961). In this volume Dodd was able to point out that no one would have crucified an itinerant preacher who went around encouraging people with general moral principles. Hunter, endorsing Dodd, writes, "Would men have crucified a Galilean Tusitala who told picturesque stories to enforce prudential platitudes? Of course they would not!"[6] Dodd saw the context of the parables to be Jesus' preaching of the kingdom that was being realized in and through his ministry. At the same time, Dodd was interested in examining the parables on two

---

[3]A. M. Hunter, "The Interpreter and the Parables," *Interpretation*, 14 (1960), 77–81; Jülicher, *Gleichnisreden*, I, 203–322; Kelley, *Significance*, 4–19.

[4]A thoughtful analysis of Jülicher is provided by Via, *Parables*, 2–22. The four major weaknesses of Jülicher's position are: a rejection of all allegorical elements; the acceptance of Aristotle's categories as a model for understanding the parables; the reduction of the parables to general moral principles; and the strict insistence on only one point of comparison for each parable.

[5]C. A. Bugge, *Die Haupt-Parabeln Jesu* (Giessen: J. Ricker, 1903) (for a view of Bugge cf. Jones, *Art*, 20); Paul Fiebig, *Altjüdische Gleichnisse und die Gleichnisse Jesu* (Tübingen: J. C. B. Mohr, 1904); *idem, Die Gleichnisreden Jesu im Lichte der rabbinischen Gleichnisse des neutestamentlichen Zeitalters* (Tübingen: J. C. B. Mohr, 1912); *Str.-B.*, I–IV.

[6]Hunter, "The Interpreter," 83.

levels: that of the ministry of Jesus and that of the early Church. Dodd understood that the Church reused the parables and at times shifted their emphases. In the Gospels we have the parables in their church setting. Dodd set out to discover the original setting of the parables in the ministry of Jesus.[7]

In his famous volume *The Parables of Jesus* (trans. 1958, rev. 1963), Jeremias pays tribute to Dodd and understands his own work as a continuation of what Dodd has done. Jeremias worked out and applied to the parables a set of ten methodological tools. With these he attempted to distinguish between the situation in the life of the early Church and the situation in the life of Jesus.[9] He criticized Dodd for concentrating exclusively on the eschatological kingdom and chose as his own emphasis the conflict aspect of the parables as reflected in the ministry of Jesus. He understood many of them to have been spoken originally in vindication of the gospel.[10]

Jeremias, more than any modern scholar, uses all of the responsibly gathered information regarding the Palestinian background of the parables. He quotes from ancient rabbinic sources as well as from the remarks of the shepherd boy who first found the Dead Sea Scrolls in 1947. Journals of travelers, observations of contemporary Western residents in Palestine and the like are all carefully screened for valuable hints toward the recovery of the original intent of the parables.[11] Combining a concern for the meaning of the parables in the life of Jesus with a study of their Palestinian background, Jeremias has given us the twentieth century's most influential work on the parables.

(2) Jones: Parables as Art

Contemporary with Jeremias' search for the original meaning of the parables in the ministry of Jesus is the work of G. V. Jones, *The Art and Truth of the Parables* (1964). His study of the parables as art forms is a significant new venture in parabolic interpretation.

Jones is one of the voices calling for some type of wider application of the parables beyond what is possible with the "severely historical" approach. Much

---

[7]Dodd's position has been criticized by many as being "severely historical." In the preface to the 1961 edition he responds to that criticism and says, "To any reader who may feel (as I know some have felt) that my severely historical treatment of the parables robs them of universal and contemporary interest, I can only repeat what I have said on pp. 146–7. By all means draw from them any "lesson" they may seem to suggest, provided it is not incongruous with what we may learn of their original intention. . . . The Gospels do not offer us in the first place tales to point a moral. They interpret life to us, by initiating us into a situation in which, as Christians believe, the eternal was uniquely manifested in time, a situation which is both historical and contemporary in the deepest possible sense" (Dodd, *Parables*, 8).

[8]Jeremias, *Parables*, 21.

[9]*Ibid.*, 113f.

[10]*Ibid.*, 21.

[11]For a more detailed review of Dodd and Jeremias cf. Kelley, *Significance*, 30–43; Jones, *Art*, 26; Scharlemann, *Parables*, 24; Via, *Dimension*, 21–24.

of Jones' book is a review of previous work on the parables. He examines the form-critical contribution, the Hebrew tradition, the discussion of symbolism and allegory. His conclusion on the last is that we must not work with rigid presuppositions that artificially restrict interpretation.[12] Jones' own views are set forth in chapters 5 and 6, entitled "The Art of Parable and the Parable as Art"[13] and "Towards a Wider Interpretation."[14] His main point is that the parables are fashioned out of the raw material of human life by a creative imagination. As a work of art a parable is not just a propositional statement "about how one should behave or how God acts,"[15] but is "independent of time."[16] The parable sets forth the truth about God and man "regardless of the passage of time or the changing environment."[17] Thus the parable achieves for Jones an "independent and 'typical' existence."[18] The broader application he calls for is possible, he believes, without allegorization. He summarizes his position by saying,

> On the whole, however, the allegorical equation is not required; a wider application of the parable is obtainable without it if what is indicated is a pattern of human behaviour, a paradigm of existence, or a picturesque account of God's relations with man. This method of extended interpretation can be described as "existential" (though not in the philosophical technical sense) because the parables concerned provide a statement about or a criticism of life dealing with concrete conditions of existence at any time.[19]

Thus Jones feels that the problem of "what it meant" *versus* "what it means" can be solved by seeing the parables as works of art with their own independent timeless existence. Yet he insists this is not true of all parables. He divides the parables into three classes. Some, he argues, are so historically bound that they have no application beyond first-century Palestine. Others have a didactic content which has *some* application beyond the original situation. The third group he calls "parables capable of more general application." The last half of his book is an exposition of the Prodigal Son as an illustration of this third type.

Thus in summary, Jones sees some of the parables as works of art having an independent timeless significance. The artistic nature of these parables allows for an application beyond the historical situation.

(3) Linnemann and Via: The Existential Perspective

The most recent thrust in parabolic interpretation is the existential. Eta Linnemann and Dan O. Via represent this view.

---

[12]Jones, *Art,* 109.
[13]*Ibid.,* 110–132.
[14]*Ibid.,* 135–166.
[15]*Ibid.,* 122.
[16]*Ibid.,* 123.
[17]*Ibid.*
[18]*Ibid.,* 125.
[19]*Ibid.,* 163.

In a recent book, *Jesus of the Parables* (trans. 1966), Linnemann has provided a discussion of the nature of parables and an exposition of eleven parables most suited to her point of view. Her approach is a combination of the presuppositions and methodologies of Jeremias, with his interest in the historical, and the existential hermeneutical approach to the parables of Ernst Fuchs.[20] What Linnemann proposes cannot be fully understood without seeing her as a part of a philosophical movement that goes back at least to Schleiermacher and moves through Dilthey, Bultmann, and the later Heidegger to Fuchs. For Linnemann, Fuchs is the most important of these thinkers. His hermeneutical principles have been fully expounded and need not detain us here.[21]

In the first section of her work Linnemann sets forth her basic principles of interpretation. She begins by distinguishing between similitude, parable, illustration, and allegory.[22] She quotes Bultmann's well-known laws for parabolic analysis[23] and then briefly examines introductory formulas. She affirms that the parables of Jesus are parables of conflict, meant to win agreement from his opposition. In this connection she writes,

> It is not enough to consider what ideas the narrator has connected with the parable; it must also be observed what ideas, images, and evaluations were at work in the hearers of the parable, in what the opposition between the narrator and his listeners consisted, and how accordingly his words must have acted on them.[24]

Here she stands with Jeremias.

In the tradition of Jülicher she affirms that there can be only one point of comparison.[25] The parable itself, she insists, is all the narrator says to his original listeners.[26]

Her debt to Fuchs is evident in her discussion of understanding, which, she says, is "guided by the way reality 'enters into language.' "[27] Again borrowing from Fuchs, Linnemann describes a parable as a "language event." She writes,

> A successful parable is an event that decisively alters the situation. It creates a new possibility that did not exist before, the possibility that the man addressed

---

[20]In her Foreword, Linnemann pays tribute to Bultmann, Jeremias, and Fuchs (*Parables*, xiii). Fuchs wrote the introduction to her book and was adviser for the work itself, which was her thesis. The influence of both Fuchs and Jeremias is everywhere evident.

[21]Richard N. Soulen, "Biblical Hermeneutics and Parable Interpretation in the Writings of Ernst Fuchs" (unpublished Ph.D. thesis, Boston University, 1964), p. 28; Paul J. Achtemeier, *An Introduction to the New Hermeneutic* (Philadelphia: Westminster, 1969).

[22]Linnemann, *Parables*, 2–8; Jeremias prefers to recognize that the Hebrew *Mashal* covered a wide range of overlapping categories; cf. Jeremias, *Parables*, 20.

[23]Bultmann, *Tradition*, 188–192.

[24]Linnemann, *Parables*, 22f.

[25]*Ibid.*, 23. Remarkably she affirms this without evidence or argumentation. In so doing she ignores the debate on this point which has continued since Jülicher.

[26]*Ibid.*, 24. Thereby, in her view, all the applications in the parables are later additions.

[27]*Ibid.*

can come to an understanding with the man addressing him across the
opposition that exists between them.[28]

She then goes on to explain that the "language event" character of the parable not
only creates a new possibility for understanding, but also forces the listener to a
decision. Even if the listener refuses the new possibility of understanding, he still
makes a decision. His choice is to reject the new understanding. This rejection then
becomes opposition.[29] Thus Linnemann builds firmly on the work of Fuchs and
yet, at the same time, goes beyond him.

Linnemann's unique advance on the existentialist interpretation of Fuchs is
her understanding of "interlocking." According to her, the parable makes a
"concession" to the opposition by representing their point of view in the parable.
The claim of the narrator is also represented. In the parable the two points of view
"interlock" and in this interlocking there is created the possibility of a new
understanding between the two sides. In telling a parable, the narrator is claiming
that one thing represents another. Linnemann writes,

> This "claiming one thing as another" together with the "concession" pro-
> duces the phenomenon of *interlocking*. In the parable the verdict of the
> narrator on the situation in question "interlocks" with that of the listener. Both
> evaluations of the situation go into the parable.[30]

At this point her line of reasoning makes a perplexing shift. She first asserts
that the "new possibility" created by the parable is a new understanding between
the original narrator and the listener. She then affirms that the listener comes to a
new understanding of *himself* which is also defined as a "change of existence" and
as a "new life." The last emphasis is easily traceable to her adviser Fuchs; but it is
not clear how she has made the shift from the one to the other, or in what way they
are related.

She concludes her discussion of the "language event" with an affirmation
that we can participate in the same event created by the first telling of the parable
through the medium of proclamation.[31] Here she shows her indebtedness to
Bultmann.

In summary, she affirms the necessity of the historical approach and
combines it with a Fuchsian-Bultmannian concept of parable as "language event"
in which we can participate through preaching.

The second recent voice in this school is Dan O. Via. In *The Parables*
(1967), Via discusses both Jones and Linnemann, pointing out deficiencies in

---

[28]*Ibid.*, 30. In this connection she explains the risk involved. The narrator risks everything "on the
power of language" (*ibid.*, 32).

[29]This understanding of parables hangs on their having been addressed to opponents. She affirms that
practically all the parables were so addressed.

[30]*Ibid.*, 27; emphasis hers.

[31]All through her discussion she affirms the need for a sound historical base for the parables. Much of
her exegesis is a wrestling with the historical question. Thus her debt to Jeremias is also clear.

both.[32] If Jeremias was interested in the historical and Linnemann in the historical-existential, then Via is concerned with the existential-aesthetic. Thus he shares Jones' concern for the aesthetic and he overlaps with Linnemann's application of existentialism. His case is well stated, and he debates with the existential philosophers and theologians on the one side and with a wide range of literary critics on the other side. No brief review can do him justice.

The first half of his work is devoted to a discussion of methodology. He is determined to move away from the "severely historical," which in his view fails to do justice to the existential and to the aesthetic. He feels that the historical work has been done, and that he can rely with confidence on Dodd, Jeremias, T. W. Manson, and others.

In his first chapter, Via discusses parable and allegory. He rejects the "one-point" approach as "artificially restrictive."[33] The one-point approach destroyed the basic unity of the parable by isolating a single element and relating it directly to the referent. Yet the allegorization of the past is also rejected. In allegory the meanings of the different elements in the parable are determined by referents *outside* the parable, not by elements *within* the parable. Yet, according to Via, parables can have allegorical elements in them without becoming allegories. He writes, "The allegorist does not begin with an image which suggests a meaning, but he begins with an idea or meaning and looks for an image to represent it."[34]

The historical approach comes under criticism because we cannot be sure what the original situation was, and because such an approach "ignores the basic human element in the parables."[35] Furthermore, the historical approach, Via feels, leaves the parable with nothing to say to the present and it ignores its aesthetic nature as a work of art.

In his second chapter Via is concerned with the problem of theological language. He affirms that the historical is important because "our efforts at translation are not to be mere sounding boards for our previously held ideas."[36] The artist writes better than he knows, and the purpose of parables is to provide a better understanding of existence.[37] The well-known existentialist categories of the necessity of knowing that existence can be gained or lost, the language-event, self-understanding, authenticity, verification analysis, functional analysis, the verification principle, inauthenticity, preunderstanding, ontic and ontological are all discussed against a background of the works of Fuchs, Dilthey, Bultmann, and

---

[32]Via, *Parables,* 23. A noteworthy recent study in some ways close to Via is J. D. Crossan, *In Parables* (1973).
[33]Via, *Parables,* 3.
[34]*Ibid.,* 6.
[35]*Ibid.,* 22.
[36]*Ibid.,* 28.
[37]*Ibid.,* 39.

Linnemann.[38] He defines the goal of interpretation as translating the text into new terms so that "the language of the text might become an event."[39] In this section Via stands squarely in the existentialist tradition of Ernst Fuchs. Exposition is hermeneutics, and its goal is a new self-understanding on the part of the listener.

Via's third chapter is on parables, aesthetics, and literary criticism. He argues that the parables are genuine works of art and that a failure to deal with this fact has led to the one-point theory of interpretation. He writes,

> From the aesthetic standpoint, to isolate one element in a literary work for special consideration breaks the unity of the work and obscures the meaning of that element by removing it from the context which provides its meaning.[40]

Yet at the same time a work of art in general and a parable in particular does not just point inward but also outward. It has meaning within itself and also beyond itself. This Via explains by borrowing an illustration from Murray Krieger, a modern literary critic. Via writes,

> If the work [of art] operates properly, it is related to the world sequentially as window, mirror, and window. First it is a set of windows through which we see the familiar world referentially. Then the windows become mirrors reflecting inwardly on each other. In this set of reflecting mirrors the familiar and the hitherto unperceived are organized in a new pattern of connections so that in this pattern there is an implicit or preconceptual existential understanding. Finally the mirrors become windows again, giving us a new vision of the world. Thus the work, being at once word and world, leads both somewhere else and terminally to itself. But even as window the second time the work still offers a pre-conceptual understanding, and the latter is conceptualized only in criticism.[41]

Thus Via makes room for the internal unity of the different elements that have meaning only in relation to each other and at the same time allows for a conceptualization of those elements. Later he summarizes his own argument by saying, "In this chapter it has been argued that a work of literary art means [i.e., has meaning] both in and through itself but that the inner, non-referential meaning is dominant."[42]

Again and again he returns to a discussion of the damage done to the parables by the one-point exegetical approach which destroys this "centripetally organized unity of form and content. . . ."[43] As an alternative he suggests that in the case of Jesus' parables, ". . . Interpretation should not isolate one point but

---

[38]For a full review of these aspects of Via's work cf. Kelley, *Significance*, 92–120.

[39]Via, *Parables*, 52.

[40]*Ibid.*, 76.

[41]*Ibid.*, 84.

[42]*Ibid.*, 86.

[43]*Ibid.*, 88. At the same time he assumes that the severely historical method necessarily goes hand in hand with the one-point approach that does this destructive work. *Ibid.*, 89.

should call attention to the total configuration, to the nature of the interconnections, and to the understanding implicitly contained therein."[44]

His own literary tools, which he wishes to use on the parables, come from the categories familiar to literary criticism. They are narrative, fiction, plot, encounter, dialogue, the protagonist's power of action, symbolism, the tragic, and the comic.

In the second half of the book he illustrates his method by interpreting a series of "tragic" and a series of "comic" parables. His remarks are divided into "historical-literary criticism," "literary-existential analysis," and "existential-theological interpretation." His main interest seems to be "literary-existential analysis."

REACTION AND ASSESSMENT: A REMAINING TASK

Having concentrated on five major voices that are still with us in the sixties and seventies, we can summarize their main emphases diagrammatically as follows:

Dodd, Jeremias	= historical	
Jones	= (historical)	aesthetic
Linnemann	= historical - existential	
Via	= (historical)- existential - aesthetic	

Dodd and Jeremias are interested in the historical, which they demonstrate to include the eschatological. Jones concentrates on the aesthetic, assuming that the historical work has already been done. He asserts a timelessness for the aesthetically constructed parable. Linnemann takes the historical seriously and works at it. To this she adds the existential. Via assumes the historical and says he is building on Dodd and Jeremias. He is grateful to Jones for initiating the discussion on the aesthetic but is critical of him for not developing it. He is grateful to Linnemann for taking the existential seriously and criticizes her for leaving out the aesthetic.

On the sweep of parabolic exegesis in this century Kelley provides a thoughtful summary. He writes,

> Each major emphasis has brought a corrective to the situation that was inherited and then has had to be corrected itself. We have no reason to believe that the pattern will be any different in the case of the existentialist approach to the parable and its latest devotee, Via. Jülicher liberated the parables from extravagant allegorization but misunderstood their nature as parables of Jesus. Historical exegesis rescued us from interpreting the parables as mere illustrations of general moral principles when it placed them in the framework of

---

[44]*Ibid.*, 93.

Jesus' ministry critically reconstructed and eschatologically described. Such rigorous historical methodology in turn has its own built-in hazard, namely, that of pre-occupation with parables as concrete and functional instruments for instruction and disputation in first century circumstances to an extent that they might have little to say to the current twentieth century situation. Via, yielding to the contemporary pressure for relevance, seeks to remedy any such deficiency by taking the parables as aesthetic objects whose enduring subject matter and translatable content is none other than an understanding of existence, in faith and unfaith, authentically and inauthentically. Our reaction to his approach is that while he may have brought parables into the present and made them eventful thereby to many moderns, he has done so at the price of considerable disservice to them both as parables and as parables *of Jesus*.[45]

In the above diagram it can be seen that a historical-aesthetic approach to the parables has not been made. The only two scholars who have asked the aesthetic question (Jones and Via) are the ones who show the least interest in the historical setting. Those who have wrestled seriously with the historical (Dodd, Jeremias, and Linnemann) have not been concerned with the aesthetic. A brief critique of each of these approaches will make clear the extent to which the historical has not been brought together with the aesthetic.

Jeremias and Dodd, with their influential works, have laid the foundation of the twentieth-century recovery of the historical-eschatological setting of the parables. Their only difficulty is that at times the raw material for a precise delineation of the culture that informs the text was not available to them. Furthermore, they provide no format for an aesthetic appreciation of the parables as art forms. This lack has at times led them to judge as miscellaneous secondary collections made by the Church, units of material that are better understood as primary unified pericopes with their own integrity. Nevertheless, anyone who struggles to understand the parables in their original setting owes these two men a debt that is beyond description.

Of the four approaches in the above diagram, Jones seems the most concerned to break out of the original historical setting. Jones has a good point. When one stands in front of Michelangelo's statue of Moses, the impression is not that of sixteenth-century Italy, but of "the angry man of God." There *is* an element of timelessness to a great work of art that helps it break out of the historical setting in which it was created. Yet in the case of the parables, if the historical is not taken seriously, they become like floating balloons, ready to follow the prevailing winds.

The difficulty with the existentialist approach generally is put succinctly by Kelley, who writes,

The danger we see in this sort of orientation is that it yields a picture of Jesus not as a wandering Jewish rabbi who instructs disciples, replies to opponents, and stimulates crowds, but rather of an existentialist theologian, wearing a

---

[45]Kelley, *Significance*, 127f.; emphasis his.

Bultmannian or Heideggerian face, who by parabolic speech dramatizes ontological possibilities for hearers.[46]

If the existentialist approach helps to illuminate aspects of the parables for a certain segment of modern man, then this approach should be discussed and evaluated in those terms. To superimpose categories involved in "what it means" back into "what it meant" is, in a sense, a new form of allegorization.

Linnemann has given some very profound insights into the nature of the way some of the larger parables of conflict must have functioned originally. In the case of the parable of the Prodigal Son, there *is* "interlocking" in the parable. The parable authentically represents the position of the Pharisees. They considered sinners to be as unrighteous as pig herders working for gentiles. Their view then "interlocks" with the view of Jesus as represented in the words and actions of the Father. A new possibility of relationship between Jesus and his opponents is opened up by the telling of the parable.

Her theory breaks down, however, when we discuss a parable directed to the disciples. All such parables she quietly ignores. Her confidence that we can participate in that event through a re-creation of it in preaching is also only a partial understanding of how the hermeneutical problem can be solved. Can we really participate in the language event of the parable in the same way that a first-century Pharisee did who stood in opposition to a Galilean rabbi?[47]

We have already questioned the appropriateness of Via's existentialist categories for a study of first-century Palestinian parables. Leaving this question aside, it must be affirmed that Via has issued a timely call for an appreciation of the parables as art forms. However, in analyzing the parables he used the categories of Western literature. Kelley observes this as he writes,

> Too hastily . . . Via hurries over the material related to parables as an Eastern form in order to determine how they stand up to scrutiny under Western standards. The latter literary tradition may be more meaningful to us in the contemporary setting but the earlier associations with a Palestinian background are of no less importance, particularly where the parables of Jesus are under discussion.[48]

Rather than looking, as Via has done, for "comic," "tragic," "the protagonist's power of action," and "plot," Eastern literature must be examined using its own literary art forms. Then when the question is asked, "What are the primary literary art forms in Eastern literature?" the almost exclusive answer is, "Stories and poems." Thus, if we would investigate the parables aesthetically, we

---

[46]*Ibid.*, 132.

[47]Linnemann only touches on this problem in passing. It is her intent to concentrate on "what it meant" and leave the hermeneutical problem outside the scope of her study. This is also our intention. However, it is our conviction that each parable has a "theological cluster" that is a part of "what it meant." This cluster we feel is translatable through preaching with the aid of the impact of the artistic elements of the parable. (Cf. pp. 37f.)

[48]Kelley, *Significance*, 130, n. 2.

must examine them to see if Eastern poetical forms occur in the text, and if the stories have a distinct literary form.

Finally, Via has been much more concerned to relate the aesthetic to the existential, rather than to the historical. Hence, not only have the aesthetical aspects of the parables not been examined in the light of their own literary forms, but in addition no attempt has been made to combine such an aesthetic analysis with a serious study of the historical setting of the parables in first-century Palestine.[49]

It is our conviction that the historical must be reexamined in the light of additional evidence from the cultural milieu of the parables. In addition the aesthetic must be viewed in the light of Oriental literary forms. This twin task is the subject of the present study.

With this in mind, we turn to a discussion of an adequate methodology.

---

[49]An excellent series of three articles on the parables in modern interpretation is provided by J. D. Kingsbury, "Ernst Fuch's Existentialist Interpretation of the Parables," *Lutheran Quarterly,* 22 (1970), 380–395; *idem,* "Major Trends in Parabolic Interpretation," *Concordia Theological Monthly* 42 (1971), 579–596; *idem,* "The Parables of Jesus in Current Research," *Dialog* 11 (1972), 101–107.

Chapter 2

METHODOLOGY (1): THE CULTURAL PROBLEM

THE BASIC PROBLEM: CULTURAL FOREIGNNESS

The parables confront the exegete with what can be called the cultural problem. When studying the apostle Paul, one is dealing with theology expressed in conceptual language. But in the case of parables, their theology is expressed in stories about particular people who lived in a given cultural setting at a specific time in history. To understand the theology of parables, therefore, we must recapture the culture that informs the text. The culture of the synoptic parables is that of first-century Palestine.[1] Palestinian Christians saw their own culture reflected in the parables and could thereby understand the teller/author's intent directly. But when the cultural base of the Church ceased to be Palestinian the parables inevitably became stories about foreigners. This "foreignness" of the culture that informs the parables we have called *the cultural problem.*

The purpose of this chapter is to set forth a methodology that will be as adequate as possible for solving this cultural problem. We will try to demonstrate that such a methodology involves (1) discussing the cultural aspects of the parables with Middle Easterners, (2) examining pertinent ancient literature, and (3) consulting the Oriental versions of the Gospels. Furthermore, once we have established as precisely as possible the culture that informs the text of the parables, there remains the question of how the interpreter is to arrive at the *point* of the parable and whether that point is simple or multiple. We will attempt to show that each parable has a "cluster" of theological motifs that together press the listener to make a single response.

---

[1]Bultmann, *Tradition,* 166.

A REVIEW OF TYPES OF SOLUTIONS TO THE CULTURAL PROBLEM

This cultural problem has been given a number of answers. Through the centuries the Church, faced with this issue, has allegorized, indigenized, universalized, existentialized, and, on occasion, given up in despair. These solutions must be examined briefly in turn.

Origen's answer was to allegorize the details of the parables and thus deny culture any role in interpretation. We are all grateful to Jülicher[2] for having discredited this exegetical method which allows the introduction of nearly anything into virtually any parable.

A second solution, used almost unconsciously, is to "indigenize" the cultural elements of the parables. In this case, the exegete assumes that first-century people thought much like himself. What does it mean for a man to knock on his neighbor's door at midnight in the first century? It is only reasonable to assume, runs the argument, that it would mean roughly the same thing as knocking on a neighbor's door today. Sooner or later, the exegete will say, "It is only reasonable to assert . . . ," to which we must ask, "Reasonable to whom?" Or he says, "It is only natural to affirm . . . ," to which we must ask, "Natural for whom?" Does the commentator mean natural for the Americans, the British, or the Germans? Once identified, the fallacy of indigenization is readily recognizable.

Plummer, for example, notes that the father in the story of the Prodigal Son turns and addresses the servants immediately after hearing his son's confession. Plummer affirms that of course this order must have been given after the two had returned to the house because no servant would run out and down the road.[3] He is apparently thinking of a nineteenth-century British butler, and does not realize that a Middle Eastern listener would naturally assume the servants had followed the father down the road. Unconsciously Plummer has read his own cultural pattern back into the parable. Far more often the exegete overlooks significant elements in a parable because they are not important to the exegete's own world.

A third method is to "universalize" the cultural elements. In this case the exegete assumes that all men are basically alike. After all, all men understand fathers, sons, and neighbors. All men experience death, separation, and suffering. In all cultures, goes the argument, the basic human relationships displayed in the parables are similar, and so a study of Palestinian culture is not really so important after all. To a certain extent this is, of course, true. There is a humanity that all men share, and there are common problems that all men try to solve. But patterns for expressing those problems or even discussing them are quite different. To "universalize" in practice becomes to "indigenize." The one who says, "All men think alike," really means, "All men think like me."

---

[2]Jülicher, *Gleichnisreden*, I, *passim*.
[3]Plummer, *St. Luke*, 375.

A fourth method is to existentialize. This, in reality, shifts the discussion from exegesis to hermeneutics. The hermeneutical question is, of course, very important, but the historical question of "what it meant" must be answered prior to a hermeneutical concern for "what it means." One cannot even intelligently discuss participation in a "language event" until it is clear *what* language event is proposed. Without the historical question, the language event becomes a creation of the exegete.

A fifth alternative is to despair. There are two aspects to this reaction. There is the question of the time gap. We are twenty centuries away from the peasant world of Palestine in the days of Jesus. Then there is the question of distance. We live in the West and Jesus and his audience were Easterners. The Western exegete must move "over" and "back." Bultmann has admitted frankly that it is impossible to recover what the parable of the Unjust Steward originally meant.[4] In the sixteenth century Tomas de Vio Cajetan held the same position.[5] The information is too scanty, so the argument goes; the path back too narrow. The original meaning of the parables in their Palestinian setting is irrecoverably lost, we are told.

It is our view that none of these five alternatives is either appropriate or necessary. Our conclusion is that the Oriental culture that informs the text of the parables can be recovered in a rather systematic fashion. This enterprise of recovering that culture we will call "Oriental exegesis."

ORIENTAL EXEGESIS: A PROPOSAL

In this section we will begin with a definition, and then proceed to examine the archaic nature of the life style of Middle Eastern peasantry. Past attempts at gaining insights from Middle Eastern peasantry will be examined, and, finally, our own experience of working with Middle Eastern people will be set forth with a description of the necessary controls.

A Definition of "Oriental Exegesis"

The culture that informs the text of the Gospel parables can be delineated in a relatively precise manner by bringing together three tools. The culture of contemporary conservative peasants must be examined to see what the parables mean in their setting. Oriental versions need to be studied to see how Oriental churchmen through the centuries have translated the text. Ancient literature pertinent to the parables must be read *with* the insights gained from these other two sources, not in isolation from them. The text must be examined against the background of

---

[4]Bultmann, *Tradition*, 199.
[5]Apparently from his *Evang. cum commen . . . Thomae de Vio Caietani in quattuor Evang. et Apostol. . . . Commentarii*, etc. (1530). Quoted by Trench, *Notes*, 324.

information gleaned from these three sources. These three tools need to be used *along with* and not in isolation from the other skills of modern scholarship.

Thus "Oriental exegesis" is a method of studying a culturally conditioned text. The method is to use the standard critical tools of Western scholarship in combination with cultural insights gained from ancient literature, contemporary peasants, and Oriental versions.

We must now examine in some detail how each of these three tools is to be used. The first of these is ancient literature.

Ancient Literature: Its Importance and the Exegete's Problem in Assessing It

Modern scholarship has been engaged for well over a century in trying to redis-cover the cultural context of the Bible. Ancient literature has been examined with precision and sensitivity for clues regarding the culture that informs the text of the parables. It is difficult to exaggerate the importance of this literature. The problem is that cultural attitudes in any literature are assumed and only rarely, if ever, explained. To examine ancient Middle Eastern literature in order to discover the cultural assumptions of a given scene is like looking for raw diamonds in a gravel pit when one has never seen a raw diamond. It is like an amateur examining an archeologist's bulk. The observer must know what he is looking for before he can see anything, even if there is a great deal to be seen.[6] Ben Sirach reports that a nobleman is known by his walk.[7] He is referring to the slow, dignified pace of the Middle Eastern patriarch, which is a sign of the patriarch's stature in the commu-nity. This fact, noted by Ben Sirach, is one of the crucial keys to the parable of the Prodigal Son. It is a key that lies available; yet heretofore it has remained unnoticed and unused.

In summary, the culture that informs the text of the parables is often illuminated by ancient literature. Somehow, the exegete must discover what he is looking for before he can search meaningfully in that ancient literature. The answer is partially found in our second tool, which will now be examined.

The Contemporary Middle Eastern Peasant and His Oral Tradition as a Tool for Recovering the Culture of the Parables

In this section we will observe the archaic nature of the life of Middle Eastern peasantry, review past attempts at gleaning insights from this peasantry, and outline the unfinished task as well as its method and controls.

---

[6]Some Johannine editor was aware of this principle when he added the phrase "The Jews do not use vessels in common with the Samaritans," in John 4:9. The editor knew his reader had a cultural problem. Our problem is the same, only much more profound.

[7]Sir. 19:30.

The Archaic Nature of His Life Style

In the south of Egypt, in the mountains of Lebanon, and in the isolated communities of upper Syria and Iraq, there are peasant communities which have lived in remarkable isolation from the rest of the world. It is not only their isolation that has enabled them to preserve ancient ways of life, however, but also that they regard changelessness as being of highest value. This principle is of great antiquity and is not unknown in the Bible. All the wisdom literature of the ancient East, including the wisdom literature of the Bible, affirmed the supreme value of changelessness. Only in the static was there meaning. This was also asserted by ancient Egyptian religion, which taught that at creation God launched Egyptian society in its totality.[8] To preserve meaning was to preserve the status quo. This identity of value and changelessness has maintained itself in Middle Eastern peasant society all through the centuries. Thus today, the finest compliment for a gentleman in the village is "Ḥāfiz al-taqālīd" (preserver of the customs).

In his famous anthropological study of the Middle Eastern peasant, Father Henry Ayrout has this to say:

> The fellaheen have changed their masters, their religions, their language and their crops, but not their manner of life. . . . Violent and repeated shocks have swept away whole peoples, as can be seen today from the ruins of North Africa or Chaldea. . . . But the fellaheen have held firm and stood their ground. . . . They are as impervious and enduring as the granite of their temples, and as slow to develop. . . . This is not merely an impression. We can see the fellah using the same implements—the plough, the *shadûf*, the *saqia* . . . the same methods of treating the body . . . many of the same marriage and funeral customs. Through the pages of Herodotus, Diodorus Siculus, Strabo, Maqrîzi, Vansleb, Père Sicard and Volney we can recognise the same fellah. No revolution, no evolution.[9]

Many villages are not connected to the outside world by any road. Access is on foot or by donkey. There is a town crier and a village weaver. Doors of streets are closed at night. A colloquial Arabic is spoken, which is sprinkled with Greek, Aramaic, Syriac, and even Akkadian words. Young girls make Astarte-type fertility figurines good enough to fool all but the professional archeologists.

Not only is the life of such peasants remarkably archaic but their intellectual life is in the form of poems and stories preserved from the past. Men gather nightly in the village for what is called "ḥaflat *samar*" (social gathering for *samar*), which is cognate with the Hebrew *shamar*, "to preserve." They are gathering to *preserve* the intellectual life of their community by the recitation of

---

[8]Henri Frankfort, *Ancient Egyptian Religion* (New York: Harper, 1961), 49.

[9]Henry Habib-Ayrout, *The Fellaheen*, trans. Hilary Wayment (Cairo: R. Schindler, 1945), 19f. M. S. Seale, after a lifetime in the Middle East, writes, "before the great transformations of modern times, the 'unchanging East' really was unchanging." Cf. Morris S. Seale, *The Desert Bible, Nomadic Tribal Culture and Old Testament Interpretation* (London: Weidenfeld and Nicolson, 1974), 21.

poems and the retelling of stories. When a village patriarch begins, "marrah ayyām al-sulṭān" (once in the days of the sultan), or "marrah ayyām al-Rūm" (once in the days of the Byzantines), or more generally, "marrah zamān" (once long ago), he becomes to a certain extent like an Englishman telling a story from the days of King Arthur's court. As such a patriarch relates some narrative out of the distant past he enters a world that *may* be culturally somewhat different from his own. Yet that ancient world, with its traditional attitudes and archaic life style, is known and preserved in these stories. Thus village life has a double layer of cultural mores. There is the culture of the peasant himself and that of the traditional oral literature he recites. Through careful and patient contact with these two layers of culture, one is able to penetrate to and understand archaic forms of culture to a remarkable degree.

The next obvious question is, Has this task not already been done? Has not the work of gleaning insights for parabolic understanding from contemporary Middle Eastern peasants not already been accomplished? It is our conviction that it has been done partially and at times imprecisely, as a review of attempts at examining this peasantry will reveal.

Past Attempts at Gleaning Insights from Middle Eastern Peasantry

In this section we will review three past types of efforts at gaining biblical insight from contemporary peasants. Jeremias has written:

> As one who was privileged to live in Palestine for some years, I can testify from my own experience how much new light has been thrown ... upon the gospels ... [by] the study of both ancient and modern Palestine. ...[10]

Jeremias has used to its fullest every scrap of responsibly gathered information from contemporary conservative Middle Eastern peasants. The difficulty is that much of the data has been gathered casually and not always precisely. The materials fall into three categories. These we have labeled (1) the view from the saddle, (2) the view from the study window, and (3) the view from the single village.

First, there is *the view from the saddle*. In the nineteenth century the Reverend W. Thomson, missionary to Syria, spent a number of years on horseback riding through Bible lands.[11] From roughly 1850 through the First World War, a virtual flood of literature was written by pilgrims, travelers, and temporary residents of Palestine. Theirs was a view from the saddle; they saw Palestine "riding through." Much was observed of significance and value. Topography, weather, the agricultural year, the way people built their houses, the way they

---

[10]Joachim Jeremias, *The Problem of the Historical Jesus*, trans. N. Perrin (Philadelphia: Fortress, 1964), 17.

[11]Cf. p. 1, n. 1. Occasionally Thomson did make cultural observations; when he did so they are excellent. His major interest was the identification of geographic sites.

farmed the ground, and so forth, were noted; and our knowledge of the Bible was enriched.

The problem of the literature of this period is that most of it was written by people who stayed in the Middle East for relatively brief periods of time. Thomson spoke Arabic fluently and spent twenty-five years in the area. By contrast, the majority of Western authors were there only for short periods, and had little knowledge of Arabic and brief exposure to Middle Eastern ways. They wrote books or articles on their return to the West that on occasion influenced the direction of parabolic interpretation to a significant degree.[12] The people who were long-term residents in the Middle East were, generally speaking, not scholars. Quite naturally they wrote devotional literature, which tended to bypass the kinds of questions scientific scholarship asks. The scholars among them like Thomson were primarily interested in the identification of biblical sites.

After the view from the saddle comes *the view from the study window*, where the author settled down in the Palestinian scene and examined much of the same material but with greater precision. The outstanding work of Dalman will probably never be surpassed. Everything that could be measured, diagrammed, photographed, or charted, he recorded. His seven volumes (1928–1942) preserve the externals of Palestinian life in a precise and admirable way.[13] However, Dalman remained the Western professor looking on from the outside. His view was "from the study window." For parabolic interpretation we need to know more than the external appearance of agricultural tools. We rather need to know the inner workings of the society of people that uses them. At the same time, E. F. F. Bishop, an Anglican missionary and Arabic scholar, was resident in Jerusalem, meeting weekly with his Western friends to discuss what the entire Palestinian scene meant to the Bible. His three books[14] have many valuable insights, mixed with much quaint reminiscence. Bishop partially moved out of his study. By his own admission much of his material came out of a discussion group that "was essentially missionary."[15] Yet Bishop had hundreds of Arab friends with whom he was in conversation; and he used Arabic versions of the Gospels for exegesis, although he never identifies which versions. However, since he was an Arabic scholar with no specialization in New Testament, his material does not engage with contemporary scholarship.

A third contribution can be called *the view from the single village*. Here we turn to two men, Abraham Rihbany[16] and N. Levison.[17] Rihbany was a Christian

---

[12]In the exegetical section we will examine in detail the case of Margaret Gibson and her influence on the contemporary understanding of the parable of the Unjust Steward.

[13]G. Dalman, *Arbeit und Sitte in Palästina* (Gütersloh: Bertelsmann, 1928–1942), 7 vols.; *Sacred Sites and Ways,* trans. P. P. Levertoff (London: SPCK, 1935).

[14]Bishop, *Jesus; idem, Apostles of Palestine* (London: Lutterworth, 1958); *idem, Prophets of Palestine* (London: Lutterworth, 1962).

[15]Bishop, *Jesus,* 20.

[16]Rihbany, *Syrian.*

[17]Levison, *Local Setting.*

Syrian peasant who emigrated to America before the First World War and became a pastor. He came from a very conservative peasant world and realized that the world of his youth was significantly different from that of the West. He wrote, "Whenever I open my Bible, it reads like a letter from home."[18] Levison was an Oriental Jew who grew up in Palestine in the nineteenth century. He became a Christian, emigrated to England, and became a clergyman there. His book, *The Parables: Their Background and Local Setting* (1926), is introduced with these words:

> My qualifications for supplying the local coloring are based upon my great privilege of having been brought up in Galilee, within sight of Nazareth and the surrounding country. . . . When I say that, up to the time I was sent to school in Jerusalem, . . . I had not seen a vehicle of any description, and that the Old Testament narratives were as intelligible as the recently written accounts of yesterday's events, it may indicate how primitive and free from change our life in Safad was.[19]

The work of both Rihbany and Levison is of great value. A difficulty with both these books is that they are for the most part not scholarly but devotional. Many of the questions, therefore, which scholarship raises are not answered. But more than this, methodologically speaking neither pastor looked beyond the recollections of his own village. It never occurred to Levison that Safad might not reflect universal attitudes across Middle Eastern peasantry. Levison apparently had not read Rihbany. We do not know from reading Levison and Rihbany whether or not their recollections can be substantiated from Syrian, Lebanese, and Egyptian villages. In spite of this drawback, the work of these two men is important because they are Middle Easterners describing their own culture, not Westerners observing them from the outside. The information they give is usually valuable. Yet it is piecemeal and partial.

The Unfinished Task: Its Method and Its Controls

In the last twenty years I have tried to glean insights from the view from the saddle, the view from the study, and the view from the individual village, with a view to working out a methodology that may help to delineate more precisely the Oriental culture that informs the text. I prefer to call this *the view from the mastaba,* the *mastaba* being the mud-brick or stone bench outside the peasant's house on which he sits and talks with his friends by the hour.

As a part of a village literacy team for five years, I was privileged to live in Oriental villages for long periods of time. Naturally, the villages themselves were among the most isolated and primitive, because they were the villages where the highest rates of illiteracy were to be found. Living in the village, I was able to become a part of the scenery and could interact with the village people not as a guest or stranger, researcher or scholar, but as an ordinary resident. With no

---

[18]Quoted in Bishop, *Jesus,* 8.
[19]Levison, *Local Setting,* x.

camera or notebook, I could watch people interacting with each other. Over a period of years, I gradually came to the realization that a new layer of perception is available when we ask a fresh set of questions of the biblical text.

The crucial questions are those of *attitude, relationship, response,* and *value judgment.* What is the *attitude* of a sleeping neighbor to a call for help in the night? What is the *relationship* between a landowner and his renters? What is the expected *response* from a father when his son requests his inheritance? What *value judgment* do the renters make regarding the steward when he suggests the reduction of rents?

I discovered that the Oriental storyteller has a "grand piano" on which he plays. The piano is built of the attitudes, relationships, responses, and value judgments that are known and stylized in Middle Eastern peasant society. Everybody knows how everybody is expected to act in any given situation. The storyteller interrupts the established pattern of behavior to introduce his irony, his surprises, his humor, and his climaxes. If we are not attuned to those same attitudes, relationships, responses, and value judgments, we do not hear the music of the piano. With the parables, the music of this "piano" contains significant aspects of the theology that called the story itself into being.

In addition to residence in the individual village, for twenty years I have proclaimed the gospel and administered the sacraments to village congregations all across Egypt and Lebanon. This has put me in touch with a wide range of village people and village pastors. What is more important, this ministry has assured a relationship of intimacy and trust that has made possible the asking of cultural questions related to the parables. Thus, I have been privileged to observe what the parables mean when seen through peasant eyes.

The primary method of gaining insight has been to engage individuals and groups in extended discussion on the meanings of the parables. The conversation usually began, "Now, if this had happened in your village in the days of your grandfather, what would it have meant?" In time I have worked out the following methodological controls:

1. The resource person must have spent at least the first twenty years of his life in a conservative, basically illiterate, isolated peasant community.

2. The primary method of collecting the information must be oral conversation in Arabic. In a "word culture" such as we have in the Middle East, nearly everything that matters takes place orally. Oriental thought is most appropriately expressed in an Oriental language.

3. The primary resource person with whom I talk must be a person whom I have known as a friend for at least five years. This guards against receiving the stylized answers of the Easterner responding to the foreigner.

4. The resource person with whom I talk must know enough about the biblical witness to understand the questions put to him.

Gradually I have been able to develop a team of about twenty-five primary resource people from Iran to the Sudan with whom I have been in conversation around key questions regarding the culture that informs the text of the parables.[20] The majority of these twenty-five are Arab pastors who themselves have wrestled with the text. The insights gained from one resource person have been shared with as wide a Middle Eastern audience as possible, to assure that they ring true with a wide spectrum of Middle Eastern people. This has been done in the course of lecturing to Middle Eastern church groups, in extended discussions with Middle Eastern seminary students and pastors, as well as through a weekly Arabic radio broadcast. During my years on the faculty of the Near East School of Theology, Beirut, Lebanon, I have been privileged to work with colleagues from Syria, Lebanon, Germany, Holland, France, England, Ireland, and America. Insights have been refined and corrected through numerous discussions with these colleagues. There has been an occasional opportunity to consult with visiting Eastern and Western scholars.

The insights gained in some cases confirm what we already know. Other known insights are refined, still others rejected, and some new raw material has been uncovered to aid in parabolic understanding.

Our third tool is the Syriac and Arabic versions of the Gospels. This additional avenue of insight into the parables will now be examined.

The Significance of the Oriental Versions for Exegesis

Oriental versions have been used for purposes of textual criticism but rarely for exegesis. It is now readily recognized that translation is inevitably interpretation. For example, anyone who translates the parable of the Unjust Steward into Arabic or Syriac must decide what word he is going to use for οἰκονόμος. There is no word in either language with the same range of ambiguity found in the Greek word. The translator *must* decide whether in his opinion the οἰκονόμος is an estate manager or a moneylender. He has to make this exegetical decision in order to translate. The decision is crucial because the entire direction of one's understanding of the parable turns on the answer given to this initial question. The translator of an Arabic or Syriac version gives his answer to this exegetical question as he translates. A second- or third-century Syriac translator will inevitably reflect in his translation his understanding of the culture that informs the text. The crucial point is that he lived in an ancient Eastern world that surely had a culture nearly identical to the culture of the parables themselves. Thus, when asking the *cultural* question, especially the older Oriental versions offer crucial raw data for exegesis.

For this study we have selected a series of eighteen Arabic and Syriac versions. The selection has been made on the basis of three factors: time, geography, and type. In regard to time, the texts selected stretch from the second to the twentieth centuries. Early versions have been given preference, but medieval and modern translations by Eastern scholars have not been ignored. The geographic origin of each text, as far as is known, has been considered in the selection. Egypt,

---

[20]A brief description of these friends and consultants is given in Appendix B.

Mount Sinai, Lebanon, Syria, Iraq, and Edessa are all represented. By "type" we refer to the fact that "church translations" have been balanced with versions produced by known Arabic and Syriac scholars, such as Hibat Allah Abu al-Faḍl Ibn al-'Assāl, the great exegete of Cairo in the thirteenth century, and the eleventh-century prince of Arab exegetes Abu al-Faraj 'Abd Allah Ibn al-Ṭayyib of Baghdad. Appendix A lists the versions selected and gives a brief description of each. Space does not permit the inclusion of all the evidence gleaned from these versions. Over a thousand texts in Arabic and Syriac were read with care, and where they are significant for an understanding of the culture of the parables here discussed this will appear in the notes.

In summary, the proposed method is to discuss the culturally oriented questions that arise from the text with as wide a sampling of carefully selected Middle Eastern Christians as possible. Major Arabic and Syriac versions will be examined minutely to see how Oriental churchmen have understood the text. With insights from these two sources in mind, pertinent ancient literature will be examined for further comparison. These three sources will be applied to the text along with the standard tools of contemporary scholarship.

The lingering question remains and will always remain: How can we be sure the Middle Eastern peasant has not changed his culture and attitudes across the intervening centuries? In answer to this, it must be said emphatically that the insight gained from the contemporary peasant must *always* be rejected if we have a more ancient or in any way more authentic alternative. If we do not have such an alternative, then the options are either to accept the cultural world view of the medieval Middle Eastern peasant (compared with ancient versions and literature), or to fall back on one of the rejected alternatives set forth above.[21] Any commentator who moves through any parable inevitably makes a series of culturally influenced judgments; the question is not, Shall we interpret, making cultural judgments as we go along, or shall we not? Rather it is, *Whose* culture shall we allow to inform the text for us?[22]

A final methodological concern is to establish an exegetical stance in respect to Jülicher's insistence that each parable has only one point. This question will now be examined.

DISCERNING THE THEOLOGICAL CLUSTER

In this section we shall attempt to show that a parable has three basic elements. First, the parable has one or more points of contact (referents) within the real world

---

[21]Above, pp. 28–29.

[22]At times I feel like a visitor who approaches a woodcarver at his bench. The carver is working away with a slightly dull chisel. The visitor pulls out a sharper chisel from his pocket and suggests, "Sir, I think this might be a better tool for the piece of work you are doing." The carpenter does not miss a stroke or look up but replies, "On what basis (tap, tap) do you think it is legitimate (tap, tap) to introduce (tap, tap) the use of chisels (tap, tap)?"

of the listener, which can be called "symbols." The second element in a parable is the "response" that the original listener is pressed to make to the original telling of the story. The third element is a combination of theological motifs in the parable that together pressed the original listener to make that response. This combination we choose to call the "theological cluster." Thus, one or more symbols with corresponding referents in the life of the listener impel him to make a single response which has in view a cluster of theological motifs.

Initially it must be said that any attempt to state in propositional terms a tightly constructed interlocking system of interpretative principles, which can be applied uniformly to all the parables of Jesus, is doomed to failure. The parables are artistically told stories that break the boundaries of all rationalistic systems.[23] The best that can be done is to outline a stance *vis-à-vis* the parables that will free them to challenge the reader to respond in terms of repentance, faith, and discipleship.

Any attempt to outline such a stance from which to view the parables must begin with Jülicher's struggle with the allegorical method. Allegory treated the parables as cryptograms that must be decoded. This evaluation of the parables Jülicher demonstrated to be utterly false.[24] He was anxious to establish and strictly maintain the unity of each parable. Each parable, therefore, could have *only* one point of comparison, one *tertium comparationis,* which Jülicher decided was some general ethical principle.

The direction of the argument is clear. Each parable has unity. That unity requires a single point of comparison; this in turn means that it carries a single significant thought. This line of reasoning must be carefully examined.

What then is meant by a point of comparison? At this juncture the discussion is greatly complicated by a confusion in terminology. Linnemann writes,

> Parables are meant to be forms of argument. It is for this reason that they have only one point of comparison. One can hardly argue several things at once. For this reason we must carefully distinguish between what a parable is arguing and what it assumes. As soon as we draw from a parable a number of different significant ideas, we can be sure that we are missing the meaning that the parable had for its first narrator.[25]

---

[23]We have accepted Jeremias' judgment where he writes, "A distinction was drawn between metaphor, simile, parable, similitude, allegory, illustration, and so forth—a fruitless labour in the end, since the Hebrew *mašal* and the Aramaic *mathla* embraced all these categories and many more without distinction. This word may mean in the common speech of post-biblical Judaism, without resorting to a formal classification, figurative forms of speech of every kind: parable, similitude, allegory, fable, proverb, apocalyptic revelation, riddle, symbol, pseudonym, fictitious person, example, theme, argument, apology, refutation, jest" (Jeremias, *Parables,* 20). Manson writes, "A parable is a literary creation in narrative form designed either to portray a type of character for warning or example or to embody a principle of God's governance of the world and men. It may partake of both natures" (*Teaching,* 65).
[24]Jülicher, *Gleichnisreden,* I, 118–148.
[25]Linnemann, *Parables,* 23.

From this quotation it is clear that "point of comparison" for Linnemann means "significant idea." Cadoux calls this point of comparison a "point of contact" and understands it quite differently. He writes,

> Allegory, being merely representative, touches that which it represents at many points, while the parable's essential function is to evoke a judgment in one field and secure its application in another; it does not therefore follow that there is only one point of contact between the story of the parable and the other field to which we carry the judgment evoked by the story. Indeed, it is comparatively seldom that it is so. The judgment elicited by the story is generally a judgment upon a more or less complex situation, and there is always a certain contact between the people and things of this situation and those of the situation to which the judgment is carried. In Nathan's parable there is obviously a certain connection between the rich man and David, the poor man and Uriah, the ewe-lamb and Bathsheba. And further than this, so long as the story of the parable is not unnaturally shaped into similarity with the features of the field to which it is applied, so long as the points of similarity grow naturally from the story, they may be multiplied with advantage, for then they assist the passage of judgment from the one field to the other.[26]

Cadoux is talking about the *referents* in the life of the listener that correspond to the different symbols in the parable.

On the surface, these two authors sound somewhat contradictory. One calls for a single point of contact, the other for many. Actually, they are discussing different aspects of the parable. For Linnemann the parable is a form of argumentation. She says, "One can hardly argue several things at once." For Cadoux the parable evokes a single judgment. To do so it may need a number of points of contact with reality outside the parable. Thus it *may* be possible to combine Cadoux and Linnemann by saying that a parable usually has a number of symbols which contribute to a single argument.

There is also a divergence between these two authors. Where Cadoux says that a parable is intended to "evoke a judgment," Linnemann holds that a parable is a "form of argument." Linnemann seems to be concentrating on the author of the parable, whom she understands to be arguing a point. Her concept calls for logic, intellectualization, and conceptualization. The debater wants to make his point and convince you intellectually that he is right. Cadoux's phrase, "evoke a judgment," focuses on a more kerygmatic note of an interaction between the author of the parable and the hearer who is expected to respond. Cadoux's focus on judgment seems more appropriate to the nature of parables; yet we prefer the word "response." The purpose of a parable perhaps is best understood as intending to "evoke a response" from the listener.

Furthermore, Cadoux's observation that a parable may have a number of points of similarity between the world of the parable and the real world of the listener is well taken. Once the interpreter has shaken himself loose from the stance

---

[26]Cadoux, *Parables*, 50f.

that sees the parable as a secret cryptogram, with a code that must be broken, then more than one symbol in the parable pointing to more than one referent in the life of the listener can be admitted with no danger to the unity of the parable. Nathan's parable[27] has three symbols which aid the teller in pressing David to make a single decision. These three symbols have corresponding referents from the real situation that called forth the telling of the parable. Their identification is obvious. However, the interpreter must not treat such identifications as the beginning of a road along which he is expected to travel and then proceed to find referents for all the elements in the parable. The exegete must look for referents only for the elements that the original listeners would have identified. These symbolic elements must contribute to the unity of the parable found in the single response the listener is challenged to make.[28]

Before proceeding we must examine and define "response" as used in this discussion of parables. Dodd writes, "The way to an interpretation of a parable lies through a judgment on the imagined situation, and not through the decoding of the various elements in the story."[29] Thus Dodd, like Cadoux, sees a parable as calling for a "judgment" on the part of the listener. This we prefer to define as a "response." What then is this response? In answer to this question Manson's definition of "parable" is helpful. He says,

> A parable is a picture in words of some piece of human experience, actual or imagined. As such it is a work of art. Further, this picture portrays either an ethical type for our admiration or reprobation, or some principle of the rule of God in the world, or it does both things at once. . . . In actual working, then, every true parable is a call to a better life and a deeper trust in God, which things are but the Godward and manward sides of a true religion, the obverse and reverse of the one medal.[30]

In our understanding of the matter, the response the listener to a parable is called upon to make covers both aspects of a parable as defined by Manson. Depending on the nature of the parable, the response of the listener may be a decision to act in a particular way or to accept a new understanding of the nature of God's way with men in the world. This latter type of response will most likely also lead the listener to act in a particular way toward his fellow man. Some parables, as Manson has indicated, involve both. Thus the line between "a new understanding of the 'rule of God in the world' " and a "decision to act in a particular fashion" is usually blurred. Manson says a parable issues "a call to a better life and a deeper trust in God." The listener's response involves hearing one or both of these calls depend-

---

[27]It is possible to make a distinction between a parable and an example story. But it is clear that the Hebrew *Mashal* and Aramaic *Mathla* covered both types of stories.

[28]Recent studies have argued that parables do have allegorical elements in them. Matthew Black, "The Parables as Allegory," *BJRL* 42 (1960), 273–287; Raymond E. Brown, "Parable and Allegory Reconsidered," *Novum Testamentum* 5 (1962), 36–45. Symbolism is probably more accurate than allegory.

[29]Dodd, *Parables*, 21.

[30]Manson, *Teaching*, 80f.

ing on the parable. This brings us to the third aspect of the parable, namely, the theological cluster.

The response invoked by the telling of the parable is informed by, or composed of, a cluster of theological themes that can be analyzed and discussed separately. Sometimes the theological themes are implied directly in what is said in the parable, sometimes they are presupposed. David hears Nathan's parable and makes the single response, "I am a sinner." At the same time, the awareness that he and Uriah are brothers under one covenant is a part of that response; so is the awareness of the holiness of God, who expects righteousness from his anointed king.[31] These different theological themes *together,* through the artistry of the parable, press the king to make his single response. The unity of the parable is to be found in that single response.

The three aspects of the parable are now clear. The parable may have a number of symbols with corresponding referents in the life of the listener. The parable calls for a single response that is usually informed by a cluster of theological themes.

With the awareness that diagrams tend to oversimplify, these three aspects of each parable may be diagrammed as follows:

I.   The telling of the   II. The listener's   III. Reflection on
     parable   response   the ground and
                                                                content of that
                                                                response

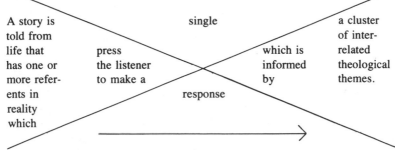

A story is   single   a cluster
told from   of inter-
life that   press   which is   related
has one or   the listener   informed   theological
more refer-   to make a   by   themes.
ents in   response
reality
which

Thus, the Pharisee, listening to the telling of the parable of the Prodigal Son, is pressed by a multiplicity of referents to make a single response to be reconciled to his "family" (which included the father and the brother). At the same time it is possible to discern a cluster of theological motifs that inform this single response.[32] In this vein, Hunter says,

---

[31] Any ancient king who assumed himself to be above the laws of his kingdom, and therefore not bound by them, would not have come to David's conclusion in similar circumstances.

[32] C. W. F. Smith writes, "It will be observed that many of the details are so apt that, once the central point is grasped, many applications may be made and deductions drawn" (*Parables,* 113; cf. also Cadoux, 50f.). Jones states, "To insist that there shall be one point and one point only, and that a

> ... In the parable there is one chief point of likeness between the story and the meaning, and the details simply help to make the story realistic and so serve the central thrust of the parable—like the feathers which wing the arrow.[33]

While it is not clear what Hunter intends with the word "meaning," his illustration is worth considering. An arrow is a single unit. But it is composed of shaft, head, and feathers. The three elements combine to form an effective missile for the bow. The feathers are not to be dismissed as an unnecessary secondary decoration. All three are essential to the nature and effectiveness of an arrow.

Thus the call for a single response does not necessarily mean a single significant idea. In a parable we find a group of interlocking themes—the "theological cluster." Different aspects of a given parable symbolize different yet *interrelated* theological themes. These combine to press for a single response.

Dodd insists that the details of a parable do not have independent significance.[34] To this we can agree. Yet the details have dependent significance, that is, they have meaning in a dependent relation to the other elements in the parable.

To approach it from another angle, Manson has written of the parables:

> ... Illustrations will not be parables in the sense that the parables of the New Testament are parables. They [illustrations] are merely the embellishment of something else, namely the chain of logical reasoning; they are the sugar-coating on the theological pill. The true parable, on the other hand, is not an illustration to help one through a theological discussion; it is rather a mode of religious experience. It belongs to the same order of things as altar and sacrifice, prayer, the prophetic vision, and the like. It is a *datum* for theology, not a by-product. It is a way in which religious faith is attained and, so far as it can be, transmitted from one person to another. It is not a crutch for limping intellects, but a spur to religious insight: its object is not to provide simple theological instruction, but to produce living religious faith.[35]

If we can accept Manson's definition of a parable as *datum* for theology, the question must be raised, Are single theological themes in the New Testament ever discussed in isolation? They may be on relatively rare occasions. Certainly such isolation is not the rule. A certain type of philosophically oriented mind is able with some effort to isolate a single theme and discuss it in depth. But in the New Testament it is much more common to find theological themes discussed in clusters. Who is to say that John 3:16 discusses only "love" or "the world" or "believing" or "perishing" or "eternal life"? This does not mean that there is no unity in this verse, but it does signify that the unity is found in a theological cluster of concepts.

In the case of the parable of the Sower, the listener is called to "hear the word of the kingdom and bear fruit." This decision to hear and bear fruit is based

---

parable shall be understood only as a whole, and not in relation to its part (which is supposed to turn it into an allegory), is pure dogmatism" (*Art*, 140).

[33] A. M. Hunter, *Interpreting the Parables* (London: SCM, 1964), 10.

[34] Dodd, *Parables*, 18.

[35] Manson, *Teaching*, 73.

on and informed by a cluster of theological motifs. Among these are:

1. The kingdom is like a seed growing slowly; it is not an apocalyptic revo-
    lutionary disruption.

2. The parable speaks of grace. The sower sows liberally even in potentially
    unfruitful ground.

3. Fruit-bearing is an essential mark of the kingdom.

4. The parable offers the listener hope. There is assurance of a harvest in spite
    of difficulties.

These theological motifs are to be understood only in tension with each
other within the unity of the parable,[36] which is centered in the *call to hear the
word of the kingdom and bear fruit.* Such an understanding does not allow for
identifying the thorns with the Jewish leaders, and the good soil with the Church. A
cluster of motifs forms the ground and content of a single response.

In summary, a parable is not an illustration but is a mode of theological
speech used to evoke a response. The parable may have a number of referents in the
life of the listener to whom it is addressed. The listener is challenged by the telling
of the parable to respond. This response is informed by a cluster of theological
motifs.

SUMMARY AND CONCLUSIONS

Knowledge of the culture that informs the text of Gospel parables is crucial to a full
understanding of them. The impact of such cultural elements has, in the past, been
discerned only partially. Significant elements of the cultural setting of the synoptic
parables can be delineated more precisely through discussion with contemporary
peasants, through minute examination of Oriental versions of the Gospels, and by
a careful study of pertinent ancient literature. These three tools must be used in
addition to the standard critical tools of scholarship. The present study seeks to
combine the use of these four tools, conjoining them with an analysis of various
literary structures used in parables. To this matter of literary structure we now turn.

---

[36]Via argues that the one-point approach is ''artificially restrictive.'' Of this approach he writes,
''Important elements in the parable may be overlooked and the meaning of the parable attenuated''
(*Parables,* 3). Jones affirms that exemplary stories ''can be invoked to illustrate several things'' (*Art,*
118); cf. also Manson, *Teaching,* 80; Jeremias, *Parables,* 131; M. Dibelius, *From Tradition to Gospel,*
trans. B. L. Woolf (New York: Scribner, 1935), 249, 253.

Chapter 3

METHODOLOGY (2): FOUR TYPES OF LITERARY STRUCTURES IN THE NEW TESTAMENT AND THEIR SIGNIFICANCE FOR THE INTERPRETATION OF PARABLES

In a recent address to the Society of Biblical Literature James Muilenburg called for a move beyond form criticism to "rhetorical criticism." He said that his primary interest was:

> ... in exhibiting the structural patterns that are employed for the fashioning of a literary unit, whether in poetry or in prose, and in discerning the many and various devices by which the predictions are formulated and ordered into a unified whole. Such an enterprise I should describe as rhetoric and the methodology as rhetorical criticism.[1]

The intentions of this chapter are in harmony with Muilenburg's interests. Since the above address the entire topic of literary analysis in biblical and non-biblical literature among linguists and biblical scholars has mushroomed enormously to the extent that even the subject of "literary structures (rhetorical criticism) in the New Testament" is a full study in itself (cf. Bibliography, section F). Here we are interested in this field as it affects the interpretation of the parables. We will attempt to (1) review briefly the history of interest in literary structures in biblical literature, (2) define our terms, (3) outline four types of literary structures in biblical literature, and finally (4) conclude some working principles for the passages under consideration.

---

[1]James Muilenburg, "Form Criticism and Beyond," *LBJ* 88 (1969), 8. Martin Kessler in a recent article has emphasized the new mood among a growing number of biblical scholars who insist on the artistic integrity of a literary product. This "new criticism" has been called in Germany *Werkinterpretation*, and it is "exemplified by ... the insistence on the formal integrity of the literary piece, the *Kunstwerk*." Cf. Martin Kessler, "New Directions in Biblical Exegesis," *Scottish Journal of Theology* 24 (1971), 320. This chapter and indeed the entire study can be seen as being in line with this new attempt to appreciate the finished literary product, the *Kunstwerk*. Morris S. Seale in a significant recent book, *The Desert Bible, Nomadic Tribal Culture and Old Testament Interpretation* (London: Weidenfeld and Nicolson, 1974), speaks of the text of the Bible and of his refusal "to carve it up, to catalogue it or to otherwise 'atomize' it" (p. 2). Furthermore this chapter is written with an awareness of the work of Leach, Levi-Strauss, Barthes, Beauchamp and other structuralists. We are not concerned here with structuralism or semiology as ideologies but with *literary* structure as outlined by Muilenburg above.

A REVIEW OF PAST SCHOLARSHIP ON THE QUESTION OF LITERARY STRUCTURES

In the eighteenth century, J. A. Bengel made brief reference to the presence of *chiasmus* in a number of passages in the New Testament.[2] His illustrations were within the proper definition of *chiasmus*, that of two lines of poetry with the second line reversing the order of the first, and thus creating an ABBA pattern.

In the early nineteenth century John Jebb wrote about certain biblical passages:

> There are stanzas so constructed that, whatever be the number of lines, the first line shall be parallel with the last; the second with the penultimate; and so throughout, in an order that looks inward, or, to borrow a military phrase, from flanks to centre. This may be called introverted parallelism.[3]

Thomas Boys of the same period looked for literary structures in the Psalms.[4] John Forbes in 1854 advanced the work of Jebb.[5] Late in the nineteenth century, William Milligan of Scotland observed structure in some passages in the Apocalypse.[6] E. W. Bullinger in the same period overworked his schemes so irresponsibly as to discredit more than to advance an interest in literary structures in biblical literature.[7] In 1925 C. F. Burney's monograph, *The Poetry of Our Lord*, was published, and it remains a major reference work in the field.[8] Burney concentrated on parallelism, accentual rhythm, and rhyme. At times he left out sections of a verse to achieve his rhythm. He can also be faulted on other specifics. Yet his work remains basic to all further discussion.

In the thirties, the subject of literary analysis in the New Testament was touched on briefly by Bultmann, Manson, Goguel, Streeter, and Taylor.[9] Of this group Manson wrote regarding the synoptic material attributed to Jesus,

---

[2]Bengel, *Gnomon, passim.*

[3]John Jebb, *Sacred Literature* (London: n.p., 1820), 53.

[4]Thomas Boys, *Key to the Book of Psalms* (London: n.p., 1825).

[5]John Forbes, *The Symmetrical Structure of Scripture* (Edinburgh: T. & T. Clark, 1854).

[6]William Milligan, *Discussions on the Apocalypse* (London: n.p., 1893), *passim.*

[7]E. W. Bullinger, *Figures of Speech used in the Bible* (London: Eyre and Spottiswoode, 1898); *idem, Key to the Psalms* (London: Eyre and Spottiswoode, 1890); *The Companion Bible* (Oxford: University Press, 1948 [1913]).

[8]Burney, *Poetry.* During the same period Cladder, Schmidt, and Loisy tried to demonstrate that the New Testament is Greek poetry and should be divided into *stichoi.* Their views were almost universally rejected by later scholarship. Cf. Hermann J. Cladder, *Zur Literaturgeschichte der Evangelien* in *Unsere Evangelien. Akademische Vorträge* (Freiburg: Herder, 1919), I; Alfred F. Loisy, *L'Evangile selon Luc* (Paris: Nourry, 1924); P. Schmidt, *Der Strophische Ausbau des Gesamttextes der Evangelien* (1921). An excellent review of the work of these men is found in Lucetta M. Mowry, "Poetry in the Synoptic Gospels and Revelation, a Study of Methods and Materials" (unpublished Ph.D. thesis, Yale University, 1946), 4. Mowry lists the Schmidt volume in her bibliography. I have not been able to locate the book or any reference to it outside of her thesis.

[9]Bultmann, *History,* 70; T. W. Manson, *Teaching,* 50–56; Maurice Goguel, *The Life of Jesus,* trans. Olive Wyon (New York: Macmillan, 1945), 296–303; B. H. Streeter, "Poems of Jesus," *The Hibbert Journal* 32 (1933/34), 9–16; V. Taylor, *Formation of the Gospel Tradition* (London: Macmillan, 1935), 88–100.

A still greater extension of the phenomenon of parallelism, and one which has not so far as I am aware been noticed as such, is to be found in the words of Jesus. Here the parallelism covers not single clauses containing each one simple idea, but still larger aggregates each of which contains many clauses.[10]

Manson concludes his discussion by saying, "Perhaps we should regard this strophic parallelism as the most distinctive characteristic of his poetry and his special contribution to the forms of poetry in general."[11]

In the forties, three authors are worthy of brief note. Olmstead, an Aramaic scholar and historian, tried to provide an English translation of the Dominical sayings, keeping in mind the Aramaic he assumed to lie behind them. He was not specifically interested in literary form, but printed lines in poetic format when he determined that the saying had poetic structure.[12]

Mowry's Yale thesis seems to be the only dissertation ever written in this country on the topic of New Testament poetry.[13] She rather arbitrarily accepts the category of accentual rhythm as essential for determining what shall be called poetry. She concludes that there are twenty poetical sayings in the synoptic Gospels. These she divides into three categories: the gnome of the wise man, the oracle of the prophet, and the psalm.[14] Mowry feels that she has determined the absolute minimum for synoptic poetry. Yet, granting her methodological principle that a couplet must have accentual rhythm to be poetry, two of her twenty pieces of poetry must be struck and her "absolute minimum" reduced to eighteen. In two cases she has indicated a stress for the verb "to be" in the present tense.[15] At the same time she insists that "retrovertability" into Aramaic is a necessary quality for a couplet to be called Dominical poetry.[16] Nonetheless, in spite of her undefended arbitrary selection of meter as determinative of what sections of the New Testament are poetry, and her putting stresses on nonexisting words, her work is useful. In a number of synoptic passages she does substantiate both parallelism and rhythmic meter.

The third author of the forties is N. W. Lund,[17] whose 428-page book produced varied reviews. McGinley was quite favorable and felt that Lund had demonstrated his point "beyond cavil."[18] H. J. Cadbury of Harvard was critical yet positive. In his opinion, Lund had rather badly overworked some of his

---

[10]Manson, *Teaching,* 54.

[11]*Ibid.,* 56. This last statement no longer stands, as a result of the discovery of the same "strophic parallelism" in the Old Testament and in Qumran, as we shall see.

[12]A. T. Olmstead, *Jesus in the Light of History* (New York: Scribner, 1942), *passim.*

[13]A DIATREX computer printout at University Microfilms, Ann Arbor, Michigan, in January, 1972, produced *no* references.

[14]Mowry, *op. cit.,* 144–235. She finds seventeen illustrations of the first category, two of the second, and one of the third.

[15]*Ibid.,* 144, 156.

[16]*Ibid.,* 133.

[17]Lund, *Chiasmus.*

[18]Laurence J. McGinley, review of Lund, *Chiasmus,* in *Theological Studies* 13 (1942), 452–54.

material but "some of the evidence is inescapable."[19] T. W. Manson has the longest review, in which he also is positive, yet sharply critical. He concludes by saying, "While it must be said that Mr. Lund has overdriven his thesis in many directions, it must still be admitted that he has a thesis. There are clear cases of the kind of arrangement he describes."[20]

Jeremias has an extended essay on chiasm.[21] Regarding it, Miesner observes,

> Jeremias (p. 152) praised Lund's work in the Old Testament as "eine Reihe guter und überzeugender Belege für Chiasmus am A T." Yet, elsewhere (p. 145) he strangely described Lund's work of over 25 years as "völlig unbrauchbar."[22]

Having worked with Lund's book for a number of years, I find T. W. Manson and H. J. Cadbury the most accurate and useful evaluations. Lund has certainly pushed his scheme too far. As Cadbury has rightly suggested, each piece of evidence must be examined on its own merits and neither rejected nor accepted *a priori*. There is no doubt that Lund broke some significant new ground in the analysis of literary structures.

For over twenty years little was done. Then in 1965 John Bligh reopened the discussion with a book on Galatians[23] in which he organizes the entire book of Galatians into interlocking structured literary forms. Now in the seventies many scholars in different fields are taking literary analysis seriously.[24]

Thus there has been a small but relatively steady stream of scholars who have worked in this area variously called chiasm or literary analysis or New Testament poetry or rhetorical criticism. Much is yet to be done. Before we can proceed to our own analysis a few terms must be defined.

A DEFINITION OF TERMS

In the absence of uniformity of vocabulary, we will define our own terms. The categories of synonymous, antithetical, and synthetic parallelisms are established and will be used on occasion. Then when parallel lines follow each other in an AA' BB' CC' DD' pattern they will be called *standard parallelism*. This form of parallelism is common to the Old Testament and is well known in the Psalms and

---

[19]H. J. Cadbury, review of Lund, *Chiasmus*, in *Journal of Religion* 23 (1943), 62f.

[20]Manson, review of Lund, *Chiasmus*, in *JTS* 45 (1944), 85.

[21]Joachim Jeremias, "Chiasmus in den Paulusbriefen," *ZNW* 49 (1958), 145–156.

[22]Miesner, *Chiasm and Paul*, 42, n. 73.

[23]John Bligh, *Galatians in Greek, A Structural Analysis of St. Paul's Epistle to the Galatians* (Detroit: University of Detroit Press, 1966).

[24]Bibliography section F. Also Miesner's bibliography, *Chiasm and Paul*, 360–65. Matthew Black's important work, *Aramaic Approach*, concentrates on two-line parallelism, alliteration, assonance, and paronomasia. He does not discuss the question of literary structure.

the Prophets.[25] It is found also in the New Testament. A clear example is in Luke 21:23–24, which is as follows:

> A   Alas for those who are with child
> A' and for those who give suck in those days
>
> B   For great distress shall be upon the earth
> B' and wrath upon this people
>
> C   They will fall by the edge of the sword
> C' and be led captive among all nations.

When parallel lines are in an A B C–A' B' C' pattern they will be called *step parallelism*. A clear example of this type which falls within this study is Luke 11:9–10, as follows:

> A   Ask, and it will be given you
>   B   Seek, and you will find
>   C   Knock, and it will be opened to you.
>
> A'   For every one who asks receives
>   B'   And he who seeks finds
>   C'   And to him who knocks it will be opened.

When the parallel lines are inverted in an A B C D–D' C' B' A' structure the pattern will be called *inverted parallelism*. This pattern can be seen clearly in Amos 5:4b–6a:

> 1   *Seek-me and-live*
>   2   and do-not-seek *Bethel*
>   3   and-*Gilgal* do-not-enter
>   4   and to-*Beer-sheba* do-not-cross-over.
>   3'   because *Gilgal* an exile shall-be exiled
>   2'   and-*Bethel* shall-come to-nothing
> 1'   *Seek Yahweh and-live.*[26]

As this field of study expands there is the need for increasing precision in vocabulary. Often the word *chiasm* is used loosely to refer to all types of literary structures, particularly those with some inversion of themes. This word properly refers to two lines where the themes are reversed in the second, such as Mark 2:27:

---

[25]It must be noted emphatically that this brief discussion is incomplete. Any well-written piece of literature has a series of interlocking correspondences that together form the artistry of the piece. We are presupposing the literary tradition of the Old Testament. The trained eye will note other patterns of correspondence that we do not discuss. We observe all through this chapter the literary pattern that appears to us to be dominant. The criterion for that dominance is the strength of the correspondences.

[26]The words connected with dashes indicate that the words so connected represent one word in the original Hebrew. In each case we shall present the structured material on the page in the above forms to aid the eye in identifying the lines that are parallel.

This particular stanza has the main point at the beginning and the end, not the middle. In the New Testament we have observed the climax more often in the center. Yet each pericope must be examined on its own ground.

```
     A                    B
The sabbath was made for man,
     B          A
not man for the sabbath.
```

If one were to draw a line connecting the A's and the B's the lines would form an X, which is the Greek letter *Chi,* hence *chiasmus.* This is often shortened to *chiasm.* We shall preserve this precise technical term for simple A B B A patterns of various types.

Extended inversions are used in so many different ways that some term is needed to cover all of them. We prefer to speak of the *Inversion Principle.* The wide application of its use will become evident as we proceed. It is possible to try to make subtle distinctions between "poetry," "heightened prose," "rhetorical prose," "nonpoetic parallelism," and the like. Obviously, "poetry" is what a given people using the word in a certain culture understand as poetry. The structures we intend to examine can be called *patterned semantic relationships.* They are at least this. Some of the material we shall examine has long been identified as poetry, some not. The material to be analyzed can be understood to fall into four basic *types,* some of which are clearly prose, others are perhaps better understood as poetry. It is to these four types that we now turn.

FOUR TYPES OF LITERARY STRUCTURES IN THE NEW TESTAMENT

Briefly stated these four are as follows:

a. Longer or shorter sections of prose that use the inversion principle for an outline.

b. Poetic sections that use a variety of parallelistic devices in a variety of forms (we have identified seven).

c. Sections that have a tight parallelism in the center but are encased with one or more sets of matching sections of prose.

d. The parables in Luke usually follow a *Parabolic Ballad* form that is distinct from the above.

Part of the complexity of this subject is because the above four are not used in isolation from one another. An author may mix his literary types and may well have done so unconsciously. Here we can only attempt a preliminary analysis with the full knowledge that much is yet to be done before these types and forms are fully understood in the New Testament. To the first of these types we now turn.

TYPE A–Prose Sections That Use Inversion as an Overall Outline

This type is perhaps the most common, and the most universal.[27] But not only in

---

[27]Miesner has fully documented the use of literary structure in classical Greek and Latin literature. Cf.

the ancient world was the inversion principle at work. Two young men today carry out the following conversation:

The Dialog

A   Are you coming to the party?
B   Can I bring a friend?
A   Boy or girl?
B   What difference does it make?
A   It is a matter of balance.
B   Girl.
A   O.K.
B   I'll be there.[28]

The Dialog with
the Inversion Showing

A   Are you coming to the party?
  B   Can I bring a friend?
    C   Boy or girl?
      D   What difference does it make?
      D'   It is a matter of balance.
    C'   Girl.
  B'   O.K.
A'   I'll be there.

Unknown to either young man, they asked four questions and then answered them in an inverted fashion. The literary structure of the discourse is A B C D—D' C' B' A'. A fascinating number of such illustrations have come to my attention and demonstrate that the use of the inversion principle is relatively universal and often subconscious. Thus as we find these in biblical literature the question must always be asked whether the inversion is deliberate. The question is of some significance. When a biblical author is using the inversion principle deliberately he often places the climax in the center. Usually he reinforces this climax by relating it specifically to the beginning and end of the structure. Usually there is a "point of turning" just past the center of the structure. The second half is not redundant. Rather it introduces some crucial new element that resolves or completes the first half. When the inversion principle is used with conscious precision most, if not all, of these elements appear and are crucial for a proper interpretation of the passage. In the little conversation given above, speaker A wants to know if his friend is

---

Chiasm and Paul, 60–69. Worthy of special note are George E. Duckworth, *Structural Patterns and Proportions in Vergil's Aeneid: A Study in Mathematical Composition* (Ann Arbor: University of Michigan Press, 1962); R. B. Steele, "Chiasmus in the Epistles of Cicero, Seneca, Pliny and Fronto," *Studies in Honor of Basil L. Gildersleeve* (Baltimore: Johns Hopkins Press, 1902), 339–352; C. H. Whitman, *Homer and the Heroic Tradition* (Cambridge, Mass.: Harvard University Press, 1958).
[28]E. A. Schegloff, "Notes on a Conversational Practice," *Studies in Social Interaction,* ed. D. Sudnow (New York: The Free Press, 1972), 78f.

coming, thus the beginning and the end are crucial for him. But speaker B is trying to communicate, "If I can bring my girlfriend, I'll come." The center of the structure is secondary for both speakers. However, in cases we shall examine, the specific features listed above will be seen prominently. What then of biblical literature?

In Daniel we can observe a clear case of our Type A—a prose inversion. The major features that repeat are as follows:

Daniel 3:13–30

The king in anger commands that SMA[29] be brought in

> Serve my God or you will be punished
> Who is the God who will deliver you

>> The God we serve will deliver us from the king
>> We will not serve or worship the golden image

>>> The fire is heated seven times

>>>> The king orders SMA bound and cast into the fire
>>>> SMA are bound and cast into the fire

>>>>> the king asks about three men bound in the fire

>>>>> the king sees four men loose in the fire
>>>>> one like a son of man

>>>> The king orders SMA to come out
>>>> SMA come out

>>> The fire did not touch them

>> The God of SMA delivered his servants from the king
>> They did not serve or worship any God except God

> Speak against the God of SMA and you will be punished
> There is no other god who can deliver in this way

The king promotes SMA in Babylon.

The use of the inversion principle is clear. The material seems to be straightforward prose. The climax is obviously the center.[30]

Barbara Thiering has observed this use of the inversion principle in the *Hodayoth* of Qumran. A clear example is in 9:29b–36b. Its structure is:

---

[29]SMA is an abbreviation for Shadrach, Meshak, and Abednego. It may be significant that there are precisely twelve full repetitions of the three names.

[30]The inversion principle has been found by Stephen Bertram to have been used in the construction of the entire book of Ruth. Cf. Stephen Bertram, "Symmetrical Design in the Book of Ruth," *JBL* 84 (1965), 165–68. A significant number of other OT passages using the inversion principle have been brought to my attention; some of the studies are as yet unpublished. In Tertullian the inversion principle has been discovered to cover entire books. Cf. R. D. Sider, "On Symmetrical Composition in Tertullian," *JTS* 24 (1973), 403–423.

Because thou hast known me from my father
and from the womb (   )[31]
(   ) my mother thou hast dealt kindly with me
from the breasts of the one conceiving me are thy mercies
and from the lap of the one rearing me (   )

> And from my youth thou hast illuminated me
> with the wisdom of thy judgments

>> and with certain truth thou hast upheld me
>> and with thy holy spirit thou hast delighted me
>> and (   ) till this day
>> and the rebuke of thy righteousness with (   )
>> and thy guiding peace delivers my soul
>> and with my steps the abundance of forgiveness
>> and infinite mercy with thy judgments of me

> and until I am old
> thou takest care of me

for my father knew me not
and my mother to thee abandoned me
for thou art a father to all the sons of thy youth
and thou rejoicest in them as the one who conceives loves her babe
and as a foster father in the lap thou carest for all thy creatures.[32]

In this translation we have followed Thiering's format. However, the first and the last stanzas are in almost perfectly balanced step parallelism. The first has:

> my father
>> the womb
>>> my mother
>>>> the one conceiving
>>>>> the lap.

The last has:

> my father
>> my mother
>>> a father
>>>> the one conceiving
>>>>> the lap.

Moving to the New Testament, a clear case of Type A is Luke 18:18–30:

1   A certain ruler asked him,   ETERNAL LIFE
> "Good teacher, what having done I shall inherit *eternal life*?"

  2   And Jesus said to him,
> "Why do you call me good?
>> No one is good but one, even God.

---

[31]These blank spaces are meant to indicate lacunas in the text.
[32]Barbara Thiering, "The Poetic Forms of the Hodayoth," *JSS* 8 (1963), 191; my translation.

You know the commandments:

Do not commit adultery	7	(loyalty to family)	
Do not kill	6		THE
Do not steal	8	(property)	OLD OBEDIENCE
Do not bear false witness	9		—fulfilled
Honor your father and mother.''	5	(loyalty to parents)	

And he said,
"All these I have observed from my youth."

3   And hearing Jesus said to him,
      "One thing you still lack.
      Sell everything you have
      and distribute to the poor
      and you will have treasure in heaven
      and come and follow me."

THE NEW OBEDIENCE
—demanded (the ruler)

4   And hearing this
      he became deeply grieved
      for he was very rich.

NEW OBEDIENCE
—too hard

5   And seeing him Jesus said,
      "How hard it is
        for those who have possessions
          to *enter the kingdom of God.*
      It is easier for a camel to go through a needle's eye
      than for a rich man
        to *enter the kingdom of God.*"

ENTER THE
KINGDOM

4'   And those who heard said,
      "And who is able to be saved?"
      But he said, "What is impossible with men
        is possible with God."

NEW OBEDIENCE
—too hard
—possible only
    with God

3'   And Peter said,
      "Lo, we have *left everything we possess*
        and *followed you.*"

THE NEW OBEDIENCE
—fulfilled (disciples)

2'   And he said to them,
      "Truly I say to you
      there is no one who has left

house	(property)	
or wife	(loyalty to family)	NEW OBEDIENCE
or brothers	(loyalty to family)	—fulfilled (any man)
or parents	(loyalty to parents)	
or children	(loyalty to family)	

      for the sake of the kingdom

1' who will not receive much more in this time
    and in the age to come—*eternal life.*"

ETERNAL LIFE

Here the material is clearly organized by use of the inversion principle. The question of eternal life occurs in stanza 1 and is repeated in stanza 1'. In stanza 2 five of the Ten Commandments have been selected but are rearranged so as to have "loyalty to family" at the top of the list and "loyalty to parents" at the bottom with the question of "property" in the center. In 2' there is also a list of five items all of which discuss the three topics singled out for attention by a special arrangement in stanza 2. The two demands required of the ruler in 3 are met by the disciples in 3'. Both the ruler (4) and the bystanders (4') find this too demanding. The parable (utilizing step parallelism) occurs in the climactic center. Obviously "inherit eternal life" (1 and 1') is identical to "enter the kingdom of God" (5). Thus a short parable is placed in the center of what we have preferred to call a "theological mosaic" constructed around the inversion principle.

In Galatians 3:5–14 the following use of the inversion principle is observable:

Galatians 3:5–14

A   Therefore he who supplies *the Spirit to you* and works miracles among you,
  is it by works of the law or *by hearing with faith?*
  Thus Abraham *"believed God,* and it was reckoned to him as *righteousness."*

  B   So you see that *it is men of faith* who are the *sons of Abraham.*
    And the Scripture, forseeing that God would *justify the gentiles* by faith
      preached the gospel beforehand to *Abraham.*
    In thee shall *all the gentiles be blessed.*
    So then, those *who are men of faith* are *blessed with Abraham* who had faith.

    C   For all who rely on works of the law are under a *curse*
      for it is written, *"Cursed* be everyone who does not abide
      by all the things written in the book of the law, and do them."

      D   For it is evident that no man is justified before God
        by *the law*

        E   because, *"He who through faith is righteous shall live."*

      D'   And *the law* does not rest on faith
        but "He who does them shall live by them."

    C'   Christ redeemed us from the *curse* of the law
      having become a *curse* for us
      for it is written, *"Cursed* is every one who hangs on a tree."

  B'   That to the *gentiles*
    the *blessing of Abraham*
    might come in Jesus Christ

A'   that the *promise of the Spirit*[33]
  we might receive through faith.

The parallels in the above inversion are as follows:

_____

[33]This structure is slightly revised from John Bligh, *Galatians in Greek,* 34. Bligh has found the inversion principle all through the book of Galatians. As with Lund, each piece of evidence must be examined on its own merits.

```
A    Spirit, faith, righteousness
  B     Gentiles, blessing of Abraham
    C     Curse
      D     Law
        E     Righteousness by faith
      D'    Law
    C'    Curse (Christ)
  B'    Gentiles, blessing of Abraham (Christ)
A'   Spirit, faith, promise.
```

All the parallels are strong and unmistakable. The climax is in the center. The center is related theologically to the beginning and the end. This is particularly clear when the two quotes in A and E are compared. The second half introduces Christ, who is the significant missing element in the first half. Unit B is internally inverted, again with the center (Abraham) repeated at the outside.

Turning to one of the later books of the New Testament, the same Form A can be found in 2 Peter 3:8–18. The structure is as follows:

2 Peter 3:8–18

1   *Do not let this one fact escape you, beloved*
    that with *the Lord one day* is as a *thousand* years
    and a *thousand years* as *one day.*

  2   He is not slow, *the Lord* of *the promise,* as some *count* slowness
      but he is *forbearing* toward you.

    3   He is not wishing that any should perish
        but that all should reach repentance.

      4   The *Day of the Lord* will come like a thief.
         Then *the heavens will pass away with a loud noise*
         and *the elements will be dissolved with fire*
         and *the earth and the works that are upon it* will be burned up.

        5   Since all these things are thus to be dissolved
           what sort of persons ought you to be in lives of holiness and
             godliness

      4'   waiting for the hastening, the coming of the *Day of God*
         because of which the heavens will be kindled and dissolved
         and *the elements will melt with fire*
         and a new heaven and *a new earth we await according to his promise*
         in which righteousness dwells.

    3'   Therefore beloved, since you wait for these things
      be zealous to be found by him without spot or blemish and in peace.

  2'   And the *forbearance* of *our Lord*
    count it as *salvation.*

    (So also our beloved brother Paul wrote to you according to the wisdom
    given him, speaking of this as he does in all his letters. There are some

things in them hard to understand which the ignorant and unstable twist to
their own destruction as they do the other scriptures.)[34]

1'   You therefore *beloved, knowing* this beforehand
      beware lest you be carried away with the error of lawless men and lose your
          own stability
      and *grow in the grace and knowledge of Our Lord and Savior Jesus Christ*
      to him be the glory both now and *to the day of eternity.* Amen.

The structure climaxes again in the center, where the reader is told (in the
1st line) that what has been described will be dissolved and that thus (the 2nd line)
he should live in holiness and godliness. This admonition to a godly life recurs in 3'
and at the end of the structure in 1'. The addition of ethical specifics is the new
feature of the second half.

The question as to whether these structures are conscious or unconscious
has not been resolved. In the case of Luke 18, where the order of the laws selected
from the Decalog has been rearranged for discernible purposes and divergent
material brought together to create the "theological mosaic," it seems clear that
the use of the inversion principle was conscious and deliberate. In the Galatians
passage, the selection of passages from the Old Testament and their arrangement in
a special order also makes the inversion almost certainly deliberate. The Second
Peter structure and the example from Daniel are more open to the possibility of
being unconscious uses of inversion.

TYPE B—Seven Poetical[35] Forms Using a Variety of Parallelistic Combinations

Before we illustrate the different forms of parallelistic structures, for clarity's sake
we will first define the forms to be discussed. The seven fall into three categories:
forms with one stanza;[36] forms with two stanzas; forms with three or more stanzas.
The forms will be labeled and defined as follows:

With one stanza:

Form I: Parallelisms formed into a single stanza that inverts single words or brief
             phrases.

Form II: Parallelisms formed into a single stanza that inverts clauses, full
             sentences, or double lines.

Form III: Parallelisms formed into a single stanza by the use of step parallelism.

---

[34]This long comment about Paul, perhaps a later gloss, has little to do with the rest of the passage and
could just as easily have appeared almost anywhere in the entire book of Second Peter.

[35]We are using the word "poetry" here rather loosely. When the parallelism between matching lines is
as precise as that found in the poetic sections of the Old Testament or that found in the *Hodayoth* of
Qumran, we choose to call it poetry. It may well be "parallelistic prose" and could be called "artistic
prose," among other things. By the word "poetry" in this section we intend to indicate a multiplicity of
correspondences and a precision in those correspondences not found in the other types.

[36]By "stanza" we intend a series of correspondences that together complete an idea or balance out a
known literary form.

With two stanzas:

> *Form IV:* A poem with two stanzas in which the second stanza is a parallel repetition of the first.

> *Form V:* A poem with two stanzas in which the second stanza begins with the theme appearing at the center of the first stanza.

With three stanzas:

> *Form VI:* Parallelisms formed into three stanzas in which the third stanza is parallel in some way to the first and the center is extended to a stanza by itself.

> *Form VII:* A parallelistic structure of three or more stanzas in which a number of the above types are combined.

Examples of each of these forms will now be examined.[37]

Form I (A Single Stanza that Inverts Single Words or Brief Phrases)

Examples of Form I are as follows:

Amos 5:24

> Let-roll-down
>> like-waters
>>> justice
>>>> and righteousness
>> like-a-stream
> ever-flowing.

Amos 5:7

> The-one-who-turns
>> to wormwood
>>> justice
>>>> and righteousness
>> to-the-earth
> casts-down.

---

[37]The supreme significance of poetry for an oral-tradition community is discussed by Nicholson, who quotes Ibn Rashiq's comment on the poet: "A poet was a defense to the honor of them all, a weapon to ward off insult from their good name, a means of perpetuating their glorious deeds and of establishing their fame forever." Cf. R. A. Nicholson, *A Literary History of the Arabs* (Cambridge: University Press, 1962), xxii. It is well known that every period of the literary history of the Bible was significantly represented by poetry. This extends into the intertestamental period with the Qumran literature. Kraft writes of the importance of the Qumran Thanksgiving Psalms "for an understanding of what New Testament writers regarded as poetry." Cf. C. F. Kraft, "Poetic Structure of the Qumran Thanksgiving Psalms," *Biblical Research* 2 (1957), 16. Seale, *The Desert Bible,* describes graphically what poetry means to an oral-tradition community; cf. pp. 18–23.

An illustration of the inversion of phrases is Amos 5:14–15a.

1   Seek-good
  2   and-not-evil
    3   that you-may-live
      4   and-he-will-be Yahweh
      4'   God-of Hosts
    3'   with-you as-you-said
  2'   hate evil
1'   and-love-good.

The theme of "Good" is placed at the outside and "God" at the center.

Note also Isaiah 60:1–3.

1   *Arise*
  2   shine
    3   because it-has-come your-light
      4   and-the-glory
        5   of-Yahweh
          6   upon-you *has-risen*
            7   for-behold darkness shall-cover the-earth
            7'   and-thick darkness the-people
          6'   and-upon you *shall-arise*
        5'   Yahweh
      4'   and-his-glory upon-you shall-be seen
    3'   and-they-shall-come the-gentiles to-your-light
  2'   and-kings to-the-brightness
1'   *of-your-rising.*[38]

Each of the seven semantic units is repeated in the second half of the poem in inverted order. The focus in the center of the structure is "darkness" (7 and 7'). This is encased in an envelope of "resurrection" (6 and 6'). The theme of resurrection is repeated for special emphasis on the outside.

A mixing of words and clauses is seen in 9:9b–10b of the *Hodayoth,* which has the following structure:

For I-know thy-truth
  And I-choose
    A-judgment-of-me
    And in-scourging-of-me
  I-delight
For I-hope in-thy-grace.[39]

This same mixing is demonstrated by Paul in Romans 10:8–10.

1   *This is the word of faith which we preach*
  2   "If you confess

---

[38]Cf. Lund, *Chiasmus,* 44.

[39]Thiering, *JSS* 8, 204; my translation. She provides a series of illustrations of this form.

```
3   with your mouth
  4   'Jesus is Lord'
    5   and believe
      6   in your heart
        7   'God raised him from the dead'
        7'   you will be saved''
      6'   for with the heart
    5'   one believes
  4'   unto righteousness
3'   and with the mouth
2'   confesses
1'   unto salvation.
```

The theme of salvation appears in 7' and 1'.

The well-known opening to John's Gospel is a Form I and appears as follows:

```
1   In the beginning
  2   was
    3   the word
      4   and the word
        5   was
          6   with God
          6'   and God
        5'   was
      4'   the word.
    3'   This one
  2'   was
1'   in the beginning with God.⁴⁰
```

The last line summarizes the beginning and the middle.

---

⁴⁰N. W. Lund, "The Influence of Chiasmus upon the Structure of the Gospels," *ATR* 13 (1931), 42:

As we indicated above (cf. n. 25) we have space here only to point out what appears to be the dominant literary structure. Yet it is significant to observe in this simple stanza two literary structures at work together reinforcing one another. The same stanza can be seen as follows:

```
1   In the beginning
  2   was
    3   the word
    3'   and the word
  2'   was
1'   with God
1   and God
  2   was
    3   the word.
    3'   This one
  2'   was
1'   in the beginning with God.
```

Form II (One Stanza with Full Clauses, Sentences, or Double Lines)

This is perhaps the most important of all these parallelistic forms. Below are five representative examples:

Amos 9:1–4

   A   Strike the-capitals until the-doorjambs shake
         breaking-them on-the-heads-of all-of-them

      B   and-the-remainder with-the-*sword*
            I-will-slay

         C   shall-not-*flee-away* among-them the-one-who-flees
             and-shall-not-escape among-them an-escaper

            D   if-they-dig *to-Sheol*
                from-there my-hand shall-take-them

               E   and-if they-*climb-up to-the-heavens*
                   from-there I-will-bring-them-down

               E′   and-if they-*hide on-the-peak-of Carmel*
                   from-there I-will-search-them-out to-take-them

             D′   and-if they-hide from-before my-eye *in-the-bottom-of the-sea*
                from-there I-shall-command the-serpent and-it-shall-bite-them

         C′   and-if-they-*go into-captivity*
             before-the-face-of their-enemies

      B′   from-there I-shall-command *the-sword*
         and-it-shall-slay-them

   A′   and-I-have-set my-eyes on-them
      for-evil and-not for-good.[41]

The semantic parallels are as follows:

   God brings judgment
     the *sword*
        no escape *away*
           no escape *down*
              no escape *up*
              no escape *up*
           no escape *down*
        no escape *away*
     the *sword*
   God brings judgment

This same use of two structures on the same lines reinforcing each other we will observe below in much greater complexity in Acts 2:23–36; cf. pp. 80–82.

[41]Revised from Lund, *Chiasmus*, 86f.

In this poetic structure there seems to be no turning point at center, yet the center is still the climax. There is no escape, *not even in heaven.*

Psalm 89:28–37

My mercy will I *keep* for him *forevermore*   KEPT FOREVERMORE
and my covenant shall stand fast with him.

His seed also will I make to *endure* forever
and *his throne* as the days of heaven.   HIS SEED, THRONE, ENDURE

If *his children* forsake my law   DAVID'S CHILDREN
and walk not in my judgments

if they *break my statutes*   THEY BREAK—STATUTES
and keep not my commandments

then will I visit their transgression *with the rod*   JUDGMENT
and their iniquity *with stripes*.

Yet my mercy will I not utterly take from him   MERCY
not prove false in my truth.

My covenant will I not break   I BREAK NOT—COVENANT
not after the thing that is gone out of my lips.

Once I have sworn by my holiness   DAVID
unto David will I not lie.

His seed shall endure forever
and *his throne as the sun before me.*   HIS SEED, THRONE, ENDURE

*It shall be established forevermore as the moon
and the witness in the sky standeth fast.*[42]   ESTABLISHED FOREVERMORE

The climax of judgment and mercy is powerfully reinforced by the inversion. Mercy also opens the poem. The point of turning occurs as usual just past center with the word "Yet."

The same form but with seven units occurs in Matthew 13:13–18 as follows:

Therefore I speak to them in parables,

1   because seeing *they see not*
and hearing *they hear not,* nor understand.

2   And *it is fulfilled to them*
the *prophecy* of Isaiah which says,

3   "Hearing *you shall hear*
and shall *not understand*

4   and seeing *you shall see*
and shall *not perceive.*

5   For this people's *heart* is become dull

---

[42]Cf. John Forbes, *The Symmetrical Structure of Scripture* (Edinburgh: T. & T. Clark, 1854), 40.

6   and the *ears* are dull of hearing

   7   and their *eyes* they have closed
   7'   lest they should perceive with the *eyes*

6'   and hear with the *ear*

5'   and understand with the *heart,* and should turn again
   and I should heal them.''

4'   But blessed are *your eyes*
   for they see

3'   and *your ears*
   for *they hear.*

2'   For truly *I say unto you*
   that many *prophets* and righteous men

1'   desired to see what *you see,* and *did not see*
   and to hear what *you hear,* and *did not hear.*[43]

A striking example of the use of inverted parallelism is in John 5:24–29:

Truly, truly I say to you,

He who *hears my word and believes* him who sent me
   he has *eternal life*   LIFE
he does not come to *judgment*
   but he has *passed from death to life.*   JUDGMENT

   Truly, truly I say to you
     the *hour is coming* and now is
       when *the dead will hear the voice of the Son of God*
       and *those who hear will live.*

       For as the Father has *life* in himself
         so he has granted the son also to have *life* in himself   LIFE
         and has given him authority *to execute judgment*   JUDGMENT
         because he is the Son of man.

   Do not marvel at this
     for *the hour is coming*
       when all *those in the tombs will hear his voice*
       and *they will come forth*

those who *have done good*
   to the *resurrection of life*   LIFE
those who have *done evil*
   to the *resurrection of judgment.*[44]   JUDGMENT

---

[43]Revised from Lund, *Chiasmus,* 233f. The author seems to have begun with the text from Isaiah. This text already had the Heart—Ears—Eyes = Eyes—Ears—Heart inversion in it. The new author adds 4' and 3' to balance the remaining sections of the OT quote and then extends the stanza to seven by adding 1 and 2 to the beginning and matching it with 2' and 1' at the end.

[44]This five-stanza poem was first noted by John Forbes, *Symmetrical Structure,* 69. Quite independently the identical structure was discovered by Lucy Brown, my former student at the Near East School of Theology, Beirut, Lebanon. A remarkable aspect of this particular structure is that the first

One of the most remarkable poetic structures in all of the New Testament is Ephesians 2:11–22. Jews and Gentiles in the flesh form the first two stanzas. Jews and Gentiles in the spirit form the last two. The center three stanzas have a threefold repetition of the ''two becoming one.'' The structure is as follows:

Therefore remember

1	that then you *the Gentiles **in the flesh*** the ones *called uncircumcised*	GENTILES (IN THE FLESH)
2	by those *called circumcised* which is *made **in the flesh** by hands*	JEWS (IN THE FLESH)

     3   that you were once *separated from Christ*
            alienated from the citizenship of Israel
            strangers to the covenants of promise

        4   having *no hope*
            and *without God **in the world.***

           5   But now in Christ Jesus *you who were once afar off*
               have been brought near in the blood of Christ.

              6   For *he is our peace*
                   who *has made **the two one***
                   and *has destroyed the dividing wall of hostility in his body*

                 7   abolishing the law of commandments and ordinances
                      that ***of the two** he might create* in himself **one new man**

              6'   *so making peace*
                  *reconciling **the two in one body*** to God through the cross
                  bringing the hostility to an end in it.

           5'   And he came and preached peace *to you who were far off*
               and peace *to those who were near*

        4'   for through him we both have *access*
            ***in one spirit** to the Father.*

      3'   *So then you are no longer strangers and sojourners*
           but *you are fellow citizens with the saints*
           and *members of the household of God*

2'	built upon the foundation *of the Apostles and Prophets* (Jesus Christ himself being the chief cornerstone in whom the whole structure is joined together) and growing into a holy temple **in the Lord**	JEWS (IN THE LORD)
1'	into which *you are* also built for *a dwelling place of God **in the spirit.***	GENTILES (IN THE SPIRIT)

Stanza 3 matches 3' with inverted parallelism,[45] the rest are step parallelisms. One additional comment in 2' brings this hymn into line with 1 Corinthians 3:11.

---

two stanzas are *realized eschatology*. The judgment has *passed* and the hour is *now* for the dead to hear the voice. In the last two stanzas we have a balancing *futuristic eschatology*.

[45]This set of six lines could be read as three separate units and not as one unit. We have kept the above

Form III (One Stanza Using Step Parallelism Rather Than Inverted Parallelism)

A clear example of this is Isaiah 55:10–11, which is structured as follows:

A   For as-it-comes-down the-rain and-the-snow from-the-heavens
  B   and-there returns-not but-waters the-earth
    C   causing-it-to-give-birth and-causing-it-to-sprout
      D   and-giving seed to-the-sower and-bread to-the-eater

A'   So shall-be my-word which goes-forth from-my-mouth
  B'   it shall-not-return to-me empty
    C'   for it-shall-accomplish that-which I-requested
      D'   and-succeed in-that for-which I-sent-it.

A New Testament example is Luke 6:20–26:

1   *Blessed* are the poor
  for yours is the kingdom of God

  2   *Blessed* are those now hungry
    for you shall be satisfied

    3   *Blessed* are those that weep now
      for you shall laugh

      4   *Blessed* are you when men hate you
(and when they exclude you and revile you, and cast out your name as evil, on account of the Son of man. Rejoice in that day, and leap for joy, for your reward is great in heaven)[46]
      for so their fathers did to the prophets.

1'   But *woe* to you that are rich
  for you have received your consolation

  2'   *Woe* to you that are full now
    for you shall hunger

    3'   *Woe* to you that laugh now
      for you shall mourn

      4'   *Woe* to you when all men speak well of you
        for so their fathers did to the false prophets.

---

form because the author all through this literary piece seems to be working with two- and three-line units.

[46]The long expansion in unit 4 is not artless. There are seven phrases. Three negatives are followed by a reference to the Son of man, which is then balanced by three positive phrases. Thus a single couplet has been expanded to form a stanza in itself. Freedman has noticed the same phenomenon in some OT parallelisms. Cf. David N. Freedman, Prolegomenon to G. B. Gray, *The Forms of Hebrew Poetry* (New York: Ktav, 1972 [1915]), XXXVI. Freedman writes, "It is as though the poet deliberately split a bicolon or couplet, and inserted a variety of materials between the opening and closing halves of that unit to form a stanza."

Form IV (Two Stanzas, the Second Parallel to the First)

This form is much rarer, especially in the New Testament. Two examples will suffice to illustrate its presence.

Acts 4:8–12

I   *Text*   *unifying themes*

A   Rulers of the people   (You rulers)
     and elders of Israel

  B   if we are being examined today   (A man—whole)
       concerning a good deed to a cripple

  B'   by what means
       this man has been saved   (How saved?)

A'   be it known to you all
     and to all the people of Israel   (All the people—know)

II

A   by the name of Jesus Christ of Nazareth whom you crucified
     whom God raised from the dead(By name of Jesus—you killed, God raised)

  B   by him this man is standing before you—whole.(By Jesus—a man whole)

    C   This is "the stone which was rejected (by you) builders(You rejected)
         which has become the head of the corner"   (Exaltation)

  B'   and there is not in anyone else—salvation   (Only by Jesus—salvation)

A'   for there is no other name under heaven given among men
     by which we must be saved.   (By name of Jesus—we must be saved)

Major relationships between stanzas

I   A   You rulers
     B   A man whole
     B'   Salvation
     A'   *All* the people

II   A   You crucified
     B   A man whole
     B'   Salvation
     A'   *We* must be saved

The second passage chosen to illustrate Form IV, Acts 2:23–26, is much more sophisticated. It is actually a "counterpoint form." The material matches in a 1–10, 10–1 pattern as well as 1–5 5–1, 1–5 5–1. We will observe the overall 1–10 first:

A   *This one* (Jesus) . . . *you crucified and killed*

  B   but *God raised him up,* having loosed the pangs of death
       (because it was not possible for him to be held by it).

    C   David says, "I saw the Lord always before me, for he is at my right hand. . . ."

       MEN, BROTHERS, IT IS NECESSARY TO SPEAK TO YOU BOLDLY

      D   that the patriarch David died and was buried
          (and his tomb is with us to this day).

        E   *Being therefore a prophet, and knowing*

          F   *that God had sworn with an oath to him*

            G   that he would set one of his descendants upon his throne

              H   *he foresaw and spoke*

                I   of the *resurrection of the Christ*

                  J   that *he was not abandoned to Hades*

                  J'   *nor did his flesh see corruption.*

                I'   *This Jesus God raised up*

              H'   of that *we are all witnesses.*

            G'   Being therefore exalted at the right hand of God

          F'   *having received from the Father the promise of the Holy Spirit*

        E'   *he has poured out this which you see and hear.*

      D'   For David did not ascend into the heavens

    C'   but he himself says, "The Lord said to my Lord, Sit at my right hand. . . ."

       ASSUREDLY THEREFORE LET ALL THE HOUSE OF ISRAEL KNOW

  B'   that *God has made him Lord and Christ*

A'   *this Jesus whom you crucified.*

    Lines A and A' are on the theme of *crucifixion.* Lines B and B' combine on *resurrection.* Lines C and C' are quotations from David. Both mention *my right hand.* In both halves of the structure, immediately after the quotation from David, there is a vocative address directed to the audience. Each address is composed of three semantic units. In the second these are reversed. This can be seen as follows:

MEN, BROTHERS   IT IS NECESSARY TO SPEAK   BOLDLY TO YOU

ASSUREDLY THEREFORE   LET THEM KNOW   ALL THE HOUSE OF ISRAEL

Or, to state it in another way, the first vocative address is put in different words, reversed, and placed in the corresponding position in the second half of the structure.[47] Lines D and D' refer to the fact that David did not ascend but died and was buried. E and E' are semantically somewhat weaker or perhaps just more subtle. Line E refers to the prophet who knew. Line E' tells the listeners that they *see and hear,* that is, that they also *know.* In line F, God makes a promise. In line F', he fulfills a promise. G and G' discuss *enthronement.* H and H' speak of

---

[47]This vocative address ties the hymn to a specific historical setting. Without it the hymn could be put into any context where an apostle was addressing Jews. Because this pair of vocatives are not a part of the discussion we have chosen not to give them identifying letters.

witness, the prophetic and the apostolic. I and I' return to the theme of the *resurrection.* J and J' are on the *death* of Christ.

This hymn has a series of expansions. The first is the apparent interpolation of "delivered up according to the definite plan and foreknowledge of God by the hands of lawless men," which appears in line A. Most of this interpolation occurs in the speech in Acts 4:28. Line B is expanded with "because it was not possible for him to be held by it," and line D is expanded with "and his tomb is with us to this day." Both of these last appear to be explanations of the text. They could be antiphonal responses. Yet they sound more homiletical than liturgical. The two quotations from David have expanded far beyond the balancing phrase, "my right hand." The first one is clearly a later expansion in that part of it appears in the poem itself in lines J and J'. In all, there are five expansions of the original poem.[48]

At the same time the same lines form two matching stanzas. This can be seen as follows:

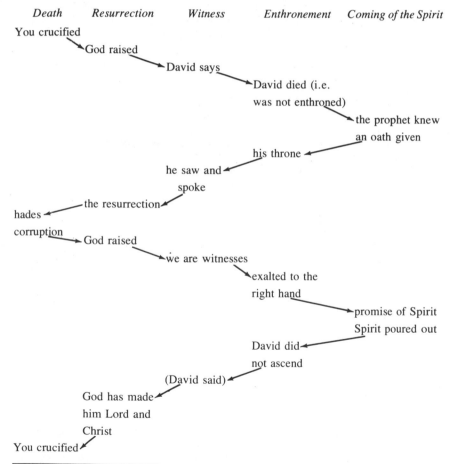

| *Death* | *Resurrection* | *Witness* | *Enthronement* | *Coming of the Spirit* |

You crucified

God raised

David says

David died (i.e. was not enthroned)

the prophet knew an oath given

his throne

he saw and spoke

the resurrection

hades

corruption   God raised

we are witnesses

exalted to the right hand

promise of Spirit

Spirit poured out

David did not ascend

(David said)

God has made him Lord and Christ

You crucified

---

[48] These would seem to indicate that the material is much earlier than the date of the composition of the book of Acts. It would also indicate that the poem had had wide use and that the final editor of the

Form V (Two Stanzas with the Center of the First Forming the Outside of the Second)

A clear case of this type is Luke 4:16–20:

A 1   And Jesus returned in the power of the Spirit to Galilee.
        And a report went forth through the whole neighborhood concerning him
            and he taught *in their synagogues*
        Being praised by all.
        And he came to Nazareth, where he had been brought up.

B 1   And he entered (as his custom was on the Sabbath) *into the synagogue*
  2   and he stood up to read
    3   and there was given to him the book of the prophet Isaiah.
      4   And opening the book, he found the place where it was written,
        5   *"The Spirit of the Lord* is upon me, because he has anointed me
          6   *to preach* the good news to the poor.
            7   He has *sent me* to proclaim to the prisoners *freedom*
              8   and to *the blind recovery of sight*
            7'   to *send forth* the oppressed ones in *freedom*
          6'   to *proclaim*
        5'   *the acceptable year of the Lord."*

      4'   And having closed the book
    3'   after giving it back to the attendant,
  2'   he sat down
1'   and the eyes of all *in the synagogue* were fixed on him.

The ideas that repeat are:

He returned—to Galilee
  the whole neighborhood
    in their synagogues
  praised by all
he came—to Nazareth

into the synagogue
  he stood up
    was given to him the book
      opening the book
        the Lord
          to preach
            he has sent me—freedom
              to the blind—*sight*
            to send forth—freedom

---

material either does not recognize the poetic structure (and thus does not restore the poem to its original form) or for some reason chooses not to restore it, or he himself is the author of the expansions. It is difficult to attribute a poem as stylistically perfect as this one to the same hand that expands it and thus destroys that original balance. Answering all these questions is beyond the scope of this study.

> to proclaim
>   the Lord

> closed the book
>   giving it back
> he sat down
> the *eyes* of all *in the synagogue* were on him

"In the synagogue" is the center of stanza 1, and this same theme becomes the beginning and the end of the second stanza. This is the distinctive feature of Form V. Also we observe that the second stanza climaxes on the theme of "opening the eyes," and at the very end of the same stanza the *eyes* are on him.

Form VI (Three Stanzas with the Third Stanza Repetitive of the First

This form will occur twice in the material discussed in the exegetical section. Here we intend only to illustrate that this form is used widely in New Testament Literature. We have selected three examples.

Luke 11:29–32

> This generation is evil, seeking a sign
>   but no sign shall be given to it except the sign of *Jonah*.
> For as Jonah became a sign to the *Ninevites*
>   so will the Son of man be to this generation.
>
>   The queen of the south will arise at the judgment
>   with the men of this generation and judge them.
>   For she came (from the ends of the earth) to hear the wisdom of *Solomon*
>   and behold something greater than *Solomon* is here.
>
> The men of *Nineveh* will arise at the judgment
>   with this generation and judge it.
> For they repented at the preaching of *Jonah*
>   and behold something greater than Jonah is here.

The stanzas are clearly A–B–A with Jonah–Solomon–Jonah.

Romans 11:17–24

> I   But if some of the branches were broken off
>   and you being a wild olive shoot
>   were grafted in their place
>   to share the richness of the olive tree
>   do not boast over the branches
>
>   (if you boast, remember it is not you that support the
>   root, but the root that supports you).
>
> II   Then you say, The branches were broken off
>   so that I might be grafted in.

True, through unbelief they were broken off
you through faith stand fast.

So do not become proud
but fear.

For if God the natural branches did not spare
neither you will be spared.

Note then the kindness and the severity of God
toward the fallen severity, on you the kindness of God

(provided you continue in his kindness
otherwise you too will be cut off).

And even they, if they do not persist in unbelief
will be grafted in

III   for God is able to graft them in again.
For if you have been cut from what is by nature a wild olive
and grafted, contrary to nature
into a cultivated olive tree
how much more these natural branches will be grafted
into their own olive tree.

The outer units are also inverted. They relate to each other as follows:

I	Branches—broken off	III	they—grafted in
	wild olive		wild olive
	grafted in		grafted in
	olive tree		cultivated olive
	branches (broken off)		natural branches—grafted in

The step parallelism is presumably the primary form because the last line of stanza III is reflected in the center of stanza II, not the center line of stanza III. This structure has two bracketed comments. The first is a comment on the question of boasting; the second is a hortatory repetition of the threat of being cut off.

John 16:20–22

Truly, truly, I say to you

I   You will weep and lament
but the world will rejoice.

You will be sorrowful
but your sorrow will turn into joy.

II   *When* a woman is in travail
she has *sorrow*
because her hour has come

but *when* she is delivered of the child
she no longer remembers her *anguish*
for joy that *a child is born* into the world.

III   So you have sorrow now
    but I will see you again

    and your hearts will rejoice
        and no one will take your joy from you.

The "Joy and Sorrow" theme dominates the first and third stanzas, while the second stanza breaks into step parallelism with an illustration that informs both the first and the last. This three-stanza Form VI often occurs in this simple form in the Gospels.

Form VII (Complex Combinations of the Above)

These structures are the most complex and the most controversial. None occurs in the parabolic material under discussion in this study. They can be observed in the work of Bligh, Lund, and Miesner.[49]

In conclusion we have observed seven forms in biblical literature that exhibit precise parallelism in their structure. The Old Testament material has long been called poetry. It is our view that much of the New Testament material which has the same forms also deserves this designation.

TYPE C—Sections That Have a Tight Parallelism in the Center But Are Encased Within One or More Sets of Prose Envelopes

A simple example of this type is Acts 5:1–6, whose structure is as follows:

But a man named Ananias with his wife Sapphira sold a piece of property, and with his wife's knowledge he kept back some of the proceeds, and brought only a part and laid it at the apostles' feet. But Peter said,

A   "Ananias, why has Satan filled your heart
    to lie to the Holy Spirit?
        (and to keep back a part of the proceeds of the land?)[50]

    B   While it remained unsold
       did it not remain your own?

    B   And after it was sold
       was it not under your authority?

A   Why have you contrived this deed in your heart?
    You have not lied to men but to God."

When Ananias heard these words, he fell down and died. And great fear came upon all who heard of it. The young men rose and wrapped him up and carried him out and buried him.

---

[49]Bligh, *Galatians, passim;* Lund, *Chiasmus,* 242–286; Miesner, *Chiasm and Paul,* 97–272. Miesner's work is worthy of special attention.

[50]The correspondences between lines in this center section are extremely tight. For this reason this explanatory aside is bracketed. It has no parallels, and is redundant.

The four couplets are encased within sections of prose. In the example of Luke 18 given above, the central parable of six lines was encased within four sets of prose envelopes. The famous 1 Corinthians 13 has at its beginning and end a discussion of gifts for the church. The four couplets of parallelism quoted above from Luke 21 also fit into this category, as does Acts 26:2–29, where ten couplets of standard parallelism are encased within six matching sets of prose envelopes, and Romans 10:9–10, which is encased in three envelopes.

TYPE D—The Parabolic Ballad[51]

The sayings of Jesus often employ a series of three-line stanzas. An example of this is in Luke 6:32–36:

1   And if you *love* those who love you
        what credit is that to you?
            For even sinners love those who love them.

2   And if you do *good* to those who do good to you
        what credit is that to you?
            For even sinners do the same.

3   And if you *lend* to those from whom you hope to receive
        what credit is that to you?
            Even sinners lend to sinners, to receive as much again.

4   But *love* your enemies
        do *good*
            and *lend* expecting nothing in return
                (and your reward will be great).

The last stanza is a three-line recapitulation of the first three.

An editor close to Matthew with his interest in rewards seems to have gone through Luke, and we find editorial comments on the question of rewards sprinkled through the structured sections of Luke again and again.

Sometimes the parables in Luke fall into step parallelism, at other times inverted parallelism is used. More often they are structured along the lines of three-line stanzas. These stanzas may or may not be inverted. Each stanza introduces a new scene or a significant shift of action. A clear example of this parabolic ballad is found in Luke 10:30–35:

A man was descending from Jerusalem to Jericho:

1 and he fell among *robbers*		COME
and they stripped him and beat him		DO
and departed leaving him half dead.		GO
2 Now by chance a certain *priest* was going down that road		COME

---

[51]John Dominic Crossan in a recent major article ("Parable as Religious and Poetic Experience," *Journal of Religion* 53 [1973], 330–358) has described the parables of Jesus as "poetic metaphors"; cf. pp. 349f. Our "parabolic ballad" can be seen as further evidence for Crossan's thesis.

	and when he saw him	DO
	he passed by on the other side.	GO
3	Likewise a *Levite* when he came to the place	COME
	and saw him	DO
	he passed by on the other side.	GO
4	And a certain Samaritan, traveling, came to him	COME
	and when he saw him	DO
	he had compassion on him.	DO
3'	He went to him	COME
	and bound up his wounds	DO
	and he poured on oil and wine.	DO
2'	Then he put him on his own beast	DO
	and led him to the inn	DO
	and took care of him.	DO
1'	The next day he took out two denarii	DO
	and gave them to the manager saying, "Take care of him	DO
	and whatever more you spend I will repay on my return."	DO

In this case the stanzas are inverted.[52] The priest was of sufficient rank to be known to have been riding, and could have taken the man to the inn. The Levite, being of a lesser rank, might not have been riding, but he could at least have rendered first aid. The Samaritan in the second half reverses the actions of the first three stanzas. It is of particular interest to note the comparison between the first and last stanza:

THE ROBBERS (1)
1. took his money
2. beat him
3. left him half dead (and will not return)

THE SAMARITAN (1')
1. spent his own money
2. cared for him
3. left him cared for and promised to return.

Some of the lines are redundant and apparently included in the story only to fill out the literary form. Note particularly the last line of stanza 2', "and took care of him."[53]

---

[52]Crossan has also observed the use of inversion in this parable. Cf. *In Parables,* 62. However, he has not observed the precise nature of the Samaritan's actions in compensating for all who came before him. The suggestion that the priest was riding an animal may be too speculative. If this is rejected we would have simple 1–2,2–3–2',2'–1'. That is, the Samaritan carries out two distinct acts. He *renders first aid* and *transports* the man to the inn. These two actions can be read as matching the two religious leaders who should have rendered aid (without the inversion of 2–3–3'–2'). Either way the parabolic ballad form is intact.

[53]Here in Luke 10:25–37 not only is the parable very carefully structured but the dialog between Jesus and the lawyer has the following form:

This parabolic ballad structure (Type D) will occur in a number of the parables under discussion in this study.

SUMMARY AND CONCLUSIONS

We have observed in the New Testament and elsewhere four types of literary structures. One of them (Type B) uses carefully balanced parallelisms and is found in seven different forms. The fourth (Type D) is a ballad type more suitable for storytelling. When the author is using a literary structure the discovery of that structure is found to be crucial for exegesis for several reasons. The structure may:

1. identify the climactic center;

2. show how the author is relating the center to the outside;

3. make clear the turning point of the passage and alert the reader to look for a significant shift of emphasis in the second half;

4. provide a crucial key to understanding by enabling the reader to see what words, phrases, or sentences are matched with what other words, phrases, or sentences in the structure;

5. demonstrate where newer material has been fitted into an older piece of literature;

Round One

Lawyer–Question 1   *"What must I do to inherit eternal life?"*

    Jesus–Question 2   "What about the law?"

    Lawyer–Answer 2   "Love God and your neighbor."

Jesus–Answer 1   *"Do this and live."*

Round Two

Lawyer–Question 1   "Who is my neighbor?"

    Jesus–The parable of the Good Samaritan

        Question 2   "Which of these three became a neighbor?"

    Lawyer–Answer 2   "The one who showed mercy on him."

Jesus–Answer 1   "Do and keep on doing this."

Again this takes us beyond the topic of this chapter. This is a dialog structure that we have not discussed. We note it only because it is a further illustration of the use of the inversion principle. A full interpretation of the parable in its Lucan setting must take into account the structure not only of the parable itself but of the dialog. Crossan (*In Parables*, 61) has observed the general form but has not noted the inversion at work within it.

6. mark off the literary unit itself with clarity (the beginning and the end are usually distinct and thus the unit is identified);

7. provide crucial evidence for textual problems.

8. The parabolic ballad literary type opens new doors for understanding the parables, and a range of New Testament problems related to them.[54]

---

[54]Miesner succinctly identifies the function of chiasm as fourfold, "Memory, beauty, meaning and textual considerations" (Miesner, *Chiasm and Paul*, 44).

AN ANALYSIS
OF FOUR PARABLES
AND TWO POEMS IN THE
TRAVEL NARRATIVE
OF LUKE

Chapter 4

THE LITERARY OUTLINE
OF THE TRAVEL NARRATIVE
(JERUSALEM DOCUMENT): LUKE 9:51–19:48

All the biblical passages selected for this study fall in the so-called Lucan Travel Narrative. The Narrative itself has a very precise literary outline that aids significantly in determining the divisions between units of the tradition and in identifying the main subject of each unit. For these reasons the structure of the Travel Narrative must be examined.

In this section we will attempt to demonstrate that 90 percent of the material in the Travel Narrative of Luke has a carefully constructed inverted outline. Some short pieces of tradition do not fit the structure and seem to have been included, usually between sections, on the basis of word association.[1]

Stagg speaks for many scholars when he says of the Travel Narrative, "it is most difficult if not impossible to outline."[2] Evans finds it "completely amorphous."[3] Yet Goulder discovered what he believed to be a "chiastic structure."[4] Our proposal is a revision and extension of Goulder's suggestion. Goulder tried to work all of the material into his structure. Some of it, we are convinced, does not

---

[1] It must be understood that this is intended to be a brief presentation of the literary structure of the Travel Narrative. A full debate with other views on the structure would be a lengthy study in itself. For a discussion and review of recent scholarship on the Travel Narrative, cf. J. H. Davies, "The Purpose of the Central Section of Luke's Gospel," *Studia Evangelica*, II(=*Texte und Untersuchungen*, Band 87), ed. F. L. Cross (Berlin: Akademie-Verlag, 1963), 164–69; Bo Reicke, "Instruction and Discussion in the Travel Narrative," *Studia Evangelica*, I(=*Texte und Untersuchungen*, Band 73), ed. Kurt Aland *et al*. (Berlin: Akademie-Verlag, 1959), 206–216; W. C. Robinson, Jr., "The Theological Context for Interpreting Luke's Travel Narrative (9:51ff.)," *JBL* 79 (1960), 20–31; Frank Stagg, "The Journey Toward Jerusalem in Luke's Gospel," *Review and Expositor* 64 (1967), 499–512; J. Schneider, "Zur Analyse des lukanischen Reiseberichtes," *Synoptische Studien. Alfred Wikenhauser zum siebzigsten Geburtstag* (Munich: Zink, 1953), 207–229; Hans Conzelmann, *The Theology of St. Luke*, trans. Geoffrey Buswell (New York: Harper, 1961), 60–73; G. Ogg, "The Central Section of the Gospel According to St. Luke," *NTS* 18 (1971), 39–53.
[2] Stagg, *loc. cit.*, 499.
[3] C. F. Evans, "The Central Section of St. Luke's Gospel," *Studies in the Gospels. Essays in Memory of R. H. Lightfoot*, ed. D. E. Nineham (Oxford: Blackwell, 1957), 40.
[4] M. D. Goulder, "The Chiastic Structure of the Lucan Journey," *Studia Evangelica*, II, 195–202.

fit. He identified six idea units. Our proposal is ten "sections" that follow a precise inverted outline. This outline is as follows:

THE STRUCTURE OF THE JERUSALEM DOCUMENT (Luke 9:51–19:48)

THE TEN DOUBLE SECTIONS (++ extra material inserted   {   EXTRA MATERIAL
                              into the sections)   {   INSERTED BETWEEN
                                                       {   SECTIONS

1. *JERUSALEM: ESCHATOLOGICAL EVENTS 9:51–56*
    (a) Day—"the days were fulfilled" 51
    (b) Death—"for him to be delivered up" 51
    (c) Fulfilment—"he sent messengers before his face" (Mal. 3:1)
    (d) Judgment—the call for fire to destroy the village (Mal. 3:5 ??)
    (e) Salvation—"the Son of man came not to destroy but to save" 55b[5]

2. *FOLLOW ME 9:57–10:12*
    (a) People come to Jesus 9:57–62
    (b) Jesus sends out the seventy 10:1–20 (++ woes on Chorazin and Bethsaida 10:13–15)

                              {   HIDDEN FROM THE WISE 21
                              { ONLY THE SON KNOWS THE FATHER 22
                              {   BLESSED ARE YOUR EARS 23–24

3. *WHAT SHALL I DO TO INHERIT ETERNAL LIFE? 10:25–41*
    (a) Dialog on the law 25–28
    (b) Love the neighbor—the Good Samaritan 29–37
    (c) Love the Lord—the story of Mary and Martha 38–42

4. *PRAYER 11:1–13*
    (a) The right content for prayer—the Lord's prayer 1–4
    (b) Assurance in prayer—the friend at midnight 5–8
                    —a poem on a father's gifts 9–13

5. *SIGNS AND THE PRESENT KINGDOM 11:14–32*
    (a) A sign of the kingdom—the dumb speak 14
    (b) Signs and the kingdom 14–26 (++ blessed is he who keeps the word 27–28)
    (c) Signs and the Son of man (Jonah and Solomon) 29–32

                              {LIGHT, DARKNESS AND THE EYE 33–36

6. *CONFLICT WITH THE PHARISEES: MONEY 11:37–12:34*
    (a) Conflict with the Pharisees, money—seven woes 11:37–54
                    (++ seven misc. sayings 12:1–12)
    (b) Money—the rich fool 12:13–21
    (c) Do not be anxious—treasure in heaven 22–34

7. *THE KINGDOM IS NOT YET AND IS NOW 12:35–59*
    (a) The kingdom is not yet—"be like men waiting" 35–48
    (b) The kingdom is now—fire upon the earth 49–53
                    —interpret the present time 54–56
                    —the judgment is near 57–59

---

[5]Cf. J. M. Ross, "The Rejected Words in Luke 9:54–56," *ExpT* 89 (1973), 85–88. With Ross we suggest a restoration of these words.

8. *THE CALL OF THE KINGDOM TO ISRAEL 13:1-9*
    (a) Repent or perish—Pilate and the Galileans 1-5
    (b) Produce or perish—the unfruitful fig tree 6-9

9. *THE NATURE OF THE KINGDOM 13:10-20*
    (a) Love and not law—the healing on the Sabbath—a woman 10-14
                   —what about your ox or ass? no reply 15-17
    (b) Humility—the kingdom is like mustard and leaven 18-20

10. *JERUSALEM: ESCHATOLOGICAL EVENTS 13:22-35*
    (f) Salvation—"will those who are saved be few . . . enter by the narrow door"
     (e) Judgment—"depart from me . . . you . . . thrust out of the kingdom"
      (d) Vision—"you will *see* Abraham and the prophets in the kingdom"
       (c) Fulfilment—the ingathering of the messianic banquet of the kingdom (Mal.
             1:11)
        (b) Death—"Herod wants to kill you"
         (a) Day—"today, tomorrow, and the third day—I am made perfect"
         (a) Day—"today, tomorrow, and the coming day—I go"
        (b) Death—"the prophet must not die away from Jerusalem"
       (c) Fulfilment—a failure of the messianic ingathering—"I would have gathered
             you under my *wings* (Mal. 4:2?) and you would not"
      (d) Judgment—a *lament* over Jerusalem "Jerusalem . . . killer . . . your house
             forsaken
     (e) Vision—"you will *not see me* until you say 'blessed is he who comes in the
             name of the Lord' "
    (f) ——————??

9' *THE NATURE OF THE KINGDOM 14:1-11*
    (a) Love and not law—a healing on the Sabbath—a man 1-4
                   —what about your ass or ox? no reply 5-6
    (b) Humility—"he who humbles himself will be exalted" 7-11

8' *THE CALL OF THE KINGDOM TO ISRAEL AND TO THE OUTCASTS 14:12-15:32*
    (a) The great banquet 14:12-24
        —the cost of discipleship 25-35
    (b) The lost sheep and lost coin 15:1-10
    (c) The two lost sons 15:11-32

7' *THE KINGDOM IS NOT YET AND IS NOW 16:1-8, 16*
    (a) The kingdom is not yet
        ——————??? (19:12-26)
    (b) The kingdom is now—the unjust steward 16:1-8
        —everyone is pressed by the kingdom 16:16

                                          ⎰THE LAW IS STILL VALID 17
                                          ⎱   DIVORCE 18

6' *CONFLICT WITH THE PHARISEES: MONEY 16:9-31*
    (a) Money—God or Mammon 9-13[6]
    (b) Conflict with the Pharisees, money 14-15[6]
    (c) Lazarus—the need for treasure in heaven 19-31

_____

[6]For a discussion of the shift of 16:9-15 see below, pp. 116f.

$$\left\{\begin{array}{l}\text{OFFENSES } 17{:}1{-}2 \\ \text{FORGIVENESS } 3{-}4 \\ \text{FAITH } 5{-}6 \\ \text{DUTY } 7{-}10\end{array}\right.$$

5' *SIGNS AND THE COMING KINGDOM 17:11–37*
    (a) A sign of the kingdom—lepers cleansed 11–19
    (b) Signs and the kingdom of God 20–21
    (c) Signs and the Son of man (Noah and Lot) 22–37

4' *PRAYER 18:1–14*
    (b) Assurance and steadfastness in prayer—the Unjust Judge 1–8
    (a) The right attitude in prayer—the Publican and the Pharisee 9–14

$$\{\text{CHILDREN AND ETERNAL LIFE } 15{-}17$$

3' *WHAT SHALL I DO TO INHERIT ETERNAL LIFE? 18:18–30*
    (a) Dialog on the law 18–21
    (b) Love for neighbor—"Give to the poor" 22–28
    (c) Love for the Lord—"We have left our homes and followed you" 28–30

$$\{\text{PREDICTION OF THE PASSION } 31{-}34$$

2' *FOLLOW ME 18:35–19:9*
    (a) People come to Jesus—the blind man 35–43
    (b) Jesus goes out—the call to Zacchaeus 19:1–9

1' *JERUSALEM: ESCHATOLOGICAL EVENTS 19:10, 28–48*
    (f) Salvation—"The Son of man has come to seek and to save the lost"

$$\{\text{THE KINGDOM OF GOD IS NOT YET } 19{:}11{-}21$$

    (e) Vision—seeing the mighty works they said, "Blessed is He who comes in the name of the Lord"
    (d) Judgment—a *lament* over Jerusalem—"They will not leave one stone upon another"
    (c) Fulfilment—cleansing of the temple—the purification of the Sons of Levi (Mal. 3:2–4)
    (b) Death—Jerusalem leaders seek to kill him
    (a) Day ——————— ???
    ("Destroy this temple and after *three days* I will raise it up again." Cf. John 2:19, where this reference to "three days" is attached to the cleansing of the temple. This tradition itself occurs in Mark 14:58; 15:29.)

    The shorter units of material that are apparently not a part of the original collection are marked. Many of these seem to have been placed in their present position because of word association with units already in the structure. Some add a special theological emphasis (cf. 16:17 as a corrective to 16:16).

    Obviously there is no "traveling" done at all and the title "Travel Narrative" is a misnomer. Furthermore, many are confused as to where the "Travel Narrative" ends. The above outline makes it clear that 9:51–19:48 is the full sweep of the document. We prefer to call it the "Jerusalem Document."

    The semantic correspondences between the units are very strong and need no comment.[7] The double ten inversion occurs both in Acts 2:23–36 and Ephesians 1:3–14. The repetition of Jerusalem on the outside and at the center gives it a prominence that is unmistakable. Death and the eschatological day are the climax of the document. There is also a suggestion of a shift at the center. In the second half of the structure the theme of humility is emphasized. This theme is formally introduced in a discussion of humility (14:7–11), which ends with the statement, "For every one who exalts himself will be humbled, and he who humbles himself will be exalted." The theme of humility is then seen in:

The Cost of Discipleship	14:25–33
The Lost Son	15:11–32
The Unjust Steward	16:1–8a
(who considers begging and digging)	
Dives and Lazarus	16:19–31
The Servant Coming in from the Field	17:7–10
The Publican and Pharisee	18:9–14
Zacchaeus	19:1–10

This theme is not necessarily dominant in each of these pericopes. It seems rather to be more prominent in the units of the lower half of the structure than in the upper half. This theme may have helped determine which of two matching units was placed in the second half and which was introduced in the upper half. The point of turning of such a structure is usually the unit just past the center. This holds true here as well. The lament over Jerusalem, reference to the death of the prophet, and the hint of the triumphal entry all occur in the second half of section 10. The shift to a special emphasis on humility we have mentioned. Another significant shift can be seen in section 8' with its call to the outcasts added to the call to Israel.

The structure raises a number of questions that are beyond the scope of this study. It is our view that a pre-Lucan Jewish-Christian theologian arranged the material into the ten-unit pattern. The arrangement itself is the result of considerable theological reflection. The climax on death and the eschatological day in Jerusalem is not an accident. Luke himself claims that he used written sources. Is it not possible that this was one of them? Luke, we conjecture, had this document available to him. He did some cautious editing, moved in some new material, and shifted two pericopes out of their original position. He then incorporated the edited document into his Gospel.

For our purposes the document with its outline is significant for delineating blocks of material and determining their main themes as understood by the

---

[7]Miesner has discovered a significant parallel to the Jerusalem Document in Acts 12:25–21:16 (cf. *Chiasm and Paul,* 273–290). The special importance of Miesner's discovery is of course that it occurs in a second volume written by Luke. At the same time the OT also has examples of large blocks of material arranged in an inverted pattern. Cf. Stephen Bertram, "Symmetrical Design in the Book of Ruth," *JBL* 84 (1965), 165–68; Edwin M. Good, "The Composition of Hosea," *Svensk Exegetisk Årsbok,* 31 (1966), 21–63.

theologian/editor of the document. Of particular interest for this study are sections 6, 7, and 8. They appear in the structure as follows:

6. *CONFLICT WITH THE PHARISEES: MONEY 11:37–12:34*
>   (a) Conflict with the Pharisees, money—seven woes 11:37–54)
>   (++seven misc. sayings 12:1–12)
>   (b) Money—the rich fool 12:13–21
>   (c) Do not be anxious—treasure in heaven 22–34

7.- *THE KINGDOM IS NOT YET AND IS NOW 12:35–59*
>   (a) The kingdom is not yet—"be like men waiting" 35–48
>   (b) The kingdom is now—fire upon the earth 49–56
>   —interpret the present time 54–56
>   —the judgment is near 57–59

8. *THE CALL OF THE KINGDOM TO ISRAEL 13:1–9*
>   (a) Repent or perish—Pilate and the Galileans 1–5
>   (b) Produce or perish—the unfruitful fig tree 6–9

8' *THE CALL OF THE KINGDOM TO ISRAEL AND TO THE OUTCASTS 14:12–15:32*
>   (a) The great banquet 14:12–24
>   —the cost of discipleship 25–35
>   (b) The lost sheep and lost coin 15:1–10
>   (c) The two lost sons 15:11–32

7' *THE KINGDOM IS NOT YET AND IS NOW 16:1–8, 16*
>   (a) The kingdom is not yet
>   ————————???? (19:12–26)
>   (b) The kingdom is now—the unjust steward 16:1–8
>   —everyone is pressed by the kingdom 16:16

> { THE LAW IS STILL VALID 17
> { DIVORCE 18

6' *CONFLICT WITH THE PHARISEES: MONEY 16:9–31*
>   (a) Money—God or Mammon 9–13[8]
>   (b) Conflict with the Pharisees, money 14–15[8]
>   (c) Lazarus—the need for treasure in heaven 19–31

All three sections have eschatological overtones but each has a different emphasis. Sections 6 and 6' discuss money, death, and the life to come. The parable of the Rich Fool in section 6 and the parable of Lazarus and the Rich Man in 6' are clearly on this topic. Then the dicussion of mammon in 16:9–13 also clearly discusses this subject. In 6' the Pharisees are linked to the discussion of money (see 16:14–15).

The eschatological warnings of sections 7 and 7' are concerned with the coming of the kingdom, not with death. Thus the overall structure of the Jerusalem

---

[8]For a defense of the shift of 16:9–15 from its present position in the text to the place seen in the above outline see below, pp. 116f.

Document requires a break between 16:1–8 and 16:9–13. This will be discussed in detail as part of the exegesis of these verses.

The eschatology of sections 8 and 8′ is related to the call of the kingdom, not death. Thus sections 7 and 7′ are closer to 8 and 8′ respectively than to 6 and 6′. This, then, means that the parable of the Unjust Steward is closer to the parable of the Prodigal Son which precedes it than to the section on Mammon which follows it. This also will be discussed in detail as part of the exegesis.

In summary, it can be stated that the Jerusalem Document does have a structure. This structure is neither historical nor exclusively theological but rather literary. By comparison with the corresponding sections, divisions between blocks of material can be made with greater precision. Dominant themes in different sections also show up more clearly. The literary structure provides new evidence toward solving a wide spectrum of synoptic problems which lie beyond the scope of this study.

Since Luke 16:1–13 illustrates in one passage the various aspects of culture and literary structure that this study attempts to set forth, this passage will be dealt with first. Luke 11:5–13 is structurally similar to 16:1–13 and will thus be studied second. The fifteenth chapter of Luke will then be considered last.

Chapter 5

EXEGESIS OF LUKE 16:1–13

THE UNJUST STEWARD (LUKE 16:1–8)

In the first part of this chapter we intend to show that the parable of the Unjust Steward is an eschatological warning to sinners. In the parable a dishonest steward discovers that his master expects obedience and judges those who fail him. The steward also discovers extraordinary mercy. He decides to risk everything on the unqualified mercy of his master. He knows that if he fails, he goes to jail; if he succeeds, he is saved. His plan was the right one and he is praised for it. The entire parable is cast in the form of a "Parabolic Ballad" (Form D). The theological cluster includes insight into the nature of God, into the crises that the kingdom brings to the sinner, and into the only hope for man's salvation.

Many commentators affirm that this parable is the most difficult of all the synoptic parables. As we have observed, the problems are so complex that both Tomas de Vio Cajetan (1469–1534) and Rudolf Bultmann declared them insoluble.[1] The multiplicity and complexity of the problems of this parable are succinctly stated by C. C. Torrey, who writes,

> This passage [Luke 16:8f.] brings before us a new Jesus, one who seems inclined to compromise with evil. He approves a program of canny self-interest, recommending to his disciples a standard of life which is generally recognized as inferior: "I say to you, gain friends by means of money." This is not the worst of it; he bases the teaching on the story of a shrewd scoundrel who feathered his own nest at the expense of the man who had trusted him; and then appears to say to his disciples, "Let this be your model!"[2]

The seeming incongruity of a story that praises a scoundrel has been an embarrassment to the Church at least since Julian the Apostate used the parable to assert the inferiority of the Christian faith and its founder.[3] Our need for a more

---

[1]See above, p. 29.
[2]Charles C. Torrey, *Our Translated Gospels* (New York: Harper, 1936), 59.
[3]Scharlemann, *Parables*, 81.

86

precise understanding of the culture that informs the text is perhaps greater in this parable than in any other. The text is in excellent condition with only a few minor variants, some of which we will note as we move through the parable.[4]

The disciples are the primary audience. In verse 1 they are addressed specifically, but the Pharisees are assumed by Luke to be included among the listeners, for in verse 14 they, too, heard "all these things."

The word "parable" is not mentioned in verse 1, but neither is it included in the parable of Lazarus except as a variant. Apparently Luke assumes that the word "parable" given in 15:3 is to cover the parables of chapter 16 as well.[5]

Three initial questions must be discussed at some length before proceeding to the parable itself. They are,

1. Is the master assumed to be an honorable man, or is he a partner-in-crime with his steward?

2. Has the steward obliged the renters to sign bills for amounts greater than the actual debts? Is his reduction of the debts merely a surrender of his dishonest "cut"?

3. Is the steward an estate manager dealing with land rentals or is he an authorized agent for a moneylender?

The interpretation of the entire parable hinges on the answers given to these three questions. We will examine each of them in turn.

Everything indicates that the master is an upright man. In the immediately preceding parable of the Prodigal Son, the father is clearly a noble man; and the sons, by contrast, are ignoble. In the parable of Lazarus the rich man is ignoble, but Lazarus is judged worthy of eternal life. One naturally assumes the same character contrast in the parable of the Unjust Steward. Furthermore, the steward is clearly labeled "unjust," yet no breath of criticism is leveled at the master. If the master were ignoble, he would have acted in a very different manner. The steward is dismissed, but not scolded, punished, or jailed.

Some scholars follow a line of argument that forces them to assert a partner-in-crime status for the master. Oesterley writes, "The lord commends the dishonesty of his steward and may, therefore, not unreasonably be regarded as belonging to the same category."[6] Derrett implies a criticism of the character of the master when he concludes that the master is pleased to acquire an unearned reputation for piety by approving the actions of his steward.[7] At the end of the

---

[4] The authenticity of the parable is almost beyond question. D. R. Fletcher writes, ". . . It hardly seems plausible that an apocryphal parable involving such obvious difficulties of interpretation should have been incorporated by the early Christian community into its traditions of the parables of Jesus." Fletcher, "Riddle," 15.

[5] The Old Syriac, the Arabic Diatessaron, the Peshitta, and Ibn al-Ṭayyib add the word "parable" to this verse in their translations. Thus these translators clearly understood this text as a parable.

[6] Oesterley, *Jewish Background,* 197. Cf. also Caird, *Luke.* Caird writes of the master, "He was, in fact, no less a son of this world than his steward" (p. 187).

[7] Derrett, "Steward," 216f. Cf. also Via, *Parables,* 159. Via suggests a "scheming businessman" for the master; cf. Arndt, *St. Luke,* 375. In contrast, Smith writes, "There is nothing in the parable to

parable the master is deceived. Were he ignoble, we would expect from him a stream of anger directed toward the steward. This does not happen. Any line of argumentation that places the person and character of the master in a bad light will need substantial support.

The second question deals with the action of the steward. There is a strong current in modern scholarship that affirms that the steward has inflated the bills to enrich himself. In the crisis of his dismissal, he subtracts his "cut" from the bills. This opinion can be traced to Margaret Gibson. In 1902 Gibson, an Arabic and Syriac scholar at Cambridge, wrote a letter in comment on this parable to the *Expository Times*. She said,

> . . . I know that at the present time, wherever Orientals are left to their own methods, uncontrolled by any protectorate of Europeans, the plan is to farm out taxes or property of any description. The steward would therefore demand from the cultivators much more than he would pay to the overlord, perhaps even double, and pocket the difference himself.[8]

Gibson shows the attitude of an imperialistic age in assuming the cultural superiority of Europeans. This assumption by itself is enough to render suspect her judgments on the "natives." Furthermore, Gibson was a resident of Cambridge and came to the Middle East only as traveler, scholar, and pilgrim. In spite of this, her almost casual suggestion was picked up and endorsed by a rather amazing list of scholars.[9] It is our view that Gibson has made a basic mistake in her evaluation of Middle Eastern customs. In light of the influence her remark has had, it must be examined with some care.

Gibson may be giving an accurate description of land renting practices in the Turkish Empire at the turn of the century. She suggests that this pattern is an appropriate frame of reference for this parable. Her exact meaning is not clear. Does she intend to say, "Middle Eastern landowners are not smart enough to keep their stewards from cheating; European control is more intelligent and can provide this safeguard"? This is obviously false, and we can assume that this is not what

---

prepare us to take an unfavorable view of the employer's character" (B. T. D. Smith, *Parables,* 109). Derrett in a more recent article (" 'Take thy bond . . . and write fifty' (Luke XVI.6). The Nature of the Bond," *JTS* 23 [1972], 438–440) discusses the nature of the bond in the parable, but again requires that the master be a partner-in-crime with his steward. His data are from the Greek world and thus do not apply.

[8] Margaret Gibson, "On the Parable of the Unjust Steward," *ExpT* 14 (1902/1903), 334. Scharlemann, *Parables,* 88, has noted that this suggestion was first made by M. Evers in "Das Gleichniss vom ungerechter Haushalter" (1901). Hermann Marx, in a revision of Evers' work published in 1908 (*Die Gleichnisse Jesu* [Berlin: Reuther & Reichard, 1908], 83), refers to this suggestion of Evers and calls it "eine höchst originelle Auffassung." Evers seems to have made his "original interpretation" independent of any insight into the culture of the area.

[9] W. D. Miller, "The Unjust Steward," *ExpT* 15 (1903/1904), 332–34; E. Hampten-Cook, "The Unjust Steward, I.," *ExpT* 16 (1904/1905), 44; Gächter, "Oriental," 121–131; C. B. Firth, "The Parable of the Unrighteous Steward (Luke xvi.1–9)," *ExpT* 63 (1951/1952), 93–95; Derrett, "Steward," 198–219; Fitzmyer, "Manager," 23–42; Stuhlmueller, *Luke,* 149.

she intends. Rather she seems to be saying, "Middle Eastern landowners agree with their agents on a fixed amount which they expect to receive from land rentals. The owners then allow their agents to inflate the bills beyond this amount to whatever the traffic will bear, even up to 50 percent." No doubt wealthy Turks owning land in Arab provinces during the last days of Imperial Turkey did function in this manner. Yet such an assumption has at least the following implications:

1. The master is dishonest.

2. He is willing to allow his steward's profits to be almost as great as his own.

3. He does not care if the leading citizens of the local community are badly cheated. Thus he has no social relationship to them.

4. The steward does cheat the debtors mercilessly on a regular basis.

5. The steward has been given tacit permission to cheat the debtors as much as he wants. He will be closely watched. If he is caught cheating the master he will be dealt with in a ruthless fashion.

6. The steward is hated bitterly by all the renters. Restoration to their good graces would be almost impossible under any conditions. Proverbially speaking, if they ever get him down they will beat him to death.

None of these assumptions fits the parable under consideration.

Gibson is correct in assuming that the renters paid something to the steward. Officially the steward received a fee from the renters. Derrett argues convincingly that the steward is a legal "agent" for the master and so acted under the Mishnaic regulations governing such agents.[10] The Mishna mentions specifically a fee to be paid by the renter to the agent who draws up the rent contracts.[11] In addition to this (judging from modern village customs), the steward will likely receive a little something "under the table" from most, if not all, of his master's renters. A token amount is considered legitimate and honorable. At feast time, harvest time, and at other important social occasions, he will likely expect some gratuity from his master's renters.[12] He is criticized only if his demands are unreasonable.

None of this appears in the accounts. What is recorded on the bills is known to the master. This is clearly evident in the Mishnaic passage cited above, which says of agents, "They may not write contracts of share-tenancies or fixed-rate tenancies except with the knowledge (and agreement) of both parties, and the tenant must pay the fee."[13] What is written on the bills is public information discussed openly in the community.

Furthermore, if the steward tries to inflate the bills, the debtors will be fully aware of what is happening. They can appeal to the master unless he is a

---

[10]Derrett, "Steward," 201–204.

[11]Mishna *Baba Bathra* x.4.

[12]The amazing flow of expensive gifts between company executives at Christmas time is a Western equivalent to the same practice.

[13]*Baba Bathra* x.4.

partner-in-crime. If the steward has been cheating the debtors to the extent of 20 to 50 percent of their bills, he will be bitterly hated by them. Once he falls from power he will have to leave the community. No further deception, even if it is to their economic advantage, will lead those debtors to welcome him into their homes.

For years I have been discussing this point with consultants from the Middle East and beyond to India. The village cultural pattern is everywhere the same. A dishonest steward has many ways to cheat. Every time he buys or sells anything he will make a "cut." But all his extra profits are "off the record." What is written on the debtors' bills he must deliver to the master.[14]

The Turkish landowner in the Middle East is vividly remembered as corrupt, ruthless, and indifferent to any suffering he or his steward might cause his renters. This total scene, however, is quite different from the one that confronts us in the parable. At the very beginning, someone cares enough about the welfare of the master to report the actions of the dishonest steward. The master is clearly a part of the community. The wealthy, distant, foreign, ruthless landowner is unknown in the synoptic parables.[15]

Finally, according to Jewish law, if an agent buys for less or sells for more than the price specified by the principal, the extra profits belong to the principal, not to the agent.[16] Thus, it must be concluded that Gibson's dated, superficial

---

[14]Part of the confusion in this regard arises because the Middle Eastern moneylender *does* ask the debtor to sign for more than he receives. The purpose of this subterfuge is to avoid the laws against exorbitant interest rates. The question of land rentals *vs.* money lending will be discussed below. The details of the parable point to the former. Making the steward into a moneylender creates new problems and inadequately solves old ones.

From antiquity comes an illustration of this money-lending practice. Josephus records how Herod Agrippa about 33–34 A.D., when nearly bankrupt, borrowed money from a banker. Josephus writes that the banker, called Protos, "complained that Agrippa had defrauded him of some money, and forced Marsyas Herod's agent `to draw up a bond for 20,000 Attic Drachmas but to accept 2,500 less." Josephus *Antiquities* xviii.6.3. Translation from *Josephus,* ed. Louis H. Feldman, Vol. IX in the *Loeb Classical Library* (Cambridge: Harvard University Press, 1965), 103.

In his translation Whiston gives a note saying, "Spanheim observes that we have here an instance of the Attic quantity of use-money, which was the eighth part of the original sum of 12%, for such is the proportion of 2,500 to 20,000." Cf. *The Works of Flavius Josephus,* trans. W. Whiston (London: Ward, Lock, n.d.), 455, n.1. Spanheim turns out to be Ezekiel Spanheim, a late 17th-century author and expert on both Greek coins and Josephus. (E. Spanheimii. Fl. Josephi . . . Opera Omnia . . . accedunt nunc primus notae . . . ineditae in universa Fl. Josephi opera . . . 1726.) This is an example of writing a larger figure than the debt owed. However, this illustration does not apply to the parable. Greek commercial law underlies the illustration. Furthermore, the money is borrowed directly from the banker Protos and not from someone he represents. Also, Herod already owed the sum of 2,500 Drachmas, so Protos is collecting previous debts. Finally, the percentages in the parable are not consistent and much higher.

[15]Luke 12:42–48 is a case in point. There the master is absent but on returning is very upset when he finds that his steward has been mistreating those under him.

[16]Horowitz, *Jewish Law,* 552. In this particular case, Horowitz is quoting from the *Mishnah Torah of Maimonides* and thus the legislation is late and may not apply. Yet it does demonstrate the working assumption that the principal knows the financial rates used by his agent.

surmise leads in the wrong direction. Her suggestion is inappropriate to the cultural elements in the parable.

The third question is that of the profession of the steward and the nature of the debts owed. There are two aspects to this question. First, is the steward a legal "agent" and, if so, is he paid or does he have to fend for himself financially? Second, is he an estate manager dealing with land rentals or a moneylender supervising cash? Under this question we will argue that the steward is a legal "agent" and most likely a *shaluaḥ* (or *shaliaḥ*). He is paid. The rich man is a landowner, and thus the steward is an estate manager. The debtors are *ḥakirīn* who have rented land for which they must pay fixed amounts of produce. We will deal with the question of "agency" first.

Regarding "agency," Horowitz gives a convenient summary of Mishnaic legislation.[17] He points out that there were three kinds of "agents." These were:

1. A general agent (*shaluaḥ*) who labored either gratuitously or for a fee.

2. A sarsor, a broker or middle man who was always a paid agent.

3. A mursheh, who was an attorney appointed by written instruction to recover property or a debt and authorized to bring suit.[18]

The general agent was "one sent." Often the task for which he was sent was a personal family affair like the arranging of a marriage.[19] In such a case it is easy to understand why the agent might not be paid. He would most likely be a member of the family or a friend of social status equal to the principal. To pay him in such special circumstances would be an insult. On the other hand, Horowitz makes quite clear that the agent was usually paid.[20]

We do not have enough information in the story to determine with finality which of the three alternatives is most appropriate to the steward of the parable, yet the *shaluaḥ* is by far the most probable. In any case, Horowitz' discussion makes it quite clear that all three types of agents were usually paid. The *shaluaḥ* could work gratuitously, but this would be an exception.

---

[17]Horowitz, *Jewish Law,* 538–568.

[18]*Ibid.,* 539.

[19]b.Tal. *Massektoth Ketanneth* 186; Horowitz, *Jewish Law,* 544.

[20]Horowitz assumes that the agent (*shaluaḥ*) is paid and notes the exception to this general assumption when he says, " 'Shaluah' is also used in a narrower sense of a gratuitous agent, one who renders services as a favor" (*Jewish Law,* 539). The same point is confirmed later in the discussion where Horowitz writes, "But when he was entitled to a fee or commission, it sometimes became a question whether he had fully performed" (*ibid.,* 541). Referring to all three types of agents in general, Horowitz says, "The agent is entitled to repayment of the ordinary, regular and customary expenses which he incurred on behalf of the principal . . . and to payment of his hire, fee or commission if it was an employment for hire" (*ibid.,* 549). This evidence is overlooked by Gächter, who states flatly, "He [the master] did not pay the steward for his services, for the steward was supposed to be in a position to gain his livelihood from those who were under him. He hired out the different portions of the master's property to cultivators. They had to pay revenues from which one part would go to the master, one part to the steward" (Gächter, "Oriental," 127). This theory of the unpaid steward who has to live by his wits is unsupported by evidence from any quarter.

In regard to the profession of the steward we must begin with the Greek word itself. T. W. Manson lists three alternatives for the word οἰκονόμος:

1. an overseer or head-servant responsible for the welfare and discipline of the rest of the household staff (Luke 12:42);

2. a bailiff or estate-manager;

3. a civic official like a city treasurer (Romans 16:23).[21]

Manson favors the second, estate manager.

All the Syriac versions for "steward" read *rab bayto,* which means "manager of the house." This is somewhat ambiguous but leaves no room for "money-lending agent." All but two of the Arabic versions have *wakīl* (estate manager).[22] Otto Michel traces the word through the LXX to the Hebrew *'asher 'al habbayit.*[23] In rabbinic literature the οἰκονόμος becomes a kind of chief slave who supervises the household "and even the whole property of his master."[24] The chief slave is called a *ben bayit.* In Luke 16, however, the steward is not sold, but dismissed. Michel suggests for Luke 16:1 "housekeeper," "estate manager," or "accountant,"[25] and suggests the Aramaic *gizbar,* which agrees with Ibn al-Ṭayyib's eleventh-century Arabic version and is still within the range of words referring to a landed estate and its manager. Thus the Greek word itself, along with its Hebrew, Aramaic, Syriac, and Arabic equivalents, points to "estate manager."

Again the Mishna provides significant information, in this case in the laws governing land rentals. There were three types of renters. These were,

1. a tenant on shares (aris or kablan) who paid a percentage of his crop to the owner;

2. a tenant who paid a fixed portion of the crop to be grown (hoker);

3. a tenant (soker) who paid rent in money.[26]

The second type fits exactly the conditions of the story. The Blackman edition of the Mishna spells out the situation in a note where a *ḥakīr* is defined as the tenant "who agrees to pay a certain quantity of produce irrespective of the yield."[27] Derrett argues at some length that the debtors cannot be renters because "the vital point is that under any such agreement the obligee *owes* nothing at all until the time for payment."[28] Derrett fails totally to see that the steward is not *collecting* the

---

[21]Manson, *Sayings,* 291.

[22]The two exceptions are the Diatessaron, which gives *qahramān* meaning "butler," "steward," or "household manager," and Ibn al-Ṭayyib, who translates "storehouse keeper." Thus in the Middle East the story has almost always been understood specifically to refer to an agricultural scene with a manager and *never* as a money-lending tale.

[23]Otto Michel, *TDNT,* V, 149–153.

[24]*Ibid.,* p. 149.

[25]*Ibid.*

[26]Cf. Horowitz, *Jewish Law,* 334; Mishna *Baba Metzia* ix.1–10.

[27]*Mishnayoth, Order Nezikin,* ed. Philip Blackman (London: Mishna Press, 1954), 223, n.2.

[28]Derrett, "Steward," 213; emphasis his.

amounts. The amounts are not *due* until harvest, but they are indeed *owing* from the day the agreement is signed. Even after the bills are changed there is no attempt to collect even the reduced amounts. In regard to Derrett's argument, we are obliged to state that he has not used Horowitz and the Mishna widely enough, and has misunderstood the very agricultural scene he is rejecting.

Having dismissed the possibility of the debtors being land renters, Derrett works out a very elaborate scheme arguing that cash debts were liquidated and reinstated in agricultural produce in order to avoid the laws of usury.[29] This is, of course, possible, but if we assume the debtors to be *ḥakirīn* there is no need to postulate such a complicated scheme of which the parable itself gives no hint.

When we ask, How do we know that the debts are usurious? Derrett answers, "Their very large amounts show that something suspicious was afoot."[30] That will hardly do as an assumption for what becomes the foundation of the entire argument.[31] Derrett also asserts that if the master were a landowner and his debtors tenants, "Jesus would have said so."[32] We would argue in the opposite direction. In an agricultural setting, with the laws and customs surrounding the *ḥakīr* well known, it would be redundant to tell peasant listeners that a rich man was a landowner and that his debtors were land renters. In the parable of the Prodigal Son, the father is a landowner. This is clear from the details. Yet this fact is not stated; it is implicit. By contrast, if the master were a banker, *then* the audience would need to be told.

The crucial weakness in the "moneylender" theory is that it of necessity implicates the master in dishonest dealings. Fitzmyer uses the "money rental" category. When he comes to the question of the master's integrity, he tries to protect the master by saying, "The master may well have been ignorant of the original transactions."[33] Granted the master does not know how much the steward is getting indirectly, but he knows *exactly* the amounts charged for rental of the large tracts of land in his estate. Even if he is a moneylender, he knows exactly where his money is, and what is due him. It is hard to imagine any type of banking anywhere in the world in any period where this would not be the case. Fitzmyer is trying to avoid making the master a partner-in-crime with the unrighteous steward. If usury is recorded in the bills, the master necessarily becomes such a partner.[34]

---

[29]*Ibid.*, 244.

[30]*Ibid.*

[31]Quite to the contrary the Oriental storyteller delights in the use of large amounts. Jesus is no exception; cf. Matt. 18:23–35.

[32]*Ibid.*

[33]Fitzmyer, "Manager," 36.

[34]Manson bypasses the entire landowner *vs.* moneylender debate by suggesting that the debtors are "buyers." He writes, "Both debtors would seem to be persons who have purchased goods from the estate and have not yet paid for them" (Manson, *Sayings,* 291). This view must be rejected in that any estate selling its oil and wheat to merchants would naturally be paid in cash, not kind. There would be no point in selling a hundred jars of oil for a hundred jars of oil. This solution creates more problems than it solves. An excellent review of the relevant data on the word steward can be read in W. L. Hendricks, "Stewardship in the New Testament," *Southwestern Journal of Theology* 13 (1971), 25–33.

An additional significant source of information on this culturally oriented question is the Arabic commentary on Luke by Dr. Ibrāhīm Saʿīd of Cairo.[35] Commenting on Luke 16:2, Saʿīd writes,

> Thus the owner requested his manager to present to him the contracts signed by the farmers and countersigned by the manager, in order to show how much was owing to the owner by each partner from the produce of his fields.[36]

Saʿīd clearly assumed that the debtors were renters and that the setting was that of an estate with land rented out to farmers.

As in the case of Luke 15, the community must be considered to be one of the *dramatis personae*.[37] The Middle Eastern peasant always thinks and acts as part of his community, not as an individual isolated from it. The general public is first mentioned in verse 1, where we are told, "Charges were brought to him." We are not told who brought these charges. Even if these were only fellow servants, clearly a wider circle of people was involved than just the master, the steward, and the debtors.

One of the more suspect cultural value judgments made almost unconsciously by many exegetes is the assumption that an Oriental master does not want to be bothered and gives little attention to his estate and almost no supervision to his manager. This is simply not true. Life has always been precarious in the East. Anyone who manages to become rich anywhere in the world naturally keeps a close watch on his source of wealth. The master in this story is specifically mentioned as such a type in that he cares enough about preserving his wealth to fire a wasteful steward.

In summary, clearly the most probable cultural setting for the parable is that of a landed estate with a manager who had authority to carry out the business of the estate. The debtors were most likely renters, *ḥakirīn*, who had agreed to pay a fixed amount of produce for the yearly rent. The steward was no doubt making extras "under the table," but these amounts were not reflected in the signed bills. He was a salaried official who, in addition, was paid a specific fee by the renter for each contract. The master was a man of noble character respected in the community who cared enough about his own wealth to fire a wasteful manager. With these relatively clear answers to our three initial questions we can proceed to the text itself.

---

[35]Dr. Saʿīd, who died in 1971 in his late 70s, was the Helmut Thielicke of the Arab world. His Arabic language was compared to that of Kahlil Gibran, the Lebanese poet. His long ministry engaged him in seminary teaching, preaching, and writing. Born about 1890, he spent his childhood and young manhood in the isolation of a tiny village in the south of Egypt. His many books include full commentaries on Luke and John. Saʿīd was a personal friend of Emil Brunner and other scholars, but publishing only in Arabic he has remained unknown outside the Arab world. As an Arabic-speaking scholar, he was competent in English, Greek, Hebrew, and French. He was only casually aware of form criticism and does not discuss it. However limited his commentaries may be in some respects, regarding the question of the Oriental culture that informs the text of the parables, his work must be taken seriously. We will take note of Saʿīd's work all through the exegesis.

[36]Saʿīd, *Lūqā*, 407. Here, as throughout, the translation of his work is my own.

[37]Cf. Derrett, "Steward," 217, and Bruce, *Synoptic Gospels*, 584. (Cf. below, pp. 167f.)

Luke 16:1–8 is carefully structured along the lines of a parabolic ballad (Type D). The structure is as follows:

A   There was a rich man who had a steward   RICH MAN—STEWARD
     and charges were brought to him   STEWARD—A RASCAL
     that he was wasting his goods.

   B   And he called him and *said* to him, "What is this I hear
       about you?   WHAT DOING?
         Turn in the account of your stewardship   FIRED AS STEWARD
          for you can no longer be steward."   OUT OF WORK

   B   And the steward *said* to himself, "What shall I do   DO WHAT?
       because my master is taking the stewardship
       away from me?   FIRED AS STEWARD
       I am not strong enough to farm and ashamed to beg.   OUT OF WORK

     C   "I know what I will do   DO THIS
         so that when I am put out of the stewardship   FIRED AS STEWARD
         they may receive me into their own houses."   NEW JOB

   B'   So summoning his master's debtors one by one   DO—ACT LIKE A
       he *said* to the first, "How much do you owe my master?"   STEWARD
       And he said, "A hundred measures of oil."   WIN FAVOR
       And he said to him, "Take your bill and sit down quickly and write fifty."

   B'   Then he *said* to another, "And how much do you owe?" DO—ACT LIKE A
       And he said, "A hundred measures of wheat."   STEWARD
       And he said to him, "Take your bill and write eighty."   WIN FAVOR

A'   Then the master commended the dishonest steward
     for his wisdom   RICH MAN—STEWARD
     because the sons of this age are wiser   STEWARD A WISE RASCAL
     than the sons of light in their own generation.

We observe seven stanzas of three lines each with one extra explanatory line in the fifth stanza. As is very often true of the Lucan parabolic form, a significant number of the stanzas begin with direct speech. The words in capitals to the right of the structure indicate something of the parallelism. In the briefest way the seven stanzas may be characterized as follows:

     Rich man, steward
         problem
         problem
           idea
         solution
         solution
     rich man, steward.

In the case of the good Samaritan there are three visitors on the road. The vineyard owner sends three times to his vineyard (Luke 20:9–16). For the great banquet there are three types of people invited (Luke 14:15–24). The nobleman who goes to the far country receives reports from three servants (Luke 19:11–27). But here there are only two illustrations of debt reductions. The reason is obvious once the ballad structure of seven stanzas is identified. Two stanzas set up the problem. The climax is in the center with the announcement of a new plan. B' and B' solve the problem created in B and B and in A' we are back to the rich man and his unfaithful steward. With this structure in mind we will proceed through the text.

The steward is summoned and addressed with the first question: (literally translated) "What this I hear about you" (with no verb to be). The word order is Semitic, idiomatic, and forceful. All of our Oriental versions maintain this identical word order. The Syriac has a present participle, "What is this that I am hearing?" which is in keeping with the Greek syntax. The implication is, of course, "I have been hearing for a long time, and I am still hearing a steady stream of things about you." It is the stock formula that a master almost always uses in such a context. The servant does not know how much the master knows and may be frightened into divulging information the master does not have. The steward, intelligent man that he is, remains silent. He has been asked a specific question by his master. His silence cannot be dismissed as insignificant.

The master then breaks the silence with the ultimatum, ἀπόδος τὸν λόγον τῆς οἰκονομίας σου. Two important questions must be answered at this point. First, Is the steward fired now or later? And second, Is the steward asked to "surrender the account books" or "get the accounts in order"?

The first question is problematic. When dealing with the debtors, the steward acts as if he is not yet fired. In verse 3 he says, "My master *is taking* the stewardship away from me." He then talks about the time "*when* I am put out of the stewardship."[38] At the same time, the present tense of the verb (i.e. "You *are* no longer able") indicates that he is fired on the spot. Manson writes, "The master takes immediate action. He orders the steward to hand over his accounts, and dismisses him from his post."[39]

In the conservative village today a steward is always fired on the spot. The owner is afraid of exactly the kind of thing that happens in this parable. If the rascal has time, he will embezzle more. The Oriental versions, without exception, make this point clear. The Old Syriac reads, "never again," and a number of the Arabic versions make the same point.[40] Furthermore, the Mishna stipulates the conditions that govern dismissal of an agent. Horowitz writes,

> The appointment and powers of the agent may be revoked at any time with or without good cause, and whatever the agent does after revocation is not

---

[38]These time references may explain why the Byzantine text changed the present tense δύνῃ to the future δυνήσῃ. The Byzantine reading is certainly in error. The present tense δύνῃ is attested by p[75] B ℵ D Θ al.

[39]Manson, *Sayings*, 291.

[40]Ibn al-Ṭayyib has "from now on"; the new Jesuit "after today"; the Diatessaron "now it is not possible." The rest of the Arabic versions have *baʻd*, which in this context also means "from now on."

binding on the principal. *It takes effect,* however, only from the time that it is brought home to the agent or the person with whom he is dealing.[41]

In the case of this steward he *is* notified. Thus legally his authority as an agent is immediately cancelled. At the same time, more generally speaking, his dismissal is in progress, and he still has some room to maneuver until he turns in the account books and leaves the building, because word of his dismissal is not out. To summarize, we observe that from the text, the Mishna, the Oriental versions, and from modern practice it is clear that the steward is fired on the spot and his authority is terminated immediately. Regarding the question of the account books, the meaning of the word ἀπόδος is clear and can be translated "surrender" or "turn in." In the modern village, a steward in such circumstances is always asked to surrender the books, never to balance the accounts. The master knows that the steward has the skill to falsify the accounts and thus they are not examined for evidence of his guilt or innocence. Gächter argues convincingly that ἀπόδος τὸν λόγον τῆς οἰκονομίας cannot mean "give an account of your stewardship" because, used in that sense, λόγος has no article.[42] Sa'īd, quoted above, understands the accounts to be written documents.[43] Thus with Gächter, Sa'īd, and Scharlemann, it can be argued that the phrase means "surrender the account books."

The listener/reader of the parable expects the steward to be silent after the first question. But after the steward is told, "You're fired; turn in the books!" the listener/reader expects a classic debate in which the steward loudly and insistently protests his innocence. There are many standard ploys he can use to try to defend himself and blame everybody else, including the master himself.[44] But, to the amazement of all, the steward is again silent. His speech, a soliloquy, is given on his way to get the accounts. He walks out having offered no defense. This silence is supremely significant in the Oriental context. The man is indirectly affirming by his silence at least the following:

1. I am guilty.

2. The master knows the truth; he knows I am guilty.

3. This master expects obedience; disobedience brings judgment.

4. I cannot get my job back by offering a series of excuses.

L. M. Friedel wrote, "Had the steward anything to say in self-defense, he would say it now, but he confesses his guilt in the briefest form possible by saying

---

[41]Horowitz, *Jewish Law,* 542; emphasis mine.

[42]Gächter, "Oriental," 127. Cf. Matt. 12:36; Acts 19:40; Rom. 15:12; Heb. 13:17; 1 Pet. 4:5. Scharlemann notes that *logos* is the official record or account kept by the manager for his master (Scharlemann, *Parables,* 84).

[43]Sa'īd, *Lūqā,* 407.

[44]Adam knew some of these; cf. Gen. 3:8–12.

nothing."[45] The steward does not reflect on how he can get his job back. All his energy is focused toward the future.

At the same time, the steward discovers at this point something else about his master that is supremely significant. He is fired but not jailed. The Mishna makes quite clear that an agent was expected to pay for any loss of goods for which he was responsible. The steward can be tried and jailed. Rather, *he is not even scolded*. The master, under the circumstances, has been unusually merciful toward him.[46] Thus, in one scene, this servant has experienced two aspects of his master's nature. He is a master who expects obedience and acts in judgment on the disobedient servant. He is also a master who shows unusual mercy and generosity even to a dishonest steward. The thoughtful listener/reader of the parable would not miss either of these facts.

Stanza three opens with the steward wrestling with his crisis, trying to find a solution. Remarkably, he considers digging. An educated man in authority is not expected to consider manual labor. We expect him to reject this as a possibility because it is beneath his dignity. Surprisingly, his only reason is his physical weakness. He also rejects begging. This, likewise, is to his credit in a society that accepts begging as a legitimate, although despised, profession.[47]

His problem is not just his next meal. Ben Sirach makes clear that the status of the perpetual guest is intolerable.[48] That he wants and needs another job is evidenced by his considering digging and begging. But since he has been dismissed for wasting his master's property, who would hire him? He needs to create a situation that will change this devastating public image. In stanza four (the climax) a plan is born. The listener/reader is not told what the plan is; rather, as in all good drama, he watches it unfold.

It is our understanding of the parable that the steward's plan is to risk everything on the quality of mercy he has already experienced from his master. If he fails, he will certainly go to jail. If he succeeds, he will be a hero in the community. Following the details of the story closely, we will try to demonstrate that this is the plan that popped into his scheming mind with the introductory dramatic aorist ἔγνων.

The key to his situation is that no one yet knows he is fired. They will find out soon enough and so he has to act quickly. Friedel writes, "For he realizes that if there is any escape from digging or begging it must be prepared now, before he hands over the account book, before he is definitely out of office."[49] First he

---

[45]L. M. Friedel, "The Parable of the Unjust Steward," *CBQ* 3 (1941), 338.

[46]The agent was liable for the loss of money or goods entrusted to him if he could not prove that they had been stolen; cf. Horowitz, *Jewish Law*, 552f. Horowitz also indicates that "his responsibility was broadly that of a bailee" (*ibid.*, 552), and at times the bailee was responsible even in the case of theft (*ibid.*, 518–526). In Matt. 8:23–35 servants are jailed for debts; how much more can a servant expect to be jailed for money irresponsibly wasted?

[47]Sir. 40:28–30.

[48]Sir. 29:21–28.

[49]Friedel, *loc. cit.*, 339.

"summons" the debtors. Only if he were still in authority would he have the right to send out lesser servants and "summon" these relatively rich and thereby important men to come and see him (their wealth is evident from the large rents owed). The assumption of such a summoning would naturally be that the steward has some important message to relay to them from the master. As it turns out, this is exactly what the steward wants them to assume. It is not harvest time. The amounts of the bills are set and outstanding but not yet due. All the details are significant. He calls the debtors in one by one because he does not want them talking to one another and asking too many questions. He is in too much of a hurry for titles. The debtors are not greeted with even "Friend" or "Sir." To the first he says specifically, "Write quickly."[50] To the second he says almost rudely, "And you."[51] He must finish before the master finds out what he is doing. This fact is crucial to the story. As we have seen, the steward was legally powerless from the moment he was notified of his dismissal. If the debtors have any way of knowing that there is any deception involved they will not cooperate. If a lesser servant enters the room and announces that the steward is fired the scheme fails. The renters may entertain suspicions (the community knows him; cf. 16:1), but as long as they have no knowledge they can and will cooperate. If they *know* or *could have known* and *then* cooperate they will be breaking faith with the master in a very serious way, and the master will no longer rent land to them. This is one of the more significant cultural factors that is ignored by nearly all commentators. The relationship between the owner of the land and his renters is a significant personal and economic relationship. In his summary of social relationships evidenced in the parables of the rabbis, Rabbi Feldman comments on the relationship between the owner of the land and his renters. He writes, "Personal relations were often friendly—sometimes quite intimate."[52] In these parables the typical evil renter is a man who cares nothing for the interests of the landowner.[53] Thus the point is made that a relationship of mutual concern was expected. In the parable of the Unjust Steward there is no criticism of the renters. They are assumed to be upright citizens of the local community. As with the master, a partner-in-crime status for the debtors must not be imported into the parable.

---

[50]This "write quickly" in the text is almost universally ignored by the commentators. We understand it to be a crucial key to a proper understanding of what is going on. He must finish before the master finds out what he is doing, but also before the renters themselves find out that it is all dishonest.

[51]This phrase, "And you," in addressing a relatively wealthy renter, is jarring to Oriental ears. The Oriental versions give the reader a slight shock with this phrase.

[52]Feldman, *Similes*, 239.

[53]Feldman gives an illustration where a renter portrayed as an unrighteous man says, "What care I for the owner of the garden?" (*ibid.*, 40). I find it hard to believe that this is unique to the Middle East. No farmer renting land anywhere in the world wants to anger the owner of the land and risk being denied the right to rent in the future. One could argue that they think there is safety in numbers. The master cannot expel *all* of them from the land lest he have no one to work it. But this, too, is inappropriate to the parable. The parallels in rabbinic similes make this clear. The relationship between renter and landowner is important as a *social* as well as a financial relationship. Furthermore, if the master is angered, he will find ways to take revenge even if he does not directly expel them.

Saʿīd significantly labels these debtors "partners."[54] Thus, from the haste of the steward and from modern and ancient custom, it is clear that the debtors assume the entire bill-changing event to be legitimate. First of all, the debtors are led to believe that the steward is still in authority. This assumption is unmistakably clear from the story itself. The steward says, "How much do you owe *my master*?" He directly asserts that he is still employed.[55] We have already noted that he *summons* them. Thus they arrive assuming that he is still in authority. The second assumption is that the master has authorized the bills and that the steward has talked him into it. This is the only assumption that fits the story. The steward asks the debtors to make the changes in their own handwriting. They accept. The amounts reach to 50 percent. We must assume that the debtors are confident that the master has approved.[56] If there is any doubt about this, as we have indicated, they will not cooperate. The risk is too great. Finally, the steward naturally takes credit for having arranged the reductions. He need say little or nothing. The bills are not due. These sudden reductions come, as it were, "out of the blue." The steward may quietly let it be known, "I talked the old gentleman into it." We can easily reconstruct the kind of small talk that would have taken place during the bill changing. After all, he, the steward, was in the fields day after day. He knew that the rain was bad, the sun hot, and the worms active. The steward thus achieves the position of a factory foreman who has arranged a generous Christmas bonus for all the workers. The bonus itself is from the owners. But the foreman is praised for having talked the owners into granting it. The last part of this assumption is also inescapable. The steward will not carry out a plan that does not reflect to his credit in a significant way. There would be no point in doing so.

In summary, then, the steward openly asserts that he is in authority. The debtors assume that the reductions are authorized; otherwise they would not cooperate.[57] The steward quietly lets the debtors know that he has arranged for the reductions. With these assumptions all the cultural elements fall easily into place.

---

[54]Saʿīd, *Lūqā*, 407.

[55]The steward's soliloquy in v. 3 has the same phrase. It is true that this idiom is his customary speech. However, in v. 5 he is speaking officially and so is, in fact, claiming a relationship.

[56]Derrett endorses this assumption and writes, "Without such a presumption no one would deal with a man through his steward" (Derrett, "Steward," 203). Derrett's point is not quite the same as ours. Derrett assumes that the agent must have had this kind of broad authority as an official part of his agency. Thus as long as his agency was not revoked he could make such reductions and, even if the master didn't like it, he would be bound to accept. But as we have seen the agency *was* revoked. Besides, the reductions are enormous and unprecedented, and even if the steward had the strict legal authority to make such reductions, the debtors could not cooperate if they knew that the master was not in prior agreement.

[57]Fletcher, "Riddle," 17, asks, "What kind of friends are these who are bought by such a device?" (that is, the device of cheating the master). Fletcher asks the right question; he gives the wrong answer. He concludes the key to the parable is irony, because obviously self-respecting debtors would not allow themselves to be bought by dishonest tricks. But as we have argued, from the debtors' point of view they are not being "bought" with dishonest tricks. They do not know there is any cheating involved. So far as they are concerned, all is aboveboard. Therefore they will cooperate, and only therefore does the steward come out as a hero.

The steward takes the bills from his drawer, cupboard, or file, observes the amount, and asks each debtor how much it is. The debtor affirms the amount written.[58] The steward then announces a reduction that, in each case, amounts to about 500 denarii.[59] That the values of the two reductions are roughly equivalent is another indication of his haste. It is much easier to subtract 500 denarii worth from each bill than to debate the fairness of a percentage with each debtor.[60]

In the case of the *ḥakirīn* the Mishna provides for reductions in the fixed rents.[61] If trees die, or blight spreads across a field, or a spring dries up, the owner is expected to make a reduction. Discussions of this kind always take place between renter and owner in the Middle East even if there is no legislation to provide for them. Usually the renter would have to request and argue for some reduction. Here a generous reduction is offered unsolicited.

Sa'īd makes the intriguing suggestion that, with the letter-symbol system of writing, the changes indicated would have been the simplest stroke of the pen. It would entail changing a ק to a ו and a ק to a ף.[62]

Stanzas three and four present the problem. Stanzas five and six reveal the solution. Stanza seven will now appear as a mirror of stanza one. The steward finishes his daring plan by gathering up the freshly changed accounts and delivering them to his master. The master looks at them and reflects on his alternatives. The master knows full well that in the local village there has already started a great round of celebration in praise of him, the master, as the most noble and most generous man that ever rented land in their district. He has two alternatives.

---

[58]The point of the questions is, "Do you agree that the amount recorded on the bill in front of me is an accurate statement of the rent agreement?" The steward is not asking for information. He has the written statement in front of him. He is establishing agreement. This important discussion between a steward and his master's renters is fascinating to observe. Often the renter is illiterate and the steward has to confirm the amount through reference to witnesses present at the time of the making of the agreement, to the time of day when it was made, the weather, contemporaneous events, a smell in the air, the place, and other such confirming particulars.

[59]Cf. Caird, *Luke*, 188. Caird writes, "The liquid measure (*bath*) was approximately 8¾ gallons, and the dry measure (*cor*) was a little under 11 bushels. The value of 50 baths of oil and 20 cors of wheat would be the same—about 500 denarii."

[60]The changes in the bills are in the handwriting of the debtors, not the steward. It could be argued that the steward orders the debtors to make the changes so that there will be nothing written in his handwriting. Thus he could claim innocence of the entire affair. But this is not likely. The bills are in his possession and what happens to them is his responsibility. More likely, requesting them to do the writing was standard practice. It assures that they have agreed to the bills as they now stand (and the steward has not tampered with them). This is apparently the point that Rabbi Simon ben Gamaliel (early second century) was worried about when he suggested the agent make out two copies of the bill. Cf. *Mishnayoth, Order Nezikin*, ed. Philip Blackman (London: Mishna Press, 1954), 223. But the renter was protected as long as he wrote the figures. This may be the reason why Simon ben Gamaliel's suggestion was rejected. Here the handwriting demonstrates that the debtors have been identified.

[61]Mishna *Baba Mitzia* ix.1, 6.

[62]Sa'īd, *Lūqā*, 408. There is also the possibility that a Greek translator of an Aramaic text of the parable may have confused the final "F" and the final "N" of his original. In the script of the times the two letters are very similar. Cf. E. L. Sukenik, *The Dead Sea Scrolls of the Hebrew University* (Jerusalem: The Hebrew University, 1954), folio 39, lines 14–17.

He can go back to the debtors and explain that it was all a mistake, that the steward had been dismissed, and thus his actions were null and void.[63] But if the master does this *now*, the villagers' joy will turn to anger, and he will be cursed for his stinginess.

Second, he can keep silent, accept the praise that is even now being showered on him, and allow the clever steward to ride high on the wave of popular enthusiasm. This master *is* a generous man. He did not jail the steward earlier. To be generous is a primary quality of a nobleman in the East. He reflects for a moment and then turns to the steward and says, "You are a very wise fellow."[64] One of the Old Testament definitions of "wisdom" is an instinct for self-preservation.[65] In a backhanded way the actions of the steward are a compliment to the master. The steward knew the master was generous and merciful. He risked everything on this aspect of his master's nature. He won. Because the master was indeed generous and merciful, he chose to pay the full price for his steward's salvation.

In the above discussion we have assumed that the "lord" of verse 8a is the master of the parable. This question must now be examined in detail.

The problem is as old as the Peshitta and has been debated all through the modern period. Obviously if the master of verse 8a is the rich man, then this phrase is the climax of the parable. If he is not, then the parable ends with verse 7. Manson notes:

> In view of the beginning of V. 9, "And I say unto you," there can be little doubt that Luke thought that "the lord" in V. 8 meant the steward's master; and this probably means that that was the way in which the words were taken by the compiler of the source on which he is here dependent.[66]

But then Manson proceeds to give the standard reason why many commentators find this Lucan understanding difficult to accept. The question is, How could a master who dismisses a steward for wasting his goods in verse 2 praise him in verse 8? Manson suggests that the only way the master in verse 8 could be the master of the story is if he heard about the steward's actions, stopped them, and "secured

---

[63]Mishna *Gittin* iv.1; Horowitz, *Jewish Law,* 542. This is against Derrett, who writes, "The debtors writing their new acknowledgements and destroying the old ones were safe." There is no evidence for his assumption that the old bills are destroyed. Derrett has overlooked the Mishnaic evidence that the agent, once notified of dismissal, was legally powerless and the principal not bound by his actions. Cf. Derrett, "Steward," 216; Gächter, "Oriental," 129.

[64]At the conclusion of his discussion Derrett notes: "That the steward's prudence was beneficial to the steward was evident; that it redounded to the master's reputation with the public was obvious. An ungracious repudiation was out of the question." Derrett, "Steward," 217. Here we are in basic agreement with Derrett. But for Derrett the issue is the master's "piety." We would insist that, rather, it is the master's generosity that is heralded in the community.

[65]See below, pp. 105f., for an extended discussion of this word.

[66]Manson, *Sayings,* 292.

himself against pecuniary loss.''[67] But if our line of interpretation above is sound, we have a quite adequate reason for praising the steward at the end of the parable.[68]

In agreement with Manson, Jeremias writes,

> The change of subject (καὶ ἐγὼ ὑμῖν λέγω) at the beginning of v. 9 seems to point decisively to the conclusion that the lord in the parable is intended. This may have been the meaning of the tradition as it lay before Luke, characteristic of whose style is the phrase ὑμῖν λέγω (with ὑμῖν preceding).[69]

Jeremias argues that Luke thought the κύριος of verse 8 was the master of the story but that Luke was mistaken. Jeremias then proceeds to present three arguments for identifying the κύριος with Jesus. They are:

1. The master of the story would not have praised a deceitful steward.

2. The absolute use of κύριος in Luke's gospel in some instances refers to God; elsewhere (except 12:37, 42b; 14:23) it always (18 times) refers to Jesus.

3. Luke 16:9 is like 18:8, where the comments of Jesus himself are clearly injected into the parable.[70]

The first of these arguments we have already discussed above. There is good reason for the master of the story to praise the dishonest steward.

Regarding the second, by "the absolute use of κύριος" Jeremias apparently means κύριος as a title without modifiers (excluding the vocative). His evidence, however, needs reexamination. The "absolute use of κύριος," as Jeremias defines it, occurs in Luke twenty-one times. Eighteen times it means Jesus, and only three times someone else. But when we look at the parabolic material, the results are as follows:

meaning: *The master of the story*	meaning: *Jesus*
12:37	12:42
12:42b	18:6
14:23	

To this list we then add the disputed 16:8, the present passage. Jeremias' case seems to be that of numerical weight, that if there are eighteen cases of the absolute use of κύριος that refer to Jesus and only three that do not, then the probability is that 16:8 refers to Jesus. But within the parabolic material this weight vanishes. Furthermore, in the same section Jeremias has already noted that Luke is dealing with traditional material.[71] In such presumably non-Lucan traditional material one

---

[67]*Ibid.*

[68]An Oriental master is often pleased that a servant is clever enough to outwit him. This point was made to me by Dr. Hassan Askari of India.

[69]Jeremias, *Parables*, 45.

[70]*Ibid.*; Crossan (*In Parables*, 110f.) clips the parable as early as v. 7.

[71]Verse 7 has a historic present, which is rare in Luke. The words for the weights and measures are Hebrew words left untranslated. The story itself is culturally quite Oriental.

must be extremely cautious about drawing conclusions based on Lucan stylistic peculiarities.

Jeremias' third argument is disputed by Fitzmyer when he writes,

> ... Jeremias along with many others (J. M. Creed, E. Klostermann, W. Grundmann, K. H. Rengstorf, J. Schmid, etc.) understand "the master" in v. 8a as Jesus. In this they appeal to the sense of v. 8b, which almost certainly reflects a statement of Jesus and seems out of place in the mouth of the master of the parable. These writers also appeal to Lk 18:6, where an observation of *ho kyrios* is recorded, who cannot be anyone else but Jesus. And in 18:8 there follows a similar introduction of a saying by *legō hymin* (see 16:9).—However, the situation in chap. 16 is not the same as that in chap. 18. There is an earlier mention of *kyrios* in 16:3, 5, whereas there is nothing similar in Lk 18. Moreover, in Lk 12:42, although the first instance of the absolute use of *ho kyrios* refers to Jesus, the second one is generic and does not refer to Him at all. . . .[72]

The Oriental versions give unambiguous, yet divergent, answers. The Old Syriac has "the master." The Peshitta makes the word refer to Jesus by translating "our Lord/master." The word is the well-known "marana" of the end of Revelation.[73] The Harclean returns to "the master." Medieval Arabic versions follow the Peshitta, but all of the nineteenth- and twentieth-century translations return to "the master," meaning the lord of the parable. Fakhūrī, in the Būlusiyah version, makes it doubly explicit by translating "the master praised *his* steward" [emphasis mine]. Saʿīd also clearly identifies the master as the rich man of the parable.[74]

Finally, if the κύριος of verse 8 refers to Jesus, the parable is left without an ending. Fitzmyer observes, "Without v. 8a the parable has no real ending. From the beginning, the reaction of the master to the manager's conduct is expected; it is finally given in v. 8a."[75]

Fitzmyer is right. As an Oriental story, the parable builds to a climax awaiting the owner's response at the end of the parable. One of Bultmann's principles for the telling of a similitude is what he calls "the law of end stress."[76] Verse 8a when read as a part of the parable is an almost perfect example of this principle. It is almost universally conceded that Luke understood the master of verse 8 to be the rich man of verse 1. There seems to be no remaining argument to

---

[72]Fitzmyer, "Manager," 27f., n.8.

[73]This shift from the Old Syriac "the master" to the Peshitta "our Lord/master" may be the result of the "spilling" of unambiguous meaning from one verse to an ambiguous word or phrase in another. Verse 9 is a clear Dominical saying. This fact may have influenced the way the Peshitta translators read v. 8. We will note other examples of this same "spilling" effect later in the exegesis of other parables.

[74]Saʿīd, *Lūqā*, 409.

[75]Fitzmyer, "Manager," 27. Furthermore the literary structure of the parabolic ballad requires that the master be the master of the story. Stanza seven balances stanza one as we have noted. In stanza one the reader is introduced to a rich man and an unfaithful steward. In the balancing stanza, stanza seven, the form requires and the listener/reader expects a return to the rich man and his dishonest steward.

[76]Cf. Bultmann, *Tradition*, 191.

deter us from accepting Luke's judgment and reading verse 8a as the climax of the parable.[77]

Many earlier commentators worried over how Jesus could use a dishonest man as an example. But this need not delay us. The Middle Eastern peasant at the bottom of the economic ladder finds such a parable pure delight. Nothing pleases him more than a story in which some David kills a Goliath.

Yet there is an unusual feature to this story. The storyteller in the East always has a series of stories about the clever fellow who won out over the "Mister Big" of his community. The remarkable feature of this parable is that the steward is *criticized* as "unrighteous" and called a "son of darkness." The average Oriental storyteller would not feel any compulsion to add such a corrective to this type of story. Thus the Western listener/reader is surprised at the use of a dishonest man as a hero. The Eastern listener/reader is surprised that such a hero is criticized.

The parables of Jesus have a surprising list of unsavory characters. In addition to this steward are the unjust judge, the neighbor who does not want to be bothered in the night, and the man who pockets someone else's treasure by buying his field. As Smith notes,

> The parable of the Unjust Steward, whose conduct goes from bad to worse, is only the most outstanding example of a class of parables, the use of which appears to be a unique and striking feature of Christ's teaching.[78]

In three of the four cases listed above, Jesus is using the rabbinic principle of "from the light to the heavy," which means generally, "how much more." That is, if this widow got what she wanted from this kind of judge (18:1–9), how much more you and God? If this man got bread in the night from this neighbor (11:5–7), how much more you from God. If this dishonest steward solved his problem by relying on the mercy of his master to solve his crisis, how much more will God help you in your crisis when you trust his mercy.

Verse 8a, moreover, has two key words that must be examined: $\varphi\rho o\nu\acute{\iota}\mu\omega\varsigma$ and $\grave{\epsilon}\pi\alpha\iota\nu\acute{\epsilon}\omega$. All the older Oriental versions translate $\varphi\rho o\nu\acute{\iota}\mu\omega\varsigma$ with some form of *ḥokmah*, "wisdom." The universality of this translation in the Syriac is significant. Clearly, for the Eastern fathers, there was no particular problem in using the Semitic word *ḥokmah* in this context.[79] Wisdom in the Old Testament, in

---

[77]The ὅτι of v. 8 can be read as a *Hoti recitative*. Gächter understands it in this light and translates, "Whereupon the master praised his dishonest steward: 'He has acted wisely' " (Gächter, "Oriental," 130). The Old Syriac and the Peshitta have the maddeningly ambiguous *d*, but the rest of the Oriental versions, without exception, have a causative. However, direct speech is usually spoken *to* someone and with a *Hoti recitative* we would expect, *"You* have acted wisely." Either way, the interpretation is not affected. If accepted, this suggestion nonetheless reinforces our observation that the first lines of the stanzas of the parabolic ballad very often have direct speech.

[78]B. T. D. Smith, *Parables*, 109.

[79]Sa'īd's commentary prints the Van Dyke-Bustānī Arabic text at the top of the page. Thus Sa'īd has to deal with *ḥokmah* in the mouth of the master praising his steward. Sa'īd writes, "He [the rich man] praises him for his *ḥikma* [Arabic; = Heb. and Aram. *ḥokmah*] and does not praise him for his high character, as if he is amazed at his superior intelligence but not pleased at the crookedness of his heart. This is demonstrated in that the master does not return the steward to his position" (*Lūqā*, 409).

certain contexts, definitely carries the idea of cleverness. Fohrer writes, "חכם can be used for a nonmoral cleverness and skill deployed in self-preservation."[80] This quality of wisdom is found as early as the Exodus account where Pharaoh urges his people to act "wisely" and kill all the Israelite children (Exod. 1:10), and as late as the illustration of wisdom in self-preservation of the ants, badgers, locusts, and lizards in Proverbs (30:24–28). This aspect of wisdom fits exactly into what is said of the unjust steward. In the Septuagint both σοφία and φρόνησις translate ḥokmah. The second is less frequent and less theologically freighted. Philo emphasized the practical qualities of φρόνησις.[81]

It seems only reasonable to assume that the original Aramaic word in this story was ḥokmah. The meaning in this context was the "cleverness and skill deployed in self-preservation."[82] The Greek translator, intending this lesser quality of wisdom, avoided the use of σοφία and translated with φρονίμως.

In harmony with this, the eschatological overtones of the word must not be overlooked. Jeremias[83] endorses Preisker's definition of φρονίμως[84] as "having grasped the eschatological situation" and argues that this meaning is specifically intended in this verse. Fitzmyer approves of Jeremias' interpretation and adds,

> ... The adverb is used precisely in this eschatological sense in the parable. The manager stands for the Christian confronted with the crises that the kingdom brings in the lives of men.[85]

In summary, the steward is praised for his wisdom, or ḥokmah. This means his skilfulness in self-preservation. He is sensitive to the hopelessness of his situation. He is aware of the one source of salvation, namely, the generosity of his master.

In discussing the parable of the Unjust Steward in the light of Qumran, Kosmala argues that the steward is not "the unrighteous steward" but rather the "steward of unrighteousness," and that this is eschatological language, referring primarily to the world that lies under the power of wickedness. He writes, "The expression οἰκονόμος τῆς ἀδικίας, therefore, describes a man who is completely bound up with this world in which ἀδικία is the ruling principle."[86] This would further indicate the eschatological thrust of the parable.

Turning to the second word (to praise) it is significant that the Old Syriac version reads shabaḥ (to praise), which is identical with the Hebrew shabaḥ. Yet, the Syriac word carries a fascinating additional meaning of "to keep in good

[80]G. Fohrer, TDNT, VII, 484.

[81]Philo Quod Deus Imm 35, quoted by R. C. Trench, Synonyms of the New Testament (9th ed., London: James Clarke, 1961), 263. Trench has a good discussion of the two words well documented from ancient sources; cf. also Trench, Notes, 333, n.b.

[82]Fohrer, loc. cit.

[83]Jeremias, Parables, 46.

[84]H. Preisker, "Lukas 16, 1–7," Theologische Literaturzeitung 74 (1949), 89.

[85]Fitzmyer, "Manager," 32, n. 21.

[86]Hans Kosmala, "The Parables of the Unjust Steward in the Light of Qumran," Annual of the Swedish Theological Institute 3 (1964), 115.

repute, to sustain the credit of.''[87] This meaning fits the steward's situation exactly. We can only speculate as to whether or not such a secondary meaning may have been a part of the original Aramaic of the parable in its Palestinian setting. The word in later Jewish Aramaic means only "to praise."

Of greater significance is the eschatological usage of the Greek word in the New Testament itself. Preisker writes, " 'ἔπαινος' signifies the acceptance or approval of the righteous by God alone in the Last Judgment.''[88] The verb form appears in the New Testament only in Paul's First Epistle to the Corinthians and here in Luke.[89] Yet, the idea of a divine master offering approval in an eschatological setting is present in Matthew.[90] Thus the Greek word, on the level of the story itself, carries the meaning of simple approval of what the steward has done. At the same time, on a theological level this word provides additional evidence for interpreting the parable as being primarily concerned with eschatology.

A summary of the theological cluster of this parable can be briefly stated as follows: God (the master) is a God of judgment and mercy. Because of his evil, man (the steward) is caught in the crisis of the coming of the kingdom. Excuses will avail the steward nothing. Man's only option is to entrust *everything* to the unfailing mercy of his generous master who, he can be confident, will accept to pay the price for man's salvation. This clever rascal was wise enough to place his total trust in the quality of mercy experienced at the beginning of the story. That trust was vindicated. Disciples need the same kind of wisdom.[91]

This brings us to verse 8b. Here we will try to demonstrate that it is a part of the original telling of the parable. It provides the necessary corrective to the approval of the unjust steward. He is praised for his wisdom in knowing where his salvation lay, not for his dishonesty. Furthermore the literary form indicates that it

---

[87]R. P. Smith, *A Compendious Syriac Dictionary,* ed. J. P. Smith (Oxford: Clarendon, 1903), 556.
[88]Preisker, *TDNT,* II, 587.
[89]1 Cor. 11:2, 17, 22a, 22b.
[90]Matt. 25:21, 34.
[91]There is a wonderful story in the oral tradition of the Middle Eastern peasantry which tells of a condemned murderer during the days of the famous sultan Saladin. The killer was condemned to death and kept crying, "I want to see the Sultan." Finally he was taken into the presence of the great Sultan where he cried out, "O most gracious Sultan, my sins are great but the mercy of the Sultan is greater." He was released.

A modern version of the same story was related to me in 1965 by one of the leaders of the Arab section of Jerusalem, a man named Abū Alfons. In 1960, the wife of a condemned spy came to Abū Alfons for advice on how to free her husband. He told her to wait outside the palace for the king's motorcade to form and then throw herself in front of the king's car. He explicitly instructed the lady *not* to plead innocence, with the warning, "You know he is guilty and so does the king. To offer excuses is to destroy all hope. Throw yourself on the mercy of the king!" The lady carried out the instructions. The Jordanian monarch knows full well how a noble king is expected to act and the spy was released. The Western reader can imagine the result if a similar event took place in front of the White House or at Number Ten Downing Street. All of this is to point out that Jesus, in using this particular theme, was appealing to a well-known aspect of Middle Eastern cultural life that was important enough to survive in medieval story and in contemporary life.

is a part of the original parable. The three lines of the last stanza balance the three lines of the first stanza.

A number of contemporary arguments must be discussed. Jeremias argues that verse 8b is a part of the series of additional interpretations that stretches from verse 8b to verse 13.[92] Fitzmyer reflects much of contemporary thinking when he comments,

> ... The saying preserved here represents an independent logion of Jesus which has been joined to the parable (either by Luke or his source). For it follows strangely on V. 8a, and indeed on the whole preceding parable.[93]

However, there is nothing strange about the presence of this comment at this place in the text. As we have observed, this comment makes it clear that the man is not being praised for his dishonesty.[94]

Jeremias and others argue that the parable was originally directed to the unconverted and then redirected to the Church at a later period.[95] This idea would give weight to the suggestion that 8b was added by the Church. However, the parable is more than an appeal to the listener/reader to act. It is also an appeal to insight and faith to understand a crucial aspect of the nature of the kingdom of God. Kosmala writes:

> The people to whom this parable is addressed cannot have been the "unconverted", they were rather people who were Jesus' followers and indeed belonged to the "converted", they were the "children of the light". The parable is introduced by the words: "He spoke to the disciples" (16:1), for what Jesus says in it is a plain criticism of the children of the light. . . .[96]

Thus the parable does not fit as a parable spoken only to the disciples, nor does it fit as a parable spoken only to outsiders. The Lucan setting is ambiguous, with disciples mentioned in verse 1 and Pharisees in verse 14. This ambiguity seems appropriate.

The subject of this pericope in the overall structure of the Jerusalem Document discussed above is the Coming of the Kingdom. In a parallel pericope in the upper half of the structure, Peter asks, "Lord, are you telling this parable for us or for all?" Thus the ambiguity surrounding the question of who is addressed in the parable is reflected in both 16:1–8 and 12:35–40.

It could be argued that verse 8b is not a part of the original parable but rather an addition attached to the parable by a Church nervous about a story that praises a dishonest steward. But as we have noted, the phraseology of 8b is distinctively Palestinian, and the Palestinian Church would have understood the parable and

---

[92]Jeremias, *Parables*, 108.

[93]Fitzmyer, "Manager," 28f.

[94]The Palestinian character of the comment has been fully documented elsewhere and need not detain us; *ibid.*, 28, n. 10; Jeremias, *Theology*, 169.

[95]Jeremias, *Parables*, 47.

[96]Kosmala, *loc. cit.*, 117f.

would not have been nervous about it. If 8b were Greek in vocabulary and inspiration this argument would be weighty. As it stands it does not follow. Thus, keeping in mind the literary structure and the other factors mentioned above, the greatest probability is that 8b is a part of the original parable.

Before we turn to verses 9–13 we must note the points of similarity between the parables of the Unjust Steward and the Prodigal Son. Many scholars have noted this connection.[97] A number of very specific points of relationship are to be noted.

1. Luke 16:1 does not tell us that a "parable" is about to be told. To get the word "parable" we have to return to 15:3. Thus Luke relates the two.[98]

2. In Luke 15 a son throws himself on the mercy of his father. In Luke 16 a servant throws himself on the mercy of his master.

3. The phrase δὲ καί in 16:1 is a favorite transitional device for Luke. It is used to show "that the parabolic discourse continues from the previous chapter."[99] The Old Syriac also uses a linking transitional phrase.[100]

4. Both the steward and the son betray a trust.[101]

5. Neither prodigal nor steward offers excuses.

6. The word "scattered" (διασκορπίζω) is applied to both. Furthermore, in the Syriac and Arabic versions, the word for the property wasted is in both stories identical.[102]

7. Both the steward and the prodigal experience extraordinary mercy from their superiors. The steward is not jailed for changing the bills; the prodigal is not punished for his having wasted the family's assets.

8. In both stories, there is a missing final scene. We do not know the final response of the older son or the final result of the steward's act.

Yet, at the same time, there is a shift to a new topic. One parable is on the topic of the gospel and the outcasts, the other is under the heading of the Coming of the Kingdom.[103] Luke 16:1–8 clearly has a number of ties to what precedes it. Later we will see that these connections are far closer than any links to what follows.

---

[97]Goulder clearly links the theology of the two parables, although he follows Derrett's interpretation and thus identifies repentance as the subject of both units (M. D. Goulder, "The Chiastic Structure of the Lucan Journey," *Studia Evangelica,* II [1963], 198). Manson wrote that the story of the Unjust Steward "may almost be regarded as an appendix to the parable of the Prodigal Son" (*Sayings,* 291). Derrett notes, "The parable [of the Unjust Steward] is a continuation of the theme started with the Lost Sheep and Prodigal Son, and not in antithesis to it" ("Steward," 199). J. A. Davidson says, "The background of the telling of the three parables in Lk. 15 seems to provide the clue to the meaning of the parable of the Unjust Steward" ("A 'Conjecture' about the Parable of the Unjust Steward (Luke xvi. 1–9," *ExpT* 66[1954], 31). Scharlemann writes, "This parable is a continuation of the theme started by the Lost Sheep and the Prodigal Son" (*Parables,* 83).

[98]Not too much can be made of this, in that the same can be said for the parable of Dives and Lazarus.

[99]Scharlemann, *Parables,* 83.

[100]The Old Syriac reads *tōb* (likewise, again).

[101]Cf. Scharlemann, *Parables,* 87.

[102]This is true of all but the literal Harclean.

[103]Cf. the discussion of the topical outline of the Jerusalem Document presented above in Chapter Four.

In this section, then, we have seen a parabolic ballad of an honorable master and his clever, dishonest estate manager. The manager is salaried, is probably an "agent," and deals with land renters who pay in kind. The steward is dismissed and admits his guilt by silence. He is not jailed and so discovers his master's mercy. He decides to risk everything on that mercy. Reductions are made in rents with the assumption of the master's approval. Praise flows from the local population to the master and to the steward. An ungracious repudiation by the master of such a "generous act" is out of the question. The steward is praised by the master of the story for his skill at self-preservation. Finally the parable returns to its starting point with a Dominical comment and provides unforgettable insight into the nature of God, the predicament of man, and the ground of salvation.

THE POEM ON MAMMON AND GOD (LUKE 16:9–13)

In this section we will attempt to demonstrate that Luke 16:9–13 is a carefully constructed poem with three stanzas on the single theme of mammon and God. The inversion principle is used in all three stanzas. Together they constitute a Form VI poem. The outer stanzas unite on the topic of mammon and God, and these relate to the climax of the entire poem which appears in the center, discussing mammon and the truth. The poem has been moved to this place in the text because it provides a corrective for the Greek reader, who may well misunderstand the parable. It is our view that Luke 16:9–13 has its own integrity and that it should be read and interpreted apart from the parable that precedes it. One of the important clues to making a sharp division between 16:1–8 and 16:9–13 is the introductory "And to you I say." Both here (16:1–13) and in Luke 11:5–13 there is a parable followed by a poem which has been confused with it. In the brief phrases that introduce each of the poems (cf. 16:9 and 11:9) we find the rare ὑμῖν λέγω, with the verb after the pronoun.

    a.   Parable

    b.   ὑμῖν λέγω + dominical poem on a related topic.[104]

The ὑμῖν λέγω can best be understood as evidence that an editor joined two units not originally occurring together.[105]

---

[104]Luke 12:22 may be a third example. There we have a parable followed by a poem, and some texts have the same "to you I say," again separating the parable and the poem.

[105]Aside from the cases discussed above, ὑμῖν λέγω is found in Luke only, in 6:27, where it again indicates a transition to a new subject. Jeremias observes that this unusual word order is characteristic of Luke's style (*Parables,* 45). In Luke there are 38 cases of λέγω ὑμῖν and only four of ὑμῖν λέγω. ὑμῖν λέγω is unknown to Matthew. Mark uses it in 13:37 (but D reverses the word order). In John it is found in 13:33 and 16:4. Cf. also 1 Cor. 15:34; 15:51; 2 Cor. 8:10; 1 Thess. 4:15; 2 Thess. 2:5; Rev. 2:24. We can observe further that in a passage with non-Lucan, highly *Semitic* features such as a historic present and Aramaic words, it is striking to find a *non-Semitic* construction where the verb surrenders its normal position at the beginning of the sentence in such an idiomatic phrase. In Luke 6:27; 11:9; and 16:9 all our Oriental versions except the literal Harclean restore the verb to the front of the phrase.

Verses 9–13 must now be examined to determine their meaning and to see if they have a unified poetic structure. Many scholars feel that these verses consist of a series of three separate interpretations of the parable added by the early Church. These three interpretations we are told deeschatologize the parable and turn it into a hortatory injunction on how to handle money.[106] Jeremias writes, "In v. 9 we have an entirely different application of the parable from that which is given in v. 8a."[107]

Scholars from Jülicher to Jeremias have noted a break in thought starting with 16:9. In fact, the scene changes quite radically. The following major differences between the steward and the man with mammon can be noted:

1. In the parable there is a master, a steward, and a problem between them. In verse 9 there is no master, no steward, and thus no problem between them.

2. The steward is penniless; he considers begging and farm labor. In verse 9 the man with mammon presumably has a significant sum of mammon. He is offered advice on how to spend it.

3. The steward makes reductions for the relatively rich. In verse 9 the man with mammon is encouraged to give to the poor (presumably).

4. The steward is dealing with someone else's money. The man with mammon is dealing with his own money.

5. The steward is already in his crisis. He is dismissed. The man with mammon is encouraged to plan for the future. His crisis is in the indefinite future.

6. The steward's problem is his own sin, and his master's expectations. The man with mammon faces the problem of the insecurity of worldly goods.

7. The steward is dealing with debts not yet due. The man with mammon is offered advice about "cash in hand."

8. We will note below a relationship between verse 9 and verse 13. In verse 13 a *servant* is mentioned. The parable speaks of a *steward*.

9. The steward is unfaithful and unrighteous. The character of the man with mammon is not criticized.

Thus it is evident that a clear separation must be made between 16:1–8 and 16:9–13.[108]

Having established a clear break between 16:8 and 9 we now intend to demonstrate that verses 9–13 are a very carefully constructed poem with a unified theme. The three stanzas have the following overall structure:

---

[106]C. H. Dodd: "We can almost see here notes for the three separate sermons on the parable as text" (*Parables*, 26); cf. John Reumann, *Jesus in the Church's Gospels* (Philadelphia: Fortress, 1968), 194.

[107]Jeremias, *Parables*, 46; cf. also p. 30.

[108]Jeremias suggests that the original audience of v. 9 may have been tax farmers "and others classed as dishonest persons" (*Parables*, 46). But the importance of the crucial message of the entire poem for any group of listeners would lead one to conclude that the wide circle of sinners, disciples, and Pharisees indicated in Luke 15:1, 2; 16:1, 14 is more appropriate as the audience for such a poem.

Luke 16:9–13

I.   MAMMON AND GOD

I say
to you: A   for yourselves make
                B   friends
                    C   from mammon the unrighteous
                    C'   so that when it fails
                B'   they may receive
            A'   you into the eternal tents.

II.   MAMMON AND THE TRUTH

            D   The one faithful in little
                  also in much is faithful

                E   and the one in little unfaithful
                      also in much unfaithful is.
If
therefore   F   in the unrighteous mammon
                      faithful you are not

                    F'   the TRUTH
                          who to you will entrust?
And
if   E'   in what is another's
                      faithful you are not

            D'   the what-is-yours
                  who will give to you?

III.   MAMMON AND GOD

            G   No servant can serve two masters.
                H   Either the one he hates
                    I   and the other he loves
                    I'   or the one he is devoted to
                H'   and the other he despises.
            G'   You cannot serve God and mammon.

This poem is preserved with no extra phrases or pious expansions. It shows a powerful and subtle unity of thought and a simplicity founded on great complexity of poetic structure. Structure and content will be examined by stanzas, then the internal relationships between stanzas will be considered. Finally, external relationships to other blocks of nearby material will be studied.

Stanza I—Mammon and God

The inverted parallelism is evident. The lines move as follows:

You

    They (friends)

Mammon[109]

Mammon (it)[110]

They

You

This stanza is an example of poetic structure type A.

In lines A and A' the dominant semantic relationship is "you." There may also be a relationship between "make" and "eternal tents." The average person in any age assumes that property (mammon) is for the "making" of "earthly tents," that is, for securing earthly life. By placing lines A and A' opposite each other, the poem says boldly that this is not the case.[111]

Jeremias has noted that the "friends" of line B may mean the angels, and that "they may receive" in line B' is a circumlocution for "God." He writes, "The 'friends' are possibly the angels, i.e. God (a conjecture which is supported by v. 9b where the 3rd person pl. alludes to the angels as a circumlocution for God). . . ."[112]

The first stanza then is a Form I poetic structure with three semantic units. Each unit has strong relationships to the parallel unit.

Stanza II—Mammon and the Truth

Verses 10–12 form the second stanza. These also offer six idea units, as does the third stanza. In contrast to Stanza I this stanza has double lines. It is an example of Form II. A number of patterns of correspondence may be noted:

First, each of the six bicola can be seen as relating to each other in this fashion:

D   faithful +

E   unfaithful −

---

[109]Hauck observes that "mammon" most likely has its origin in the root '*mn*. It means generally, "that in which one trusts," and specifically, "property and anything of value" (F. Hauck, *TDNT*, IV, 388). Mammon is here called "unrighteous." Manson notes succinctly, "All money gets dirty at some stage in its history" (*Sayings*, 293). Ben Sirach has some significant things to say about how "a peg will stick in the joint between two stones, and sin will wedge itself between selling and buying" (Sir. 27:2). Fitzmyer defines the use of the word in this pericope as "The tendency wealth has to make men dishonest" ("Manager," 30, n. 15).

[110]The Byzantine text reads ἐκλίπητε, but both Western and Alexandrian texts have a singular referring to mammon. Both readings refer to death.

[111]The phrase "the eternal tents" is a throwback to the tabernacle. No suggestion of impermanence is meant. Ps. 61:5 reads, "I will dwell in thy tabernacle forever."

[112]Jeremias, *Parables*, 46, n. 85. However, Jeremias prefers the meaning "good works." Many other scholars have noted the possibility of "that they may receive you" meaning God or the angels. Trench, over a century ago, listed both "angels" (as in the parable of Lazarus) and "God" as possible alternatives (cf. *Notes*, 339). Manson notes, "In the Rabbinical writings it is a common way of avoiding the mention of the divine name to use the verb in the 3rd person plural, just as in this verse" (*Sayings*, 293). Cf. also Oesterley, *Jewish Background*, 200; Fletcher, "Riddle," 24; B. T. D. Smith, *Parables*, 112.

F   unfaithful −

F′   faithful +? (a wistful "faithful")

   E′   unfaithful −

D′ faithful?? +? (a wistful "faithful")

Unit D speaks of faithfulness while D′ talks of a hoped-for faithfulness. E and E′ are on the theme of unfaithfulness. In the center mammon and the truth are contrasted.

Then the definite and indefinite pronouns form a striking eight-unit pattern:

D   the one (faithful in little)

      the one (faithful in much)

E   the one (unfaithful in little)

      the one (unfaithful in much)

F   you (with mammon unfaithful)

F′ you (entrusted with the truth?)

E′ you (unfaithful with another's)

D′ you (entrusted with yours?)

Furthermore, the first two bicola have an internal structure. The first of them (D) is chiastic. The second (E) has its two lines parallel to each other.

D   The one faithful in little

      also in much is faithful

E   and the one in little unfaithful

      also in much unfaithful is.

The poet is careful not to use the same poetic device twice in a row.

The center of the stanza has a play on words in Aramaic. The climax of this type of poetry is always the center. Thus, the center of this stanza is the heart of the entire poem. In this center, words rooted in *'mn* are used in a remarkable way. Substituting the appropriate Aramaic words the verse reads,

if therefore in the unrighteous *mamon*

'amen you are not

the *'emunah*

who will *yeyminken*?[113]

---

[113]Hauck, *TDNT*, IV, 388. Hauck writes, "The original Aramaic of the saying in Luke 16:10f. would thus contain a pun, for πιστός, πιστεύσει, τό ἀληθινόν also belong to the stem אמן." In regard to the word ἀληθινόν, we are faced with a number of alternatives. However, all the more likely candidates have *'mn* at their root. Bultmann opts for *'mt*; cf. *TDNT*, I, 249.

To summarize, this second stanza is a highly artistic example of Form II. The climax in the center is clear and striking. The stanza is intact.

Stanza III—Mammon and God

The inverted parallelisms in these six lines are clear. They are: "Two Masters, Hate, Love—Love, Hate, Two Masters." The stanza alone is another example of Form II.

Relationships Between Stanzas I and III

Three specific relationships tie the two outer stanzas together. They are:

1. Each stanza has six idea units.

2. Both stanzas I and III are enclosed with "you."

   A   you

   A′   you

   G   servant (by implication, "you")

   G′   you

3. The strongest relationship between the two outer stanzas is the repetition of the "God and mammon" theme. They are treated differently, but nevertheless the two subjects are the same.

Relationships Between the Two Outer Stanzas and the Center Stanza

We have noted that "God and mammon" is the main point of the first and last stanzas. The center of such constructions has a particular prominence, and thus stanza I has "mammon" as its focus while stanza III centers on "love and devotion." The second stanza has a double center with "mammon" and "the truth." The centers of all three stanzas thus stand opposite to each other in the following fashion:

    I   MAMMON ⌐

    II   MAMMON ⌐

             THE TRUTH ⌐

    III   LOVE AND DEVOTION

In summary, the internal unity of Luke 16:9–13 is strong and artistically satisfying. The three stanzas unite to form a single Form VI poem. The overall theme centers around God, mammon, and the truth. The two outer stanzas tell the reader that mammon is for building treasure in heaven and that you cannot serve

both God and mammon.[114] The climax in the center stanza warns the listener that
he may not be trusted with the truth unless he proves trustworthy with mammon.

What then is to be said about the origin of this poem? The following points
can be made with some confidence:

1. The poem is a unit and must have been shaped into its present form by a single
    poet of remarkable skill.

2. The inverted parallelism used here was common to the writing prophets.

3. The presence of an Aramaic word and an Aramaic wordplay demonstrate that
    the material came from the earliest level of the tradition.

4. Because it is poetry, its preservation in an oral tradition for half a century is no
    more problematic than the preservation of the oracles of Amos.

5. Verse 9 is so obscure that, as Fletcher has said, "presumably nothing so
    obscure would have been introduced into the tradition and erroneously attrib-
    uted to Jesus."[115]

6. Luke attributes the material to Jesus of Nazareth. There seems to be no
    remaining argument to keep us from accepting Luke's judgment.

One final question remains. If 16:9–13 is a separate subject related to but
clearly distinct from the parable of the Unjust Steward, then why is it placed
directly after the parable? We would suggest that Luke has moved it here for two
reasons: first as a corrective for the non-Oriental reader; second because of the
close word associations with the parable. But before examining these two reasons
we must observe its suggested original place in the Jerusalem Document (travel
narrative).

The first part of the discussion centers around the crucial verse 16. This
verse reads, "The law and the prophets were until John: since then the good news
of the kingdom of God is preached καὶ πᾶς εἰς αὐτὴν βιάζεται." This last
phrase is often translated, "and everyone enters it violently," or, "everyone
presses into it." This is to take the verb βιάζεται as a deponent thus having an
active meaning. Schrenk admits, "Philologically possible is the pass.: 'Every man
is pressed into.' " This passive reading he then dismisses as "artificial."[116] However, Hibat Allah Ibn al-'Assāl in his great critical edition of 1252 translates, "and
everybody because of it is under pressure."[117] Ibn al-'Assāl has taken the verb as a

---

[114]Manson has rightly suggested: "The point of this saying [v. 9] is . . . that by disposing of worldly
wealth in the proper way, one will have treasure in heaven. The true parallel to this verse is in such
sayings as Mt. 6[19ff.]; Mk. 10[21]; Lk. 12[33f.]" (*Sayings,* 293). Luke 12:15 is one of the few places in
Luke where possessions are discussed, although the word mammon is not used in the Greek nor
in most of the Oriental versions. The Syriac versions use a different word. But the Arabic texts have
the identical word, thus tying the passages even more closely together. Then in the narrative section in
Luke 12:32–34, the theme of treasure in heaven is clearly very close theologically to Luke 16:9.

[115]Fletcher, "Riddle," 19.

[116]G. Schrenk, *TDNT,* I, 612.

[117]Cf. British Museum Oriental Ms. No. 3382 Folio 252. Ibn al-'Assāl was one of the greatest scholars
of his century and this version of the Gospels was his greatest work. It is a critical edition that uses a

passive and read the εἰς as a causative. Significantly, one of the clear cases of the causative use of εἰς is in the Jerusalem Document at Luke 11:32.[118] Ibn al-'Assāl puts both of the traditional translations mentioned above in his apparatus; the first he traces to the Coptic, the second he finds in an Arabic version translated from the Greek. We have seen that Luke 16:1–8 is a warning to the listener that the kingdom has come and that he is in the crisis of decision regarding it. 16:16 as translated by Ibn al-'Assāl brings this verse theologically into line with the parable in a profound way. By contrast then the poem on Mammon, God, and the Life to Come is, theologically, related profoundly to the parable that follows (Lazarus and the Rich Man). In the text of Luke we now have the pericopes in the following order:

> *Eschatological warning*
>   16:1–8—the unjust steward
>
> *Money and the life to come: the Pharisees*
>   16:9–15
>
> *Eschatological warning*
>   16:16
>
> (Verse 17 seems to have been added by Jewish Christians close to Matthew who were nervous about the statement on the Law in verse 16. Verse 18 on divorce seems to have nothing to do with the context.)
>
> *Money, and the life to come*
>   16:19–31

It is our view that the original Jerusalem Document had the two discussions of *money and the life to come* together and the two *eschatological warnings* together. That is, Luke has moved Luke 16:9–15 ahead of 16:16. When 16:9–15 is moved back to its presumed original position the balance of the Jerusalem Document seen above is restored.[119]

We are then obliged to ask, Why did Luke move them? As we have suggested, his first reason was to provide a corrective for his Greek readers. The parable is an esoteric Oriental parable which Theophilus is bound to misunderstand. He, Theophilus, will no doubt think Jesus is encouraging dishonesty. Luke does his best as an editor. He moves a poem on faithfulness with money to a position immediately following the problematic parable,[120] thus hoping to protect Theophilus from a potentially serious misunderstanding.

That the poem on Mammon is theologically very close to the parable of Lazarus and the rich man has long been noted. Manson writes, ''We may leave the

---

series of twenty-eight symbols to refer to variant readings and translations which he found in Greek, Coptic, and Syriac versions. He includes the full range of omissions, interpolations, and substitutions to which he makes reference in his apparatus. His translation of this verse first drew my attention to this possibility, which is grammatically legitimate on the basis of the Greek and makes profound sense in the context of the chapter.

[118]Bauer-A., G., *Lexicon*, 229.

[119]See above, pp. 116f.

[120]Cf. Creed, *St. Luke*, 205.

question open whether this verse [v. 9] would not stand more appropriately as the moral of the parable of Dives and Lazarus.''[121] If our theory is correct, then this poem on Mammon in fact originally introduced the parable of Lazarus to which it is theologically close.

Luke's second possible reason for moving verses 9–15 ahead is word association. It is well known that in the synoptic Gospels pericopes are often placed together because of word association.[122] Hiers has noted the very strong word association between verse 4 and verse 9.[123]

a.   in order that whenever I shall be turned out   (v. 4)
     in order that whenever it fails   (v. 9)

b.   they may receive me into the houses of them   (v. 4)
     they may receive you into the eternal tents   (v. 9)

However, word association does not necessarily indicate that the two units of material brought together have the same subject; nor does it suggest that the compiler necessarily intended them to be understood as being on the same subject.[124]

There are at least two good reasons, then, why the poem on Mammon is placed directly after the parable of the Unjust Steward, although divergent in subject from it.

To summarize, we have seen in this section that the parable of the Unjust Steward is a parabolic ballad followed by a three-stanza poem on Mammon. The parable in an unforgettable backhanded way illuminates, from a unique angle, the splendor of the grace of God in which alone the believer must trust. The poem on Mammon speaks of the relationship between faithfulness with money, God, and the truth. The poet wonders if any dishonest man can be trusted with God's truth. When the two passages are read as a single subject, both are put out of focus. All the evidence points to each unit having its own special message and style. Theories that suggest the second block of material to be a gradual collection of early Church comments on the parable prove to be inadequate to the structural and theological nature of the material. The poem is the work of a skilled Palestinian poet in the first century. There remains no reason to doubt that the author was Jesus of Nazareth.

---

[121]Manson, *Sayings*, 293; cf. Creed, *St. Luke*, 305.

[122]Cf. Luke 17:20–21, and 22–37 under the topic of ''lo here, lo there''; Luke 11:14–23 and 24–26 under the topic of ''demons''; Luke 11:27–28 and 29–32 under the topic of ''hearing and repeating through preaching''; Luke 12:22–31 and 32–34 under the topic of ''fear.''

[123]Richard H. Hiers, ''Friends by Unrighteous Mammon: The Eschatological Proletariat (Luke 16:9),'' *Journal of the American Academy of Religion* 38 (1970), 30–36.

[124]Gächter, ''Oriental,'' 131, n. 40, writes, ''St. Luke may have received the parable with this catchword composition from tradition; this is more likely than that he himself created the somewhat incongruous sequence of the *logia* of Jesus.'' The literary structure of the Jerusalem Document offers more reasons for the order of the logia in it than Gächter has seen. But he did notice the use of ''catchword composition.''

Chapter 6

EXEGESIS OF LUKE 11:5-13

THE FRIEND OF MIDNIGHT (LUKE 11:5-8)

The parable of the Friend at Midnight is a parabolic ballad with some of the features of the poetical Form IV. It has two stanzas of six units each, and each stanza inverts. In this section we intend to demonstrate that this parable opens with a question expecting an emphatic negative answer. The question can be paraphrased, Can you imagine having a guest and going to a neighbor to borrow bread and the neighbor offers ridiculous excuses about a locked door and sleeping children? The Middle Eastern listener responds, "No, I cannot imagine such a thing!" The parable climaxes around the question of the "sense of honor" or "blamelessness" of the man asleep, which leads him in the night to fulfil the host's request. "Importunity" is best understood as an inappropriate foreign element, which has "spilled" into the parable from the verses immediately following it. The cultural elements of the parable fall into place once the key word ἀναίδεια is properly understood. The parable teaches that God is a God of honor and that man can have complete assurance that his prayers will be heard. Finally, a poem on a different aspect of the subject of prayer (11:9–13) is placed after the parable. In this section we will examine the parable and in the next section comment on the poem that follows it.

The overall structure of the Jerusalem Document[1] places this passage in clear parallel to Luke 18:1–14. There, as in 11:1–13, originally separate units of the tradition have been assembled by the compiler. Bultmann rightly identifies three separate units, verses 1–4, 5–8 and 9–13.[2]

Our first task is an examination of the literary structure of the parable, which is as follows:

---

[1]See above, pp. 80ff.

[2]Bultmann, *Tradition*, 324. Thus in the case of this passage it is readily recognized that a parable is followed by a related yet distinct piece of the tradition which may have had no original relationship to it.

And he said to them,

> Can any one of you imagine having a friend and going to him at midnight

(WHAT WILL NOT HAPPEN)

A 1   and saying to him, "Friend, *lend me* three loaves   REQUEST (GIVE)
    2   for a friend of mine has arrived on a journey
REASON FOR REQUEST
        3   and I have nothing to set before him."   APPEAL TO DUTY
        3'   And will he answer from within, "Don't bother me.
DUTY REFUSED
    2'   The door is now closed and my children are in bed with me.
REASON FOR REFUSAL
1'   I cannot get up and *give* you anything"? REQUEST REFUSED (GIVE)

  I tell you   (WHAT WILL HAPPEN)

B 1   though he will not *give* him anything NOT ANSWER REQUEST (GIVE)
    2   having arisen   ARISING
        3   because of being his friend NOT FOR FRIENDSHIP'S SAKE
        3'   but because of his avoidance of shame
BUT FOR HONOR'S SAKE
    2'   he will get up   WILL ARISE
1'   and *give* him whatever he wants.[3]   REQUEST GRANTED (GIVE)

A number of features of the parable appear once the structure is seen. We observe that the outside lines of each stanza unite around the theme of *giving*. The center of each stanza climaxes on the topic of *honor*. To understand this more clearly the culture of the story must be examined with care. As in the case of two-stanza poems (Form IV) where the second stanza is patterned after the first, the climax of the entire literary piece is the center of the second stanza. This is especially clear here where we have translated the key word under discussion "avoidance of shame." The details of the text and its culture must now be examined with care.

The parable of the Friend at Midnight begins with the familiar τίς ἐξ ὑμῶν. This characteristic phrase occurs three times in Q,[4] four times in Luke's special source,[5] and once in John.[6] This phrase, says Jeremias, "Does not seem to have any contemporary parallels."[7] Jeremias argues convincingly that the phrase "seeks to force the hearer to take up a definite standpoint."[8]

An older view understood the interrogative of τίς ἐξ ὑμῶν to have been lost in the prolonged sentence.[9] Jeremias understands the question to run on

---

[3]As in all the literary structures in this study, the above reflects the Greek word order.
[4]Matt. 6:27 parallels Luke 12:25; Matt. 7:9 parallels Luke 11:11; Matt. 12:11 parallels Luke 14:5.
[5]Luke 11:5; 14:28; 15:4; 17:7.
[6]John 8:46.
[7]Jeremias, *Parables*, 103.
[8]*Ibid.*
[9]Plummer, *St. Luke*, 298; Arndt, *St. Luke*, 297.

through verse 7, and to expect an emphatic negative answer.[10] A careful examination of all the occurrences of this phrase in the New Testament sustains Jeremias' view.[11]

A number of the texts using this phrase would need some adjustment in the traditional translation to make them into questions expecting emphatic negative answers. But in each case such a shift makes lucid sense. Luke 14:5 would read:

> Can any one among you imagine a son falling in a well and he shall not immediately draw him up on the Sabbath day?

And Luke 15:4 would be translated:

> Can any one among you imagine having a hundred sheep and having lost one of them, not leaving the ninety-nine in the wilderness and going after the one that is lost?

Other texts with this phrase are already translated in a way that expects a negative answer; for example, Luke 17:7 (RSV):

> Will any one of you who has a servant plowing or keeping sheep, say to him when he has come in from the field, "Come at once and sit down at table"?

Understanding the phrase $\tau \acute{\iota} \varsigma \ \acute{\epsilon} \xi \ \acute{\upsilon} \mu \tilde{\omega} \nu$ in Luke 11:5 as expecting an emphatic negative answer is crucial to the interpretation of this parable. Jesus is asking, "Can you imagine going to a neighbor, asking for help to entertain a friend and getting this response?" The Oriental responsibility for his guest is legendary. The Oriental listener/reader cannot imagine silly excuses about a closed door and sleeping children when the adequate entertainment of a guest is the issue. To understand this, the presuppositions of the Oriental scene must be noted in some detail.

Contemporary exegetical literature is full of references to the need to travel by night because of the heat. This is true in the desert areas of Syria, Jordan, and Egypt. It is not customary in Palestine and Lebanon, where there is some elevation inland and a breeze from the sea along the coast.[12] Thus the arrival of the friend at midnight is unusual.

Rihbany may be responsible for the idea found in many modern works that three loaves are a meal for one person.[13] This is true of the very small Syrian loaves; it is not true of the bread eaten in the rest of the Middle East. One type of such bread is thin, flat, and nearly two feet across. Other kinds are round, raised,

---

[10]Jeremias, *Parables,* 103, 157.

[11]Jeremias has not examined the John 8:46 reference, which does not introduce a parable. Yet it also expects a negative answer. James 2:15–16 has the phrase also, and again it does not introduce a parable but yet expects a negative answer. 1 Pet. 4:15 is a statement, not a question.

[12]This is another example of confusing peasants and bedouins of the desert. In the summer it is customary for the bedouin to travel at night because of the intense heat. For the peasant, especially in Palestine, traveling at night would be exceptional.

[13]Rihbany, *Syrian,* 215.

but much larger than the Syrian variety. A guest is given one unbroken loaf, which is often more than he will eat. The host, as Rihbany rightly observes, "needed to put before his guest more than the exact number of loaves for one adult meal."[14]

Jeremias claims that the Palestinian peasant bakes every day and that "it is generally known in the village who has some bread left in the evening."[15] The Indian peasant bakes every day, but the Middle Eastern peasant does not. Our experience confirms Bishop, who writes,

> It looks too as if the house in question [the sleeper's house] had recently completed baking a batch of loaves—sometimes enough to last for a week or more at a stretch. . . . His [the host's] supplies were finished till the family's dough had been taken to the village oven [the next morning].[16]

Village women cooperate in bread baking, and it is known who has baked recently. There may be some bread left in the host's house, but he must offer the guest a complete unbroken loaf. To feed a guest with a partial loaf left from another meal would be an insult.

The host *must* serve his guest and the guest *must* eat. Rihbany writes, "He [the host] must set something before him, whether the wayfarer is really hungry or not."[17] More than this, the issue is not food as such, but rather food adequate for the occasion. Sa'īd writes, "He [the host] has the responsibility of the magnanimous Oriental host to prepare to offer the guest that which is beyond his ability to provide."[18]

The crucial element in this initial portion of the parable is that the guest is guest of the *community,* not just of the individual. This is reflected even in the complimentary language extended to the guest. He is told, "You have honored *our village,*" and never, "You have honored me."[19] Thus the community is responsible for his entertainment. The guest must leave the village with a good feeling about the hospitality of the village as a community.[20] Again Rihbany writes, "Owing to the homogeneous character of the life in the East, borrowing has been developed there into a fine art."[21] In going to his neighbor, the host is asking the

---

[14]Rihbany, *Syrian,* 215. Sa'īd observes that one is for the guest, one for the host, and one for "the angel of the table," which he claims is a rabbinic custom. He gives no documentation. Sa'īd, *Lūqā,* 30.

[15]Jeremias, *Parables,* 157. Jeremias documents this last observation with a reference to A. M. Brower, *De Gelijkenessen* (Leiden: Brill, 1946), 211.

[16]Bishop, *Jesus,* 176. My own discussions with a wide range of Palestinians and Lebanese confirm Bishop against Jeremias.

[17]Rihbany, *Syrian,* 214.

[18]Sa'īd, *Lūqā,* 300.

[19]The guest is also told, "You have honored our house," but the reference to the larger community is dominant. The individual is never mentioned.

[20]This attitude is clearly reflected negatively in Luke 9:51–55. It is the community at large that has rejected them and John wants revenge on the community as a whole, not on a person or even a family.

[21]Rihbany, *Syrian,* 214f. While living in primitive Middle Eastern villages, we discovered to our amazement that this custom of rounding up from the neighbors something adequate for the guest extended even to us when we were the guests. We would accept an invitation to a meal clear across the village, and arrive to eat from our own dishes which the villagers had borrowed quietly from our cook.

sleeper to fulfil his duty to the guest of the village.[22] As long as the request is modest enough, refusal is unthinkable. In this case, the request is the humblest element of the entire meal, namely, the bread that will be dipped into the common dish.

Bread is not the meal. Bread is the knife, fork, and spoon with which the meal is eaten. The different items of the meal are in common dishes. Each person has a loaf of bread in front of him. He breaks off a bite-sized piece, dips it into the common dish, and puts the entire "sop" into his mouth. He then starts with a fresh piece of bread and repeats the process. The common dish is never defiled from the eater's mouth because he begins each bite with a fresh piece of bread. The bread must be flavored with something for the meal. In absolute desperation the bread is dipped into a dish of salt. Thus the Oriental phrase "eating bread and salt" means the eaters were in abject poverty and had nothing with which to flavor their bread except salt. The host of the parable asks for bread. Everybody knows that he also needs to borrow the meal itself that will be eaten with the bread. This becomes clear in the last line of the parable.

Sa'īd comments on the host's confidence that his request will be granted. This confidence, says Sa'īd, is based on three things:

1. He (the host) is a host and not a borrower. He is not asking for anything for himself.

2. He goes to one friend in order to honor a second friend.

3. He is asking for the food of bare subsistence.[23]

The host starts his rounds. He will gather up the greater portion of the meal from the various neighbors. He will also borrow the best tray, pitcher, cloth, and goblets that the neighborhood has to offer.[24] That he has a whole list of needs is seen at the end of the parable, where the sleeper gives him "whatever he needs."

The host has plenty of food. Olives are gathered at harvest time and preserved in salt for the year; also stored are grape-molasses and cheese (most of which is made when the cows are fresh). All of the family's food supplies are gathered and prepared on a yearly basis and stored in a raised loft at the end of the one-room peasant dwelling. When the host says, "I have nothing," he is speaking idiomatically and means, "I have nothing adequate to serve my guest so that the

---

[22]The structure of the stanza places this appeal to duty in the climactic center.

[23]Sa'īd, *Lūqā,* 300f. The word for "bare subsistence" is *al-kafāf.* It is a very strong word in Arabic and means that which is just enough to keep a man from starving. Sa'īd means the borrower is asking for the humblest item possible, the bread with which to eat.

When a host is being complimented on his meal he will try to turn the compliment by remarking, "This meal is nothing but bread and salt." He means, "Before you, my noble guests, the best I have to offer is only your ordinary fare, indeed, only as bread and salt. You deserve far better."

[24]If we reject allegory and assume an authentic detail in John 2:6, we would have there an illustration of jars gathered from the neighbors for the large gathering. The average family would have only one.

honor of our village will be upheld.''[25] Again the appeal to community duty is the main point.

With this background in mind, verse 7 becomes clear. Verses 5 through 7 are together the extended question that expects an emphatic negative answer. Jesus is saying, ''Can you imagine having a friend and going to him with the sacred request to help you entertain a guest, and then he offers silly excuses about sleeping children and a barred door?'' The Oriental listener/reader knows the communal responsibility for the guest and responds, ''No, we cannot imagine it.''[26]

A great deal has been made of the fact that the children are asleep and the door bolted. But these are weak considerations. The door bolt is not very heavy. Even if the children do stir, they will fall asleep again. The hypothetical excuses suggested are so unthinkable, they are humorous.[27]

A few scholars argue for some ambiguity regarding the subject of πορεύσεται. Jeremias understands verses 5–7 as follows:

> Can you imagine that, if one of you had a friend who came to you at midnight and said to you, ''My friend, lend me three loaves, because a friend has come to me on a journey, and I have nothing to set before him'', you would call out, etc.[28]

Thus Jeremias has understood φίλον as the antecedent to the verb πορεύσεται.[29] However, a nearly identical construction occurs in an unambiguous form in Luke 17:7. A comparison of the two texts is revealing. Luke 17:7 reads:

> Will any one of you—who has a servant—say—to him (the servant)

---

[25]Manson has caught some of this. He writes, ''The contents of the larder are inadequate to the claim of hospitality'' (*Sayings*, 267). Jeremias thinks the host intends to return the bread (*Parables*, 257). To return anything as insignificant as three loaves of bread would be an insult. It would be like an American housewife returning a borrowed tablespoon of sugar. On the other hand, the sleeper *will* get back what he has lent (which turns out to be much more than just bread, as v. 8 indicates). When the sleeper has a guest he will also make the rounds to provide a sumptuous meal and will most certainly stop at this neighbor's door. Jeremias concludes that the focus of the story is that ''God helps as unconditionally as the friend did'' (*Parables*, 105). This remark is puzzling in that in his major discussion of the parable (pp. 157–59) he does not refer to the ''unconditional'' nature of the transaction. Granted the sleeper does not ask for anything back and demands no payment. Nevertheless, it is clearly understood that the present host is available to return the favor in an emergency. This aspect of the cultural situation simply is not applicable theologically and no lesson is to be drawn from it.

[26]Cf. Jeremias, *Parables*, 158. The details of the hypothetical complaint are authentic. The sleeper is irritated. There is no title (cf. Manson, *Sayings*, 267). The peasant home in Palestine is one room with most of the room in a raised portion for the family. The children are asleep with the parents on this portion. The door is closed just prior to retiring (Rihbany, *Syrian*, 215f.). The reference to ἤδη here means ''for some time''; cf. Jeremias, *Parables*, 176.

[27]Rihbany knows the sleeper's answer is inadequate. He writes, ''The man within runs counter to the best Syrian traditions in his answer'' (*Syrian*, 215). Without the awareness of an alternative, Rihbany then tries to make sense out of the traditional understanding of the text.

[28]Jeremias, *Parables*, 158.

[29]Creed makes the same identification, which he admits makes for ''an awkward change of subject'' (*St. Luke*, 157).

τίς δὲ ἐξ ὑμῶν   δοῦλον ἔχων ἐρεῖ αὐτῷ

Luke 11:5 is roughly similar:

τίς ἐξ ὑμῶν   ἔξει φίλον πορεύσεται αὐτόν
                                        (the friend)

Thus the antecedent of the verb "to go" is "you," not "friend." It is, thus, much more likely that the "friend" is the sleeper, and the listener to the parable is expected to identify with the host, not the sleeper.[30]

The significance of the passage hangs on the meaning of the key word ἀναίδεια in verse 8. In Christian usage the word came to have two meanings: "shamelessness" (a negative quality) and "persistence" (a positive quality). We will need to determine if the second meaning properly applies linguistically and theologically to the text.

In ancient Greek literature the word meant "shamelessness." From Archilochus in the seventh century B.C. through Plato, Sophocles, Herodotus, and Pindar in the fifth, to Demosthenes in the fourth, all references point to "shamelessness."[31]

In Epictetus (A.D. 50–130) there is a significant use which joins ἄπιστος with ἀναιδής. Epictetus is offering advice on the necessity of rejecting externals which destroy the purpose of life. His listener asks about what position he will hold in the city. Epictetus answers,

> Whatever position you can, if you maintain at the same time your fidelity (πιστόν) and sense of shame (αἰδήμονα). But if when you wish to be useful to the state, you shall lose these qualities, what profit could you be to it, if you were made shameless (ἀναιδής) and faithless (ἄπιστος)?[32]

Thus the word in early second-century usage was clearly a negative word which could be linked with ἄπιστος. There is no sense in Epictetus of "persistence."

Turning to the papyri, Moulton and Milligan give three examples. In one, a man proves himself ἀναιδής by levying contributions on the inhabitants. A second, from A.D. 49, refers to people who "shamelessly refuse to pay" (ἀναιδευόμενοι μὴ ἀποδῶναι). The third reads, "At the hands of the greedy (πλεονεκτικῶς) and shameless (ἀναιδῶς) the authorities have had enough."[33] Once again the quality referred to is strictly negative. Again there is no suggestion

---

[30] All our Oriental versions in an unambiguous fashion identify the listener with the host. In the parallel parable of the Unjust Judge, the listener is again identified with the petitioning widow, not the judge.

[31] This is true of the adjective and the abstract noun. Cf. Henry G. Liddell and Robert Scott, *A Greek-English Lexicon*, rev. H. S. Jones and R. McKenzie (Oxford: Clarendon, 1940), 105.

[32] Epictetus *Enchiridion* xxiv; for the Greek text cf. *Simplicii Commentarius in Epicteti Enchiridion*, ed. Iohannes Schweighaeuser (Lipsiae: in Libraria Weidmannia, 1800), 232; the English translation is slightly revised from *The Discourses of Epictetus*, trans. George Long (n.p.: A. L. Burt Company, n.d.), 432.

[33] J. H. Moulton and G. Milligan, *The Vocabulary of the Greek Testament* (Grand Rapids: Eerdmans, 1930), 33; my translation.

of "persistence."[34] Preisigke gives two illustrations of ἀναιδής, which he translates *schamlos* and *rücksichtslos*.[35]

From early Christian literature, Lampe gives ἀναιδεύομαι, which he translates "lack shame" and "behave shamelessly," and ἀναιδίζομαι, which he lists as "act with impudence."[36]

In the Greek of the canonical Old Testament the form ἀναιδής is associated with "impudence of face" or "sternness of face."[37] In the Aramaic portion of Daniel, the prophet, on hearing that the king has ordered the death of the wise men of Babylon, asks cautiously, "Why has the severe (harsh) decree come out from the face of the king (ἡ γνώμη ἡ ἀναιδής)?"[38] The Aramaic word is *ḥaṣaf*. The significance of this reference is that this same Aramaic word is the Syriac word for ἀναίδεια that appears in all the Syriac versions and has (or perhaps acquires?) the secondary meaning of "persistence." Clearly the Daniel text does not have any hint of this meaning.

The other unusual reference in the LXX is Jeremiah 8:5. The text talks of "perpetual apostasy" (*meshubah niṣṣaḥat*), which is translated in the LXX as ἀποστροφὴν ἀναιδῆ. Thus we have one clear reference to ἀναίδεια meaning "continual" or "perpetual," although it still occurs in a negative context. There is the possibility that the LXX translator is giving an interpretative translation and understands "perpetual apostasy" as "shameless apostasy." Yet the LXX reading of Jeremiah 8:5 can be accepted as a precedent for the later Christian usage. Ben Sirach has both the adjective and the abstract noun. In all cases the reference is negative and means "shameless."[39]

In summary, then, in the LXX ἀναίδεια is overwhelmingly negative and, with one possible exception, means "shameless" or "defiant, angry, harsh."

Moving to Josephus, the word exclusively means "shameless" or "impudent" as far as we have been able to trace. Marcus translates it "shamelessness."[40] Thackeray uses "impudent."[41] Again, the quality referred to is negative. With one exception, it has no reference to continuity or persistence.

The problem is that in the parable of the Friend at Midnight, the negative meaning of "shamelessness" is problematical. Is it "shameless" for the believer to take his requests to God in prayer? Surely not. To make sense out of the parable,

---

[34]In the second of these, "persistent" would make sense. However, Moulton and Milligan translate it "shameless."

[35]Friedrich Preisigke, *Wörterbuch der griechischen Papyrusurkunden* (Berlin: Selbstverlag der Erben, 1925), I, 88.

[36]G. W. H. Lampe, *A Patristic Greek Lexicon* (Oxford: Clarendon, 1961), 103.

[37]Prov. 25:23; 7:13; Deut. 28:50; Eccl. 8:1; Dan. 8:23. The Hebrew words are עַז זֵעַ עָם. The adverb occurs in Prov. 21:29. Dogs are described as ἀναιδεῖς τῇ ψυχῇ in Isa. 56:11.

[38]Dan. 2:15. So Theodotion. The LXX has πικρῶς.

[39]Cf. Sir. 23:6; 26:11; 40:30, for the adjective, and 25:23 for the abstract noun.

[40]*Josephus*, trans. and ed. R. Marcus and ed. A. Wikgren (Cambridge: Harvard University Press, 1963), 427 (*Ant.* xvii.119).

[41]*Josephus, the Life*, trans. H. St. J. Thackeray (London: William Heinemann, 1926), I, 131; also *Wars* i.224.

the Church apparently felt the necessity of taking a negative quality (shamelessness) and turning it somehow into a positive quality. The answer that finally achieved almost universal acceptance was "persistence." The victory of "persistence" over "shamelessness" was so complete by the twelfth century that Euthymius, a Greek monk, was able to define ἀναίδεια as τὴν ἐπιμονὴν τῆς αἰτήσεως.[42] It is not possible to ascertain precisely how and when this shift took place, but some of the lines of movement can be noted.

In the Latin the move involves a change of vocabulary. *Improbitatem*[43] gradually gives way to *importunitatem*,[44] which finally becomes dominant. In the Coptic versions two words appear, *las* and *matlas*. Both mean primarily "shamelessness," but both acquire the additional meaning of "persistence."[45] Did the Coptic, like the Greek, acquire this additional meaning primarily, if not exclusively, as a result of this text? Is the same true of the Syriac *ḥaṣaf*?

The Arabic versions unanimously give "persistence" as a translation.[46] Thus, in all the versions examined, the problem of the negative "shamelessness" which appears in the parable of the Friend at Midnight was solved by changing the meaning of ἀναίδεια to "persistence."

This solution to the problem is inadequate contextually, theologically, linguistically, and stylistically. Persistence in prayer is one of the dominant themes of the parable of the Unjust Judge. The woman is persistent. She finally gets an answer. However, unlike the widow of Luke 18, the host in Luke 11 (as traditionally interpreted) is given an answer immediately. The answer is, No! Presumably the "knocker" persists until the sleeper is forced to change his mind. The synoptic teaching about prayer is that the pious are to be persistent *until* an answer is given. But once they receive an answer, are they to cajole God to get him to change his mind if the answer displeases them? Or, rather, are they to respond with "Thy will be done"? Cadoux comments on the persistence that supposedly will influence God to change his mind and writes, "If such a parable were spoken today with such a meaning, it would be condemned as clumsy, misleading, dangerous and irreverent."[47] Saʿīd avoids the problem by saying, "The persistence is not to get God to deal compassionately with us, but rather to prepare us for

---

[42]Cf. Bruce, *Synoptic Gospels*, 548; no reference given.

[43]Old Latin d f i l q vg.

[44]BF c ff[22] r aur.

[45]The information on the Coptic versions has been kindly gathered for me by Professor Wahīb G. Kāmil of the Coptic Institute of Higher Studies in Cairo. He has checked the versions available to him and quotes from two Coptic-Arabic Dictionaries, *Qāmūs Qalādiyūs Labīb*, 251, and *Qāmūs Kirām*, 151.

[46]At the same time, in the eleventh century, Ibn al-Ṭayyib in his commentary tries with some difficulty to make sense out of "shamelessness." Cf. Paris Ar. 86, folio 131. The last case of its appearance to my knowledge is in the 1252 text of Ibn al-ʿAssāl, who lists it in the margin.

[47]Cadoux, *Parables*, 36. Cadoux has identified the problem. His solution is to divorce the parable totally from its Lucan context and from any relation to the parable of the Unjust Judge. He concludes that the point of the parable is ethical instruction. A man may be justified in straining one relationship for the sake of another (*ibid.*, 152). This kind of radical surgery, as we shall see, is unnecessary.

receiving his blessings."[48] This may be good theology, but it is questionable exegesis. Yet Saʿīd does recognize the problem. Clearly, turning ἀναίδεια into "persistence" creates severe theological difficulties.

The story has *no* record of any persistence aside from this debatable word.[49] Traditionally we assume that he persists in his knocking. In fact, the borrower does not knock at all; he calls. To knock on a neighbor's door in the night would frighten the neighbor. A stranger knocks in the night; a friend calls. When he calls, his voice will be recognized and the neighbor will not be frightened. The poem that follows the parable (vv. 9–13) has in it a clear reference to persistence and to knocking. This poem is most likely the source of the shift from "shamelessness" to "persistence." The idea of persistence has probably "spilled over" from the following poem. The parable itself does not say he persisted in anything.

Finally, the idea of persistence does not fit the structure of this second stanza of the parable. The key to the problem is the identification of the antecedents of some of the prepositions and nouns. For clarity's sake we shall observe again the inversion of this second stanza, this time concentrating on the subject of each line.

I say to you,   *The subject of each line is:*

B 1	if he will not give to him	the sleeper
2	having arisen	the sleeper
3	because of being a friend of his	the sleeper
3'	but because of his (ἀναίδεια?)	?
2'	he will arise	the sleeper
1'	and will give him whatever he needs.[50]	the sleeper

It is clear that the entire stanza is talking about the sleeper and that line 3' should also apply to him. Whatever the disputed word means it applies to the man in bed, not the host outside the door. Furthermore the matching line in the first stanza of the parable (A–3') speaks of the sleeper's potential refusal of duty. Here we expect a discussion that relates to the same man and the same topic. Thus we have two problems in our traditional understanding of this line. We have a mistranslation of the key word ἀναίδεια and have applied it to the wrong man.

To summarize: theologically speaking, persistence after an answer is given is not consistent with the synoptic understanding of prayer. The story has no record of any repetition of the act of calling for help. The poetic structure requires that

---

[48]Saʿīd, *Lūqā*, 301.

[49]Some of the Latin fathers were apparently aware of this, because a number of the Latin texts add *et se illa persevera verit pulsans*. Cf. c ff2 i l vg^cl. The Dutch Liege Harmony went one step further and reads, "He continues knocking and shouting" (quoted in Black, *Aramaic Approach*, 291). The Greek present imperative "stop bothering me" clearly implies that the action has begun, but it tells us nothing about how long the action has been in process.

[50]The inverted nature of the sentence was observed by Bengel, who wrote, "The arrangement of the words is studied δώσει, ἀναστάς, ἐγερθεὶς, δώσει: though he will not *give, rising up,* yet *being aroused he will give*" (Bengel, *Gnomon,* I, 446). Black, *Aramaic Approach,* 59, lists this verse as an illustration of asyndeton. Ἀναστάς is unnaturally placed after the opening phrase even though it precedes it in time. The resulting awkward construction is necessary for the literary balance.

ἀναίδεια be applied to the sleeper. The problem of "shamelessness" in a text about prayer has been recognized. The traditional solution has been to read "persistence" into verse 8. This solution is inadequate.

Modern scholarship has recognized that ἀναίδεια means basically "shamelessness." Four different solutions have been proposed for the problem created here by this meaning.

The first is to accept the translation of shamelessness and apply it to the host. A few scholars working with this solution assume that he is shameless in his initial coming at night.[51] Others combine "shameless" with "persistent." The host is shameless in coming at night, and shameless in persisting. They translate ἀναίδεια, then, as "shameless persistence."[52]

Also within the scope of this solution are those who soften "shamelessness" to "boldness" and thereby turn it into a positive quality. The shift is subtle but significant. They argue that we are to come boldly to God in prayer and that this in particular was an essential message for the timid Gentile Christians. Harris writes, "Such a teaching would have special relevance for Gentile Christians who did not have the heritage of Jewish piety."[53]

The difficulties of these solutions are severe. As we have seen, the word ἀναίδεια does not, through the first century, mean persistence, and there is no reference to any persistence in the story. The shift from a negative "shamelessness" to a positive "boldness" is imaginative but unsupported. (Why was παρρησία not used if this was the intent of the text?)

A second solution is offered by Levison, a Palestinian Hebrew Christian, who observes that ἀναιδής is related to 'zz, which includes the idea of "strengthening." He suggests that some form of 'zz is likely behind the Greek. Thus he concludes that the idea of "strengthening" is the point. Levison writes, "He [the sleeper] will not rise to give it [the bread] to him because he is his friend, but in order to strengthen, fortify, or encourage him."[54] Levison specifically denies that this parable has anything to do with the parable of the Unjust Judge.[55] He thus makes the sleeper out to be a noble-hearted man concerned for his friend in need. This evaluation of the character of the sleeper is extremely questionable. If he will not offer aid for friendship's sake, how is he to be made over into a nobleman? The parable hints at excuses he would like to use; but, as we shall see, he does not use them. The literary structure of the Jerusalem Document specifically relates the two parables of the Friend at Midnight and the Unjust Judge.[56] The

---

[51]Bengel, *Gnomon*, I, 446; N. Geldenhuys, *Commentary on the Gospel of Luke* (Grand Rapids: Eerdmans, 1951), 326.

[52]Cf. Jülicher, *Gleichnisreden*, II, 273; B. T. D. Smith, *Parables*, 147; Leaney, *St. Luke*, 187; and many others.

[53]O. G. Harris, "Prayer in Luke-Acts" (unpublished Ph.D. thesis, Vanderbilt University, 1966), 87f.

[54]N. Levison, "Importunity? A Study of Luke XI.8," *The Expositor*, Series 9, 3(1925), 460; also Levison, *Local Setting*, 78–84.

[55]Levison, "Importunity?" 459.

[56]See above, pp. 80f.

judge cares nothing for the woman and the sleeper cares nothing for the host. The sleeper does not like the host and will not help him for friendship's sake. Clearly we are dealing with a man of ignoble character. Levison clearly recognizes the problem of "persistence," but his solution must be judged inadequate.

A third solution is offered by Anton Fridrichsen. He writes,

> Contrary to all that customary explanation has made it mean, this word [ἀναίδεια] in this context can only be interpreted: he [the petitioned one] will fulfil the request because of *his* own shamelessness, namely, that which will be brought to light through his refusal. Thus he will help him, not because of friendship, but so that by any means he will not be judged specifically or generally to be an ἀνὴρ ἀναιδής.[57]

Fridrichsen accepts "shamelessness" as a negative quality. He applies it to the sleeper, not to the borrower. He recognizes the crucial fact of a community with its pressures and understands the text to mean that the sleeper does not have shamelessness, does not want it, and acts so as to avoid it. Yet this solution flounders on the αὐτοῦ. If the text reads "because of shamelessness" the sleeper did so-and-so, this would be an excellent solution. However, we are informed of "his shamelessness," which clearly describes a quality that the sleeper already has, not one he wants to avoid. Fridrichsen has dismissed the idea of "persistence" and has rightly seen that the quality in question applies to the sleeper. He is also aware of the presence of the community. Yet his solution is inadequate.

Jeremias does not reject "persistence" but accepts Fridrichsen's solution. Jeremias refers to Fridrichsen and writes, "for the sake of his (own) shamelessness, that is to say, that he may not lose face in the matter."[58] The difficulty here is that Jeremias has made a subtle, yet extremely significant shift from a negative quality to a positive quality. When he quotes Fridrichsen and says, "for the sake of his (own) shamelessness," we are dealing with a negative quality. When Jeremias adds his own comment, "that is to say, that he may not lose face in the matter," he has shifted to a positive quality of supreme importance in Oriental life. This shift may be subtly implied in Fridrichsen. Jeremias makes it explicit. If I understand these men correctly they are saying,

Fridrichsen: He acts to avoid a quality of shamelessness which he does not have.

Jeremias: He acts to preserve a quality of honor which he does have.

Granted, the two ideas are the opposite sides of the same coin; nevertheless, we are left in the dark how this shift is to be made. We are back to the same problem the fathers faced in the early centuries. How is the negative "shamelessness" to be changed into a positive quality appropriate to a parable teaching something about prayer? We are convinced that both Jeremias and Fridrichsen are wrestling with the

---

[57]A. Fridrichsen, "Exegetisches zum Neuen Testament," *Symbolae Osloensis* 13 (1934), 40; my translation.
[58]Jeremias, *Parables*, 158.

right issue, and that Jeremias has jumped to the right conclusion. We will now try to demonstrate that there is evidence for this "leap" to a positive quality such as Jeremias has made.

In any language "d" and "t" are very close linguistically, and this relates to one possible solution to our problem. The Westerner pronounces both of these letters by touching his tongue to the roof of his mouth just above the teeth. The Middle Easterner touches the tongue to the teeth themselves rather than the roof of the mouth. This brings the two sounds even closer together. In commenting on the dentals Wright says, "ד often interchanges with ת, as in the Hebrew radicals תור and דור, Arabic [tār] and [dār]."[59] He further comments,

> ד and ת undergo a slight modification in Hebrew and Aramaic, when immediately preceded by a vowel. In this position they receive a sound nearly approximating to th in that and think respectively.... I should remark that where ד and ת are retained in modern Syriac of Urumiah, their sound is hard, and very little difference is perceptible between them.[60]

The same conclusion is documented by O'Leary, who says:

> In Mandaean t frequently becomes d, and so very generally in Aramaic transcription from the Greek, but here it must be remembered that in medieval and modern Greek t is often sounded as d, thus ἀρτάβη = ארדבא....[61]

This confusion is evident in the New Testament from Luke 16:6, where some texts have βάτους[62] while others read βάδους.[63]

Is it not possible that this same confusion has occurred in Luke 11:8 and ἀναίδεια was originally ἀναίτιος? This would make the text read, "Because of his *blamelessness* he will arise and give to him what he wants." This is exactly the sense that Jeremias has suggested and provides a possible understanding of how the text could be read in this fashion. Negatively, unlike Luke 16:6, here in Luke 11:8 we have no manuscript evidence for such a change from d to t. Suggestions of this kind are easy to make and attractive, but must be accepted only with great caution.

There is also another alternative. The word ἀναίδεια etymologically is the word αἰδώς with an alpha privative. Αἰδώς has two meanings:

1. Sense of shame, sense of honor, self-respect
   (a positive quality)

2. Shame, scandal (a negative quality)

---

[59]W. Wright, *Lectures on the Comparative Grammar of the Semitic Languages* (2nd ed., Amsterdam: Philo Press, 1966), 53.

[60]*Ibid.*, pp. 53–55.

[61]De Lacy O'Leary, *Comparative Grammar of the Semitic Languages* (London: Kegan Paul, Trench, Trubner, 1923), 55.

[62]p75 B Θ E F G H S V U Ω.

[63]p1,22,52 א B C L T Z Δ Ψ Origen.

In the Greek language $\dot{\alpha}\nu\alpha\acute{\iota}\delta\epsilon\iota\alpha$ negates the first, not the second. Thus we have:

$\alpha\dot{\iota}\delta\acute{\omega}\varsigma$	+ alpha privative =	$\dot{\alpha}\nu\alpha\acute{\iota}\delta\epsilon\iota\alpha$
meaning: a sense of shame (a positive quality)		meaning: without a sense of shame (a negative quality)

However, in Semitic languages, to my limited knowledge, there is no word that covers both "shame" and "sense of shame," the first negative and the second positive.

Shame is an extremely important quality in Eastern culture generally. Some areas of life are governed by law, but much of life is controlled by the "shame" (negative) that is avoided because of the individual's inner "sense of shame" (positive). The first is negative and is to be avoided at all costs; the second is positive and is to be encouraged. The importance of the concept of shame in the East is partially indicated in that there are special words for "shame" and other quite different words that mean "sense of shame."

Jeremias refers to one of the weighty Semitic words referring to "a sense of shame" (*kissuf*),[64] which he connects to this parable, perhaps rightly so if our line of reasoning can be substantiated. For an Aramaic-speaking person "shame" was, so far as we can tell, exclusively a negative word. What the translator of this story from Aramaic to Greek may have intended was:

$\alpha\dot{\iota}\delta\acute{\omega}\varsigma$	+ alpha privative =	$\dot{\alpha}\nu\alpha\acute{\iota}\delta\epsilon\iota\alpha$
Meaning: shame (negative)		meaning: avoidance of shame (positive)

In English we achieve this same shift with the word "blameless." Thus:

blame	+ negation =	blameless
(negative)		(positive)

Thus, what our text may represent is a literal translation from the Aramaic.[65] The translator began with a negative, added an alpha privative, and had what was for him a positive quality (avoidance of shame). The *kissuf* suggested by Jeremias is precisely the "avoidance of shame" suggested above. This possibility fits admirably into the cultural pattern of the story. The sleeper knows the borrower must gather up the essentials for the banquet from the various neighbors.[66] If the sleeper refused the request of anything so humble as a loaf of bread the host would

---

[64]Jeremias, *Parables*, 158, n. 27.

[65]We are not here assuming an original Aramaic text or an Aramaic gospel, but merely that the material is Palestinian in culture, which in turn assumes Aramaic words and phrases at the heart of the material. Cf. Gustav Dalman, *Jesus-Jeshua* (New York: Ktav, 1971 ĺ929). Moulton noted, "In Luke, the only NT writer except the author of Heb to show any conscious attention to Greek ideas of style, we find (1) rough Greek translations from Aramaic left mainly as they reached him, perhaps because their very roughness seemed too characteristic to be refined away." James H. Moulton, *A Grammar of New Testament Greek*, I, *Prolegomena* (Edinburgh: T. & T. Clark, 1906, 3rd ed. 1908), 18.

[66]This is against Jülicher, who argues that the host is obliged to continue knocking because there is nowhere else he can get help (*Gleichnisreden*, II, 273). On the contrary, the host can go to any home in the village except the houses of those with whom he may be currently feuding.

continue on his rounds cursing the stinginess of the sleeper, who would not get up even to fulfil this trifling request. The story would be all over the village by morning. The sleeper would be met with cries of "shame" everywhere he went. Because of his desire for "avoidance of shame" he will arise and grant *whatever* the borrower wants.

This usually neglected detail at the end of the parable provides fairly conclusive evidence against ascribing any "persistence" or "shamelessness" to the host. If the host was shameless in his request, or if he continued knocking or calling until the sleeper finally had to get up against his will and fulfil the request to get rid of the host, then certainly the sleeper would have granted the three loaves of bread and *no more*. If the request was granted in anger or irritation there would have been no giving him "whatever he wants." That the host received much more than the bread is evidence that the entire transaction was completed in a spirit of good will.

Although *kissuf* is a good prospect for the original Aramaic word in the story, *tam* and *naqi* must also be considered. These words then put us into the family of $\check{\alpha}\mu\omega\mu\rho\varsigma$, $\check{\alpha}\mu\epsilon\mu\pi\tau\rho\varsigma$, $\dot{\alpha}\mu\dot{\omega}\mu\eta\tau\rho\varsigma$, and $\dot{\alpha}\nu\alpha\dot{\iota}\tau\iota\rho\varsigma$, which brings us to the same word suggested above. *Naqi* as an Aramaic abstract noun (*neqqiyuth*) means "respectability" or "dignity," which is an intriguing possibility.

The theological cluster of this parable includes two major items. The first deals with *the nature of God*. The parable said to the original listener/reader, "When you go to this kind of a neighbor everything is against you. It is night. He is asleep in bed. The door is locked. His children are asleep. He does not like you and *yet* you will receive even more than you ask. This is because your neighbor is a man of integrity and he will not violate that quality. The God to whom you pray also has an integrity that he will not violate; and beyond this, he loves you."[67]

The second theme in the theological cluster is *assurance for man*. Again we are in the range of *a minore ad maius*. If you are confident of having your needs met when you go to such a neighbor in the night, how much more can you rest assured when you take your requests to a loving Father?

In summary, the parable of the Friend at Midnight is seen to be an Oriental story of a man who knows his request in the night will be honored even by a neighbor who does not like him. The key to the parable is the definition of the word $\dot{\alpha}\nu\alpha\dot{\iota}\delta\epsilon\iota\alpha$. This word took on the meaning of "persistence." It is here more appropriately translated "avoidance of shame," a positive quality. The literary structure of the entire parable makes clear that this quality is to be applied to the sleeper. Thus the parable tells of a sleeping neighbor who will indeed preserve his honor and grant the host's request and more. Even so, man before God has much more reason to rest assured that his requests will be granted.

---

[67]Our cultural presuppositions in the last half of the 20th century tend to make us uneasy about seeing "the preservation of honor" as a virtue that is appropriate to God. Given the importance of this concept in the Eastern value system, it would be surprising if Jesus did not use such a quality as a prime virtue for the Father. The center of each stanza climaxes on the question of honor.

THE PARABLE/POEM ON A FATHER'S GIFTS (LUKE 11:9-13)

We will try to demonstrate in this section that Luke 11:9-13 is a parable composed of three unforgettable comparisons. This parable is then encased in two stanzas of Form III poetry (step parallelism). It is a mixed parable/poem construction, yet the three stanzas together make up a three-stanza unit which approximates the poetic Form VI. The poem is most probably addressed to the opponents of the gospel, and affirms that a Heavenly Father gives good gifts to *all* his children.

Luke 11:9-13 is best understood as a separate pericope and not as originally a part of the parable of the Friend at Midnight.[68] At least four reasons lead to this conclusion:

1. Both in Luke 16:1-13 and here in 11:5-13 a parable is followed by a related pericope having a different literary style, and the two pericopes are connected with the peculiar Lucan phrase "and to you I say."

2. There are four special shifts in setting and emphasis between 11:5-8 and 11:9-13.

3. The parable has one literary form; verses 9-13 have a distinctively different form.

4. The poem is addressed to the disciples; the poem speaks to the opponents of the gospel.

These must be examined in turn.

We have already observed the very unusual phrase "and to you I say" (with the verb occurring last). This is again evidence of someone tying together two pericopes that were not originally one literary unit.

A second reason for separating the parable from the parable/poem is the shift of setting and emphasis between 11:5-8 and 11:9-13. Four specific shifts are clear. They are:

1. In the parable a neighbor deals with a neighbor; in the poem a father deals with his son.

2. In the parable there is no one asking for something good and receiving something bad. In the poem this is the burden of the imagery.

3. In the parable there is no reference to persistence. So far as we know the host asks only once. In the poem continued action is implied by the present tenses of the verbs.

4. In the parable the friend *calls* to his neighbor; in the poem *knocking* is introduced.

These specific shifts of imagery and emphasis make clear that the poem in 11:9-13

---

[68]This is recognized by many scholars: cf. Bultmann, *Tradition,* 324; Jeremias, *Parables,* 90; Jones, *Art,* 141, 149. Jones sees it as a new parable and calls it the parable of "the child asking for bread" (*ibid.*).

is a separate block of material. The style of 11:9–13 must now be examined in detail. We will attempt to demonstrate the following literary structure:

And to you I say

1		*ask,* and it shall be *given* to you	
	2	seek, and you shall find	2ND person
		3 knock, and it shall be opened to you.	

1'		For everyone who *asks* receives	
	2'	and the one who seeks finds	3RD person
		3' and to the knocker it shall be opened.	

And will any one of you

A   if the son *asks* the father for bread,
A'   will he *give* him a stone?

B   or a fish, instead of a fish
B'   will he *give* him an eel (snake)?

C   or if he *asks* an egg
C'   will he *give* him a scorpion?

If therefore

4		you being evil	
	5	you know good gifts	2ND person
		6 to *give* to your children	

4'		how much more the Father	
	5'	out of heaven Holy Spirit	3RD person
		6' shall *give* to those *asking* him.	

Burney has identified the first and the third stanzas as poetry.[69] We agree, but see them as the outer stanzas of a three-stanza poem.

The first stanza is a clear example of step parallelism. The pattern is: ask, seek, knock—ask, seek, knock.[70] The present tenses of the imperatives imply continued action and can be translated, "keep on asking, seeking, knocking." The emphasis on "everyone," which is reinforced in the Old Syriac, can be understood as an appeal to the outcasts; even they will receive if they ask. It could also be spoken in defense of the universality of the gospel. Jesus could be saying to the Pharisees, "Everyone who asks will receive, even sinners, not just the so-called righteous."[71]

---

[69]Burney, *Poetry,* 67, 82.

[70]In the Old Syriac the first three lines rhyme at the end and the second three at the beginning, with a repetition of "everyone" at the start of each line.

[71]Jeremias has assumed that the emphasis on "asking" springs from "the experience of the *beggar*" (*Parables,* 159; emphasis his). Rather, the background of this language is life in the East in general. Asking is a part of life on all levels of society. Jesus is using language from the daily interchange of social and economic life. In the Middle East, the beggar's profession is recognized as legitimately ordained of God but his position is nevertheless despised. Cf. Sir. 40:28–30; these words are overlooked by Jeremias, *loc. cit.,* n. 35.

The second stanza contains a textual problem. Both the Nestle-Aland and the Bible Society critical texts prefer two figures rather than the three.[72] Yet there is significant textual evidence from all the major families to include the bread-stone image in some form as part of the Lucan text.[73] Matthew 7:7–11 has the same poem that we are considering here. In the Matthean version the central stanza has only two figures, the stone-bread and the fish-serpent. If all three figures are included in the Lucan text for textual and poetic reasons, the Lucan version is left somewhat longer than the Matthean. This latter situation seems to be relatively frequent. In this study we observe the two other cases where a block of material common to Luke and Matthew is abbreviated in Matthew.[74]

T. W. Manson points out that the question of the original form of the poem must include a discussion of "Q." He writes,

> The three short (two-stress) lines in v. 10 answer to the three lines in v. 9; and the triple form is carried into the short parable which follows (vv. 11f.), although there is serious doubt about the text. . . . Many scholars regard it as an assimilation of the text of Lk. to that of Mt. But the question whether it stood in Lk. is distinct from the question whether it stood in Q; and, leaving the text of Lk. on one side, we have three points in the parable. The first is attested by Mt. (and Lk.?), the second by Mt. and Lk., the third by Lk. alone. The evidence for the place of the first point in Q is at least as good as that for the third; and the fact that the poem is in a triple form favors a three-fold parable.[75]

In another connection Manson also observes that we have to deal with "one of the favorite practices of the first Evangelist, abbreviation, which he carries out even at the expense of poetic form."[76]

When Manson refers to the triple form of the poem, he is talking only about verse 9. When we observe that verse 13 also has a triple form and that the poem on mammon in Luke 16:9–13 consists of three stanzas with a double three in each stanza, Manson's point is further strengthened. Thus it can be accepted that the stanza originally had three double images.[77]

One naturally suspects some kind of special relationship between the contrasting items suggested in each of the double lines. Sa'īd is again helpful. He writes,

> Bread, fish, and eggs are the ordinary food of a common man. . . . A round stone looks like a round loaf (Luke 4:3), and there is little outward difference

---

[72]*Novum Testamentum Graece*, ed. Eberhard Nestle and Kurt Aland (editio vicesima quinta, Stuttgart: Württembergische Bibelanstalt, 1964), 181; *The Greek New Testament*, ed. Kurt Aland *et al.* (2nd ed., Stuttgart: The United Bible Societies, 1968), 256.

[73]Alexandrian (א L), Caesarean (Θ), Western (D^gr Sy^c), Byzantine (A E F G H).

[74]Matt. 18:12–14 parallels Luke 15:3–10; Matt. 6:24 parallels Luke 16:9–13. If Luke is expanded to fit Matthew, why is Matthew not expanded with the egg-scorpion image to fit Luke?

[75]Manson, *Sayings*, 81.

[76]Manson, *Teaching*, 53.

[77]All our Oriental versions except Sy^s have three double images. Again the Old Syriac has closer sound correspondences than the Greek. In this second stanza in each case the second line begins with "lmu" and ends with "leh."

between the snake of the sea which is a kind of fish and a snake of the land which is an ordinary snake . . . and the scorpion all folded up looks like an egg.[78]

Bishop quotes Masterman regarding the *Barbut* (*clarias macamcracanthus*), a type of fish in the Sea of Galilee that can reach five feet in length, crawl on land, and has the appearance of a snake. Bishop mentions that it is among the unclean fish.[79] It seems quite likely that this is the "snake" of the story. The fisherman would regularly catch both edible fish and the eel-like creatures which would be cast back into the sea as unclean and nonedible. If a son asked for a fish would his father give him a "snake" out of the sea?

In addition to the visual correspondence here suggested, there is also the possibility of some auditory correspondence. In the Old Syriac given above "fish" is *nuno* and snake is *hewyo*. Six of our oldest and finest Arabic versions have fish as *hūt* and snake as *hayyah*. This word for snake is common but *hūt* is a rare word for fish. It is fairly obvious that the common word *samak* has been rejected and *hūt* selected for its assonance with *hayyah* (snake).[80]

Thus there is good evidence that the second stanza had three double images in "Q" and perhaps in Luke. The three images are brief antithetical parallelisms. Each of the couplets has the same message. A son will unfailingly receive from his father and the gift will be good.

In the third stanza we are faced with a textual problem that fortunately does not affect the clear poetic structure.[81]

Arndt explains ὁ ἐξ οὐρανοῦ as being a contraction of ὁ ἐν οὐρανῷ ἐξ οὐρανοῦ.[82] Yet there is some good textual evidence for omitting the ὁ.[83] This reading, popular in the early versions, is also represented in the Arabic.[84] With this omission the text reads in many of the Syriac and the Arabic texts, "How much more the father from heaven gives holy spirit." This would in turn lead to a slight shift in the word placement in the last three lines of the final stanza. The following would be required:

$$4'\quad πόσῳ\ μᾶλλον\ ὁ\ πατὴρ$$

$$5'\quad ἐξ\ οὐρανοῦ\ δώσει\ πνεῦμα\ ἅγιον$$

---

[78]Sa'īd, *Lūqā*, 303.

[79]Bishop, *Jesus*, 83, quoting from E. W. G. Masterson, *Studies in Galilee* (Chicago: University of Chicago Press, 1909), 45; cf. also Jeremias, *Parables*, 226.

[80]The Arabic versions are of course late, but the translators must have either sensed a wordplay in the Syriac they were translating, or remembered a wordplay in local vocaublary. Vat. Borg.Ar. 95 is from an early Greek ms. and no. 71 of the same collection from the Old Syriac. Both make this wordplay. Ibn al-Ṭayyib translating from the Peshitta also has this correspondence.

[81]Matt. 7:11 has the gift as simply ἀγαθά. Luke has apparently changed this to πνεῦμα ἅγιον, or to ἀγαθὸν δόμα, or to δόματα ἀγαθά. The Matthean form is simpler and quite likely more primitive. The shift in Luke may be to provide a smooth transition into the discussion of Beelzebub. Cf. Cadoux, *Parables*, 76.

[82]Arndt, *St. Luke*, 298. Arndt offers no documentation for his suggestion.

[83]p[75] ℵ L X Ψ it[a2,d,f] vg syr[c,p] cop[sa,bo] arm geo.

[84]Both Ibn al-Ṭayyib and Ibn al-'Assāl have, "The father gives from heaven."

6′   τοῖς αἰτοῦσιν αὐτόν.

The second line is thus left excessively long. At the same time, line 5 places
διδόναι after ἀγαθά, which allows for the following construction of that stanza:

4   εἰ οὖν ὑμεῖς πονηροὶ ὑπάρχοντες

5   οἴδατε δόματα ἀγαθὰ

6   διδόναι τοῖς τέκνοις ὑμῶν.[85]

Following this word order of lines 4, 5, and 6 we may cautiously speculate that an
original Aramaic of lines 4′, 5′, and 6′ may also have had the verb "to give" at the
head of the final line. This would require moving δώσει ahead two words in the
final stanza. With the awareness of what Manson calls the "many rash acts" that
have been committed *metri causa*,[86] making such a minor shift of word order
leaves the six lines as follows:

4   εἰ οὖν ὑμεῖς πονηροὶ ὑπάρχοντες

5   οἴδατε δόματα ἀγαθὰ

6   διδόναι τοῖς τέκνοις ὑμῶν

4′   πόσῳ μᾶλλον ὁ πατὴρ

5′   ἐξ οὐρανοῦ πνεῦμα ἅγιον

6′   δώσει τοῖς αἰτοῦσιν αὐτόν.

Even without this slight shift of word order the balance of

Giver

gift

receiver

is still intact for each stanza. The shift merely provides a more symmetrical
semantic balance.

Thus the third stanza is also a carefully constructed example of step
parallelism. The principle of *kal va homer,* common to the Dominical sayings, is
again employed. The theme centers on the quality of the gifts. The one who asks of
God can be assured of even better gifts than those a father gives his son.

A number of striking features tie the first and last stanzas together. The
structure of ABC-A′B′C′ appears in both. There is also a clear case of *inclusio.*

---

[85]The earlier position in the sentence for the verb "to give" in lines 4′, 5′, and 6′ is preferred in Semitic
word order, but the later position in lines 4, 5, and 6 maintained itself all through the Syriac versions
only to lose it in the Arabic. This would indicate that with the Syriac versions this word order was
maintained for some reason other than the normal order of the sentence. It is our suggestion that poetic
balance is the reason. As the sense of the poetry was lost, the Semitic sentence structure gradually
dominated and the Arabic word order is the result. The position of the verb in line 5′ remained
unchanged in all our Oriental versions.

[86]Manson, *Teaching,* 53.

The verbs "ask" and "give" both occur in line 1 and most likely both were in line 6'. Both verbs either occur or are implied in each of the three illustrations in the center stanza. Thus, in a very artistic fashion these two verbs unite the entire poem. If "Holy Spirit" is an editorial change, the original poem may well have had the simpler "good things." In an original Aramaic this would give two stresses to each of the six lines in the third stanza to match the rhythm of the first stanza. But most striking of all, the first three lines of the first stanza are addressed to the second person. Each line is directed to "you." Then lines 1'2'3' are directed to the third person. The same shift from second to third person occurs in the third stanza. Lines 4, 5, and 6 are specifically addressed to "you." Then again the last half of the third stanza (lines 4'5'6') shifts to the third person.

The second stanza is naturally the climax. It combines in vivid imagery the major thrust of each stanza. These are as follows:

Stanza I—*all* will receive.

Stanza II—*all* will receive and the gift will be *good*.

Stanza III—the gift will be *good*.

The images of this second stanza are simple and striking. They are constructed so that even if the listener remembers only one of them it is enough. He will have the two major emphases of the overall poem.

The question must now be raised: To whom was this material originally addressed? Was it spoken to the disciples, to the crowds, or to the opponents of the gospel? The problem focuses on the introductory phrase τίς ἐξ ὑμῶν. Jeremias argues that it "generally introduced sayings of Jesus addressed to opponents."[87] The texts themselves indicate a broader usage than Jeremias allows. The seven occurrences in the synoptic Gospels fall into the following categories:

1. Texts clearly addressed to the opponents of the gospel
    The ox falling into a pit on the Sabbath
    (Matt. 12:11 par. Luke 14:5)
    The Lost Sheep
    (Luke 15:5)

2. Texts that are clearly addressed to the disciples
    The discussion on unworthy servants[88]
    (Luke 17:7)
    Anxiety and the lilies of the field
    (Matt. 6:27 par. Luke 12:25)

---

[87]Jeremias, *Parables*, 145.

[88]It could be argued that Luke 17:7 supposes an economic level beyond the disciples of Jesus, but not so. In the East, families of remarkably modest means engage servants. Down through the lower middle class, servants are the accepted pattern. Anyone with enough money to own a boat would naturally have a servant. There is no evidence that the original followers of Jesus were entirely of the poorest of the poor. In any case, the Matt. 6:27 text is clearly intended for the disciples.

3.   A text addressed to the multitudes
The building of a tower[89]
(Luke 14:28)

Thus, in the case of Luke 11:5–8 and 11:9–13, the introductory phrase τίς ἐξ ὑμῶν does not automatically determine the setting for us.

We must then ask, Is it possible to determine the intended audience of this poem? In our view, the internal evidence of the texts themselves and the external structure of the Jerusalem Document both point to a setting of disciples for the parable and opponents of the gospel for the poem. The first has been discussed above; the second will now be examined.

In the case of the poem on a Father's Gifts, the internal evidence seems to point to a hostile audience. Jesus addresses the listeners as ὑμεῖς πονηροὶ ὑπάρχοντες, which is most likely addressed to the Pharisees.[90] In addition to the "you being evil" phrase, which is clearly addressed to opponents, the entire first stanza can perhaps best be understood as being addressed to these same opponents. "*Everyone* who asks, receives," can be in defense of sinners and publicans receiving. The admonition to ask, seek, and knock sounds very much as though Jesus is talking to those who have not yet done these things.[91]

The overall structure of the Jerusalem Document, as we have seen, connects Luke 11:1–13 with 18:1–14. In the latter passage the compiler of the material has indicated that the parable of the Unjust Judge was spoken to the disciples.[92]

---

[89]Jeremias' attempt to understand all these texts under the first heading is unconvincing (*Parables*, 103, 145). Arguing that τίς ἐξ ὑμῶν is addressed to the opponents of the gospel, Jeremias does not discuss how this can hold true for the parable of the Friend at Midnight, which he admits teaches that God is a God "who hearkens to the cry of the needy and comes to their help" (*Parables*, 159).

[90]Cf. Matt. 12:34. Jeremias argues that the polemical nature of lines 4–6' is obvious because of "the change from the second to the third person" (*Parables*, 144f.). His point is that only in addressing opponents would Jesus shift to the third person and thus avoid saying, "shall give to *you* who ask him." The difficulty is that Jeremias has not observed the poetic structure which balances the first and third stanzas. In the first stanza, as we have noted, this same shift takes place from second to third person. Yet there it is clear that the line addressed to the second person, "Ask and it shall be given to you," is balanced with the line addressed to the third person, "For everyone who asks, receives." Therefore, the shift from second to third person in lines 4–6' cannot be used to argue for "opponents of the gospel" as the original hearers.

[91]It must be granted that a precise delineation of audience cannot be made in the case of this poem. There is, in lines 1–3, the element of assurance that an answer will be given. This theme is most appropriate for the disciples, not the opponents of the gospel. The topic of assurance provides a smooth transition from the parable to the poem. In like manner, the theme of eschatology appeared both in the parable and in the poem in Luke 16 and provided a smooth transition from one to the other. Yet like the poem in Luke 16, this theme of assurance of an answer, which connects this poem in Luke 11 to the parable, is not the main thrust of the first stanza of the poem. The main point of the stanza is that *all* men shall receive. We have noted that the Old Syriac gave this "all" a threefold repetition. The Pharisees think that only *some* who call on the name of the Lord will be saved, but Jesus insists that "*everyone* who asks, receives." Again the parallel with the parable of the Publican and the Pharisee is helpful.

[92]The "theme" of Luke 18:1 goes back to 17:22. Furthermore, the introduction and the conclusion of the parable point to a disciple audience.

Then the parable of the Pharisee and the Tax Collector is clearly addressed to the opponents of the gospel.[93] Luke 11:1–13 may have been compiled with the same division in mind, that is, with the first half of the unit (11:1–8) addressed to the disciples and the second half (11:9–13) to a Pharisaic audience.[94]

Thus internal as well as external evidence points to a Pharisaic audience for the poem on a Father's Gifts. In conclusion and summary, the parable/poem on the Father's Gifts, which follows the parable of the Friend at Midnight, is stylistically divided into three stanzas with each stanza containing three double lines. As such it approximates a Form VI poetic structure. It is most probably addressed to the opponents of the gospel. The parable/poem dramatically states that a gracious father always grants good gifts (Holy Spirit) to *all* who seek him. The poem is stylistically and theologically distinct from the parable that precedes it. There is no reason to doubt that both have equal antiquity in the tradition, and have been brought together by a compiler of the Jerusalem Document with no intention that the second should be understood as a commentary on the first.[95] As in the case of Luke 16:9–13, a poem of this quality, with close semantic correspondences uniting the whole, must come from the mind of a single poet. It is theoretically possible that an anonymous poet in the Palestinian community has recast different strands of traditional material into a poem of his own creation. It is much more likely that the author is Jesus of Nazareth.

---

[93]The editor in Luke 18:9 states specifically that the parable is spoken to "some who trusted in themselves that they were righteous and despised others." Internally the parable substantiates the accuracy of this setting. The outcast publican's prayers are heard.

[94]Jeremias has observed the relationship between Luke 11:9–13 and the parable of the Pharisee and the Tax Collector in Luke 18. Of the former he writes, "The usual attack of the opponents of Jesus on his proclamation of the gospel to the despised may most naturally be suggested as its occasion. Publicans pray to God (Luke 18:13f.), and he listens to them—shocking! But Jesus replies: 'Your eyes are closed against the fatherly goodness of God. Consider how you behave towards your children. If, although you are evil you know how to give good gifts to your children, why are you unwilling to believe that God will give the gifts of the New Age to those who ask him?' " (*Parables*, 145).

[95]Jeremias understands Luke 11:9–13 as a group of logia "used by Luke as the application of the parable," and feels the point of the parable "has been distorted by this expansion" (*Parables*, 105). The distortion comes about (as in the case of Luke 16:9–13) when we read the poem as a conclusion to the parable. It seems clear that this was not the intent of the compiler himself even as he certainly did not intend the parable of the Pharisee and the Publican to be read as the conclusion to the parable of the Widow and the Judge.

Chapter 7

EXEGESIS OF LUKE 15[1]

THE LOST SHEEP AND THE LOST COIN (LUKE 15:4–10)

In this section we intend to demonstrate that Luke 15:4–10 is a single unit in the form of a double parable, and that each half of the double parable has a literary structure. The cultural elements will be reexamined with the literary structures in mind. We will first examine the Lucan setting and then proceed to the Lost Sheep and the Lost Coin.

The Lucan Setting (15:1–3)

Some modern scholars feel that the setting given to the Lost Coin, the Lost Sheep, and the Lost Sons is secondary and yet historically accurate.[2] Jeremias, on the other hand, argues that Luke 15:1–3 is a part of the Evangelist's source and not the product of his redactional efforts.[3] Jeremias also understands the introduction to be historically accurate, so that the *Sitz im Leben* of this set of parables is not the presentation of the gospel so much as the "defense and vindication of the gospel."[4] Jeremias' point is clearly affirmed in verses 2 and 3. Jesus is presented as defending his association with sinners. If it can be agreed that the setting is historically accurate, the question of its being primary or secondary is of little importance. The more important question is that of the cultural significance of table fellowship. This question must now be examined.

Table fellowship anywhere in the world is a relatively serious matter. This is especially true in the Middle East. In his most recent statement Jeremias says,

> To understand what Jesus was doing in eating with "sinners," it is important to realize that in the east, even today, to invite a man to a meal was an honour. It

---

[1]For a brief popular discussion of some of the material in this chapter cf. Kenneth Bailey, *The Cross and the Prodigal* (St. Louis: Concordia, 1973).
[2]Dodd, *Parables*, 193; Linnemann, *Parables*, 69.
[3]Jeremias, *Parables*, 100.
[4]*Ibid.*, 124.

was an offer of peace, trust, brotherhood and forgiveness; in short, sharing a table meant sharing life. . . . Thus Jesus' meals with the publicans and sinners . . . are an expression of the mission and message of Jesus (Mark 2:17), eschatological meals, anticipatory celebrations of the feast in the end-time (Matt. 8.11 par.), in which the community of the saints is already being represented (Mark 2.19). The inclusion of sinners in the community of salvation, achieved in table-fellowship, is the most meaningful expression of the message of the redeeming love of God.[5]

In the East today, as in the past, a nobleman may feed any number of lesser needy persons as a sign of his generosity, but he does *not* eat with them. However, when guests are "received" the one receiving the guests eats with them. The meal is a special sign of acceptance. The host affirms this by showering his guests with a long series of compliments to which the guests must respond. Jesus is set forth in the text as engaging in some such social relationship with publicans and sinners. Small wonder the Pharisees were upset.[6]

In addition to "eating with sinners" there is the possibility that Jesus was himself hosting sinners. The accusation, "This one receives sinners and eats with them," is closely parallel to Mark 2:15f. In this Marcan text Jesus is clearly the host for the meal. The same may be true in Luke 15:2. In Luke the verb δέχομαι often does imply hospitality.[7] The προσδέχομαι of 15:2 is synonymous with the simpler form.[8] If this is the intent of 15:2, it is very significant inasmuch as the guest is assumed in any Oriental banquet to be bringing honor to the house in which he is entertained. The order of the traditional rounds of compliments mentioned above makes this clear. The host begins by referring to the honor brought to his house by the guests. The guests can then respond either by invoking the honor of God on the noble host or by affirming that they, too, have received honor by being in the host's presence. Even if modern village banquet customs are judged too recent to be used as evidence for ancient banquets, it can certainly be affirmed that for Jesus to *host* sinners would have been a much more serious offense to the Pharisees than merely to eat with sinners informally or to accept their invitations, as in the case of Zacchaeus of Jericho.[9] Thus, as host or guest, it is little wonder that Jesus' table fellowship with sinners offended the cultural and theological sensitivities of the Pharisees. The importance of the issue for both Jesus and his opposition is reflected in the fulness of his defense recorded in Luke 15:4–32.

In summary, Luke 15:1–3 is seen as an authentic setting for the parables

---

[5]Jeremias, *Theology*, 115f.

[6]A rabbinic injunction stated, "The wise say, 'Let not a man associate with sinners even to bring them near to the Torah' " (*Mechilta* 57b on Exod. 18:1; quoted from Montefiore, *Rabbinic*, 355). Jeremias points out that for the Pharisee, entertaining the non-Pharisee was "if not entirely forbidden, at least protected by very scrupulous limitations" (*Jerusalem*, 267).

[7]Luke 9:5; 9:53; 10:8, 11; 16:4, 9; 22:17.

[8]W. Grundmann, *TDNT*, II, 57.

[9]Both acts are clearly an offense to the Pharisees, as reflected in the διεγόγγυζον of Luke 15:2 and 19:7. Yet to host sinners would most likely be the greater offense.

that follow. The issue is Jesus' welcome of sinners to table fellowship either as fellow guest or as host. This issue is of crucial importance for Jesus and for his opponents. The parables of 15:4–32 are a defense of Jesus' actions. To the first part of this defense we now turn.

The Parable of the Lost Sheep (15:4–7)

These verses are a parable cast into the Form VI poetic structure. Further research is required before it will be possible to determine whether this is poetry or merely parallelistic prose. For this study we will assume the latter, observing however that the three-stanza poetical form is used. In this section the structure of the parable will be examined and the pertinent cultural elements set forth. We will attempt to understand the theology of the parable in the light of these two aspects.

In the three-stanza form the first stanza is semantically related to the third, and the second stanza often uses a different poetic device from the outer two. The structure of the parable is as follows:

A   What man of *you,* having a hundred sheep

B   and having lost *one* (*ḥadh*) of them

C   does he not leave the *ninety-nine* in the wilderness

   1   and go after the *lost* one

      2   until he *finds* it, and having *found* it

         3   he places it upon his shoulders *rejoicing* (*ḥedhwa*)?

           4   And coming *to the home*
                 he calls *to the friends* and neighbors

         3'   saying to them, *rejoice* (*ḥedhwa*) with me

      2'   because I have *found* my sheep

   1'   which was *lost*.

A'   I say to *you* that thus there is more *joy* (*ḥedhwa*) in heaven

B'   over *one* (*ḥadh*) sinner
       who repents

C'   than over *ninety-nine* righteous persons
       who need no repentance.

The semantic correspondences between the parallel lines are as follows:

1   which man of you (a direct address to the audience)
2   one
3   ninety-nine

     A   the lost
       B   find
         C   joy
           D   restoration

      C'   joy
    B'   find
   A'   the lost

1'   I say to you (a direct address to the audience)
2'   one
3'   ninety-nine

Although to our knowledge this poetic structure has not been previously identified, the presence of literary structures generally in the parables has been noted. Jones refers to "thought-rhyme" or "kolometric harmony," and lists this parable as an example.[10] B. T. D. Smith discusses the tendency toward "schematization" and the love of "parallelism and of formulas" in the parables of Christ.[11] In a recent article Giblin approaches Luke 15 from the same perspective and notes:

> ... Closer attention to literary structure reveals wondrously the theological finality of a given work. Perhaps the interrelation of certain structural elements in a reasonably large and well-defined unit like Lk 15 will reveal to one who studies its compositional features as a *whole* a number of interesting and profitable theological insights.[12]

Giblin gives his own structural analysis of the Lost Sheep and the Lost Coin. He comments that the material has a "remarkable parallelism of structure."[13] Thus the literary structure given above is in line with hints stemming from other studies.

The structure itself is similar to Luke 11:9–13. Both have three stanzas. In both, the first stanza is reflected in a slightly different form in the third. In both, the outer two stanzas use step parallelism. There is a direct "to you" reference to introduce stanzas I and III in both poems. Three semantic units are prominent in the outer stanzas of both. Both use a poetic device in the center that is different from the outside. The climax of each is in the center.

At the same time there are some differences. In this parable on the Lost Sheep the outer stanzas are not doubled. The center has its semantic units inverted rather than in parallel.[14] Seven semantic units appear in the center rather than six. In spite of these variations, the overall structure of the parable identifies it structurally with Luke 16:9–13 and 11:9–13.

The semantic correspondences between *you, one,* and *ninety-nine* which link stanzas I and III need no further comment. In addition to the semantic correspondences, there is a striking play on words tying these stanzas together.

---

[10]Jones, *Art,* 73–75. The usual spelling is "colometric."
[11]B. T. D. Smith, *Parables,* 37.
[12]Giblin, "Luke 15," 18.
[13]*Ibid.,* 19. Giblin concentrates on parallelisms between the Lost Sheep and the Lost Coin. These certainly do exist. It is our view that the internal parallelisms are more precise and more important.
[14]A three-stanza structure with inverted parallelism in the center stanza was observed in Luke 16:9–13.

Matthew Black has noted a paronomasia in an underlying Aramaic of this parable between "one" (*ḥadh*) and "joy" (*ḥedhwa*).[15] This auditory correspondence runs through the entire poem and strengthens the unity of the three stanzas. *Ḥadh* occurs in the first stanza, *ḥedhwa* in the second, and both words in the third. Furthermore, the *ḥedhwa* (joy) is at the climactic center of the poem. Thus the two outer stanzas are linked by semantic and auditory correspondences.

This brings us to a consideration of the center stanza. The parables of Jesus are known for their naturalness and life-like qualities. Yet before and since Archimedes, anyone who finds anything cries out, "I have found it!" The natural thing for the shepherd of the parable to have said would be, "I have found my sheep." Instead we have a long, somewhat unnatural statement which is clearly constructed to provide the inversion of ideas that will fill out the parallelistic form and climax on "joy at restoration" in the center of the parable. This center must now be examined with care.

Matthew Black notes in his chapter on "Semitic Poetic Form"[16] a series of texts in the Old Syriac which have striking poetic correspondences between lines. He feels these Old Syriac readings "may well have preserved the true translation of the original Aramaic."[17] The center of this poem here in Luke 15:6 may be another illustration of Black's suggestion. In the Old Syriac this center reads,

wa'eto lebayteh

waqro lerohmaohi

which gives close grammatical and auditory correspondences between the lines.[18] Furthermore, lines C' and B' have a double auditory rhyme in the Old Syriac.[19]

To summarize the structural elements in this section, the parable uses a Form VI structure. It has strong auditory as well as semantic correspondences. Both inverted and step parallelism are used. The climax, which is "joy in restoration," is highlighted by the parallelistic structure and by the word-rhyme between "one" and "joy." This brings us to a consideration of the cultural aspects of the parable.

---

[15]Black, *Aramaic Approach,* 184. Thus v.7 in Aramaic would include, "there is more '*ḥedhwa*' over '*ḥadh*'...." Black notes other poetic associations in the same passage that appear too faint to be convincing.

[16]*Ibid.,* 143–185.

[17]*Ibid.,* 159.

[18]The Greek text does not have καί at the beginning of the second line. The Old Syriac, the Peshitta, and most of the Arabic versions do have the copula. The additional word "the neighbors" in the Greek text interrupts the structure. Both p[75] of the Alexandrian family and Θ of the Caesarean omit it. It may have spilled in from the parable of the Lost Coin. Turner observes that occasionally the poetic structure of a passage "helps the textual critic"; cf. Nigel Turner, *Syntax,* Vol. III of James H. Moulton, *A Grammar of New Testament Greek* (Edinburgh: T. & T. Clark, 1963), 346.

[19]These are:

ḥedaw 'ammi
deshekht 'erbi

The telling of a parable about a shepherd in an address to Pharisees has a special problem. Moses was accepted as a shepherd. A Midrash on Exodus records a story of Moses searching out a lost kid and being told by God that he will lead Israel.[20] Kings were referred to by Ezekiel as shepherds (Ezra 34), and God himself was thought of as a shepherd (Ps. 23). Thus the figure of the shepherd was a noble symbol. By contrast, flesh-and-blood shepherds who in the first century wandered around after sheep were clearly '*am ha' are*ṣ and unclean. For the Pharisee, a "sinner" was either an immoral person who did not keep the law or a person engaged in one of the proscribed trades, among which was herding sheep.[21] Derrett observes the incongruity of despising shepherds in the flesh and approving of them in allegories. He writes,

> The shepherd was despised socially on account of his flocks' eating private property, whatever prestige the occupation of shepherd might have in the eyes of allegorists.[22]

It is difficult to know how the rabbis managed to revere the shepherd of the Old Testament and despise the shepherd who herded the neighbor's sheep. But this seems to have been the case.

If we accept that the parable was addressed to Pharisees (15:1–3), then the parable begins with a shock to their sensitivities. Any man who believed shepherds were unclean would naturally be offended if addressed as one. Yet Jesus begins, "Which one of *you* having a hundred sheep . . . does not he leave. . . ." Thus this beginning can be understood as an indirect and yet very powerful attack on the Pharisaic attitudes toward proscribed professions. To show deference to their feelings in this matter he would have had to begin the parable something like this: "Which man of you owning a hundred sheep, if he heard that the hired shepherd had lost one, would he not summon the shepherd and demand that the sheep be found under threat of fine?"[23] It can be seriously questioned whether any Pharisee would ever take up the task of a shepherd under any condition. Thus the decision to address Pharisees as shepherds is a culturally and theologically conditioned decision of some significance.[24]

---

[20]Midrash on Exodus, *Shemoth Rabba* iii.1, quoted by Oesterley, *Jewish Background,* 181.

[21]Jeremias, *Parables,* 132; *Jerusalem,* 304. Herdsmen appear twice on the rabbinic lists of proscribed trades. Jeremias notes, "most of the time they were dishonest and thieving; they led their herds on to other people's land . . . and pilfered the produce of the herd" (*Jerusalem,* 305, also 310f.).

[22]Derrett, "Prodigal Son," 66, n. 1.

[23]The modern Christian has a kindly attitude toward Rahab. But woe to any preacher who begins his sermon, "Now which one of you ladies, if she does so-and-so."

[24]In the East, the social status identified with particular professions is a very serious matter. Major Jarvis, the British governor of Sinai in the thirties, notes the sharp distinctions between classes. A camel driver was very careful not to be known as a fisherman, and if caught fishing would point out to the visitor that he was a camel driver, *not* a fisherman (C. S. Jarvis, *Desert and Delta* [London: John Murray, 1938], 217; *idem, Three Deserts* [London: John Murray, 1936], *passim*).

In an isolated Egyptian village of Der al-Barsha in 1958–59 I tried to introduce a brick machine into the village. The mud bricks are still made as in the days of Moses. A wall built of them lasts only a

Another cultural factor needs consideration. The text says, "Which one of you having a hundred sheep. . . ." Aramaic, like Syriac and Arabic, has no verb "to have" and thus the Greek ἔχων is translated in all our Oriental versions with *lah*.[25] My Palestinian, Syrian, and Lebanese shepherd friends all agree that anyone wealthy enough to own a hundred sheep will hire a shepherd, or let some less affluent member of the extended family take care of them. The average family may have five to fifteen animals. A number of families get together and hire a shepherd. The shepherd may own some of the animals and be from one of the families. Thus, in the case of a small herd of about forty animals, the shepherd leading them may be their sole owner.[26] In the case of a hundred sheep the shepherd is probably not their sole owner. The verb in question (ἔχω) in the New Testament can mean "hold in one's charge or keeping."[27] Thus, "have a hundred sheep" can mean "be responsible for a hundred sheep" and need not necessarily mean *own* a hundred sheep.

This does not mean that the shepherd in this parable is a "hireling." The extended family owns the sheep. The shepherd is not a "hireling" nor a "stranger."[28] He is a member of the extended family and naturally feels responsible before the entire family clan; any loss is a loss to all of them. This understanding of the culture clarifies the joy in the *community* reflected at the center of the parable. In short, the extended family loses if a sheep is lost; the whole clan rejoices if the lost is found. This element of "rejoicing" in the parable also needs examination.

The parable/poem, reinforced by its structure, tells the listener/reader that the shepherd rejoices twice: once when he finds the sheep (3), and a second time in community, back in the village (3'). The first occasion of rejoicing is remarkable. My shepherd friends in upper Galilee confirm Stuhlmueller's insight, "A lost sheep will lie down helplessly and refuse to budge. The shepherd is forced to carry it over a long distance."[29] Surprisingly, this shepherd *rejoices* in the burden of restoration still before him. This theme is prominent in this first parable and drops entirely out of sight in the second. It reappears in 15:11–32.[30] Sa'īd observes that the shepherd placed the sheep on his shoulders, "knowing that the hard work is yet before him."[31] This theme of the burden of restoration is important to note. The story does not end with the finding of the sheep. After the sheep is found it must be restored. It is the restoration with its implied burden and expressed joy that is the center of the second stanza and thus the climax of the entire poem.

---

few years and then cracks and falls. The brick machine produced bricks easily five times as strong. The young men in the village were without work and a ready market for the bricks was assured. The project was a complete failure, because brickmakers are of a lower class than farmers.

[25] There is a verb "to own" in all these languages. It is not used in any of these versions.

[26] This smaller herd would be the background of John 10:11.

[27] Bauer-A., G., *Lexicon*, 33b.

[28] Cf. John 10:11.

[29] Stuhlmueller, *Luke*, 148.

[30] Goebel, *Parables*, 198.

[31] Sa'īd, *Lūqā*, 294.

A minor, yet significant turn of phrase is the reference to the shepherd having himself lost the sheep. The listener/reader expects a passive, "if the sheep was lost," which would exonerate the shepherd from any blame.[32] Rather, the shepherd is clearly assumed negligent in his duty as a shepherd. He "loses" the sheep; the verb is an aorist active participle.

A further problem is posed by the phrase *"in the wilderness"* (Luke 15:4). The shepherd leaves the flock "in the wilderness." He then returns to "the house" with the lost sheep on his shoulders. The parable has few details, yet they are sufficient to allow a reconstruction. The roving tribesmen keep sheep in the open at night. Peasants, living on the edge of the pasture lands, bring the sheep to the courtyard of the family home at the end of each day. The reference to "the house" in the parable confirms that we are dealing with peasant shepherds. Levison writes,

> I have never seen in Syria, Palestine or Mesopotamia a flock attended by a single person. Two, and even three, shepherds are commonly employed. When one sheep is lost and the shepherd goes to seek it, the other shepherd takes the flock home. On arrival, the neighbors would at once notice the absence of the shepherd or they would be told of it, for apart from the possibility of the loss of the animal, it is often a question of the safety of the man. Should he encounter a wild beast, a single-handed shepherd, with only his stick and sling, is in a perilous predicament. The finding and bringing home of the lost sheep is, therefore, a matter of great thanksgiving in the community.[33]

The text, then, can mean "he left the flock while they were still in the wilderness." The point is that the shepherd counted the flock while they were still in the wilderness (not after they got back to the village), and after discovering that one was missing, he naturally departed from them "in the wilderness," leaving a second shepherd to guide the flock back to the village.[34] Thus the leaving of the

---

[32]Colloquial speech all across the Middle East is united in this regard. When any accident or misfortune is reported by the person involved, or by a third person, the passive is always used unless the speaker deliberately wants to blame the person in the story. Thus, the man who misses a train says, "The train went from me," rather than, "I missed the train." The student says, "The pencil went from me," not "I lost the pencil." The waiter says, "The dish fell," not "I dropped the dish." The parable of the Lost Sheep occurs in Matthew as well as Luke. The Matthean version reflects this expected pattern of speech and reads, "If one of them goes astray" (Matt. 18:13), which is the normal expression. The Lucan text *deliberately* blames the shepherd. This is striking and is quite likely original (see further below) inasmuch as Jesus is addressing the Pharisees, who are called on in the parable to identify themselves with the shepherd. If they do this, they see themselves as responsible for having lost the wandering sheep.

[33]Levison, *Local Setting*, 152f. Rihbany also discusses the shepherd and his helper (*Syrian*, 300). We recall that both these authors grew up in Middle Eastern villages.

[34]I am told by Palestinian shepherds that no man can care for a hundred sheep permanently by himself. He has no feed for the sheep. They must be led out each day. No man can count on perfect health 365 days a year (not to mention his family and community duties).

Bishop confirms that under no circumstances is a flock left unguarded in the wilderness (E. F. F. Bishop, "The Parable of the Lost or Wandering Sheep," *ATR* 44 [1962], 50). Thomson wrote of shepherds, "They never leave their helpless charge alone" (*The Land*, I, 299). The Oriental versions, sheep in the wilderness need not be understood as an unauthentic element in the story. At the same time it must be observed that the ninety-nine *are* left hanging. We can assume all we like but we are not told of their return to the village. We know the lost sheep got home; we do not know what happened to the ninety-nine. We will return to this point later.

The shepherd rejoices in community. As we have noted above, this joy in community is quite likely due to two factors. First, the community rejoices in hearing that the shepherd is safe. Second, the herd is most likely owned by these same friends and neighbors. Bishop writes, ''There is the invitation to friends and neighbors in the village, who were concerned in what was likely a communal loss.''[35] The lost sheep is a community loss. The recovered sheep is an occasion for joy for all the neighbors. Even so, the sinner is lost from the community, and it is natural to expect communal joy at his recovery, not ''murmuring'' as in Luke 15:2.

Summarizing the significant cultural aspects of this parable, we have observed that Jesus makes a decision to oppose Pharisaic attitudes toward proscribed professions when he addresses them as shepherds. The shepherd in the story may not own all the sheep but still is not a hireling. Joy occurs twice in the parable. There is joy at finding the sheep, irrespective of the burden of restoration, and joy in community at the success of restoration. The shepherd is blamed for the loss of the sheep, and his leaving the sheep in the wilderness is not necessarily incongruous with Palestinian sheepherders' customs.

Before examining and summarizing the theological implications of the structural and the cultural factors discussed above, we must deal with the problem of the relationship between this version of the Lost Sheep and a similar parable that occurs in Matthew 18:12–24. The intent of this section is to demonstrate that the Lucan version is more original. The poetical and cultural elements of the parable already discussed will be the focal points of the discussion.

---

without exception, have no difficulty with the text as it stands. Had the text not fit the shepherd world as they knew it, they could very easily have moved the phrase ''in the wilderness'' ahead two words and left the verse to read, ''and leaving the ninety-nine, he went out in the wilderness.'' This alternative was not taken.

Bishop (*loc. cit.*) argues that the Semitic grammar underlying the Matthean account allows us to assume that the shepherd leaves the ninety-nine and *he* goes into the wilderness. He admits Luke cannot be read this way without some transposition. His understanding of the Matthean account is unconvincing. Bussby makes the intriguing suggestion that the Aramaic *turah* (mountain) has been confused during the oral tradition with *durah* (enclosure). Bussby quotes W. Wright as saying that the Aramaeans pronounced the ''d'' like the ''t,'' which could lead to the confusion; cf. F. Bussby, ''Did a Shepherd Leave Sheep Upon the Mountain or in the Desert?'' *ATR* 45 (1963), 93f. This is a reasonable proposal. My only difficulty with it is that, as indicated above, the Oriental versions have not sensed a problem. The Syriac could easily have changed the words back or shifted the word order if the Greek text had not fit the pastoral scene as they knew it.

[35]Bishop, *Jesus*, 166. The ms. Vat. Borg. 71 reads ''*They* called his friends and neighbors,'' indicating that the family and close friends rush out to bring the neighbors. This kind of interpretive comment reflects the communal nature of life that again and again informs the parables significantly. The shepherd is not an isolated individual but part of an extended family.

There is sharp disagreement among scholars over the question of which version of the Lost Sheep is more original, Luke's or Matthew's. Jeremias argues that the Matthean version is addressed to the Christian community, advising it to seek out the lost Christian apostates, while Luke's version is spoken in defense of Jesus' welcome of sinners and is directed against his opponents. Jeremias feels the Lucan situation is clearly more original.[36] Bultmann, on the other hand, is relatively confident that Luke's "fuller form" is secondary to the briefer Matthean version.[37]

Eta Linnemann follows Bultmann in her full discussion of the problem. She presents five major arguments in an attempt to prove the secondary nature of the Lucan version. These are:

1. Luke has "when he finds it," while Matthew gives "if he finds it." Linnemann feels that the "if" is more realistic and thus more original, and that by illuminating the uncertainty, the Church has allegorized the "good Shepherd" into the parable.

2. In Luke 15:5 the shepherd lays the sheep on his shoulders. This detail, she asserts, is a decorative expansion.

3. The shepherd cannot come back to the inhabited area, having left his unguarded herd alone in the wilderness. This detail in the Lucan version is seen as unauthentic.

4. To celebrate with the neighbors is unnatural for a shepherd.

5. The Lucan conclusion is "an allegorical exposition."[38]

These five arguments will be examined in turn.

With regard to the first, searching "until he finds it" does not exhibit an unnatural situation. The shepherd of Palestine has indeed to search "until he finds it" in the sense that he either has to bring back a live animal or bring back its remains as proof that he has not sold it.[39] Furthermore, on this point the Matthean version may actually be in harmony with the Lucan version. Matthew 18:13 has the particle ἐάν. Occasionally in the New Testament this particle is the equivalent of "when."[40] John 12:32, for example, reads, "and I, ἐάν I am lifted up." Here the meaning is clearly "when."[41] The Old Syriac also used a particle in Matthew 18:30 that can mean either "if" or "when," but means primarily "when." Burkitt

---

[36]Jeremias, *Parables,* 40. John's shepherd images are also addressed to opponents; cf. John 10:6, 19.

[37]Bultmann, *Tradition,* 171.

[38]Linnemann, *Parables,* 67–70.

[39]Cf. Amos 3:12. Because the sheep when frightened lies down and puts out a loud, incessant bleating, finding it is not considered impossible. The ground it travels in a day is not extensive and the assumption is that the sheep can be found if the shepherd is diligent. The sheep is too heavy for a wild animal to drag a great distance. Rihbany tells of an old shepherd of his acquaintance who never lost a sheep. He writes, "Whether the unfortunate sheep was yet alive or whether it had died, Yousef, as a good and faithful shepherd, always carried it back to the fold" (*Syrian,* 308).

[40]Bauer-A., G., *Lexicon,* 210.

[41]Cf. John 14:3; Heb. 3:7; 1 John 2:28.

translates the phrase, "and at what time he hath found it."[42] Thus searching "until he finds" the sheep is a fully authentic detail, and both the Matthean and Lucan versions can be understood to assume the shepherd searches until the sheep is found.

Linnemann has failed to notice that the Lucan version specifically blames the shepherd for the loss. The Matthean version, with its passive, leaves in doubt who is responsible. If, as Linnemann has argued, the Lucan version was allegorized to fit the church's image of the Good Shepherd, then this allegorizing was done in the most clumsy fashion possible.

Luke 15:5b reads, "He lays it on his shoulders, rejoicing." Linnemann understands this phrase to be a "decorative accretion." However, she has failed to see the structure of the parable that requires a repetition of the theme of "joy." This structure makes it clear that the phrase in question was not added after the composition of the parable.

At the same time, "joy at restoration" occurs at the center of the poem. "Restoration" alone is at the exact center and this is encased within a double reference to "joy."[43] Thus, *joy* is a part of the poem's climax. Furthermore, the theme of "joy," with its wordplay on "one," is clearly prominent in the entire poem-parable. Linnemann works with Jülicher's one-point-only approach to parables. Having decided that the single theme is that the one is more valuable than the ninety-nine, her hermeneutical principle does not allow her to see any theological significance in any of the other details of the parable. Thus, it is easy to dismiss as an accretion that which turns out to be a crucial part of the climax of the entire parable. The author is not just filling out a literary form when he repeats the theme of joy. The double repetition of "lost" may be for artistic and not theological reasons. But with "joy" appearing in the climax and also used in a wordplay that unites the poem, the double theme of joy is theologically significant as well as being artistically authentic. This significance will be examined briefly at the end of our discussion of the Lost Sheep. Thus, Linnemann's dismissal of Luke 15:5b as secondary to the original parable is seen to be destructive of the literary form and disruptive of the climax of the parable.

Linnemann states in her third argument that a Palestinian shepherd would not return "to the house" after finding his sheep. This position confuses the bedouin and the peasant. The bedouin lives in the wilderness and does not return to a village at night. The peasant-shepherd *does* return the sheep to his home in the village each evening.

The supposed "unnaturalness" of the shepherd's celebration with his

---

[42]F. C. Burkitt, *Evangelion da-Mepharreshe* (Cambridge: University Press, 1904), I, 103. The Peshitta changes to an unambiguous phrase that reads only "if." The Arabic versions use the particle *idha*, which also means both "if" and "when." The Syriac particle is *modi*. The Coptic Gospel of Thomas Logion 107 has the shepherd search "until he found it."

[43]In like manner, the Acts 2 poem examined above had the two related themes of cross and resurrection in the center. The cross was in the exact center and was encased within the closely related theme of resurrection.

friends is a cultural misjudgment of the scene. Village men gather almost nightly to discuss the events of the village, recite poetry, and tell stories from the oral tradition. It is fully as natural for the shepherd to call in his friends for a little celebration as it is for the woman in the parable of the Lost Coin.

Linnemann's final argument is that the Lucan conclusion is an "allegorical exposition." However, the final three lines of the parable-poem are required for the poetical structure, as we have noted, and contain the Aramaic wordplay on "one" and "joy."[44] The Matthean version has no discernible poetic structure and the Aramaic wordplay has disappeared. These features must be taken into consideration in any comparison between the two versions of the parable. In any case, a "hint of allegory" need not necessarily identify a text as secondary.[45] In fact, it may not be allegory at all, but rather symbolism. Thus, the so-called allegorical exposition in Luke 15:7 is required for the poetic structure and the Aramaic wordplay.

Finally, the question of the source of the Lucan version being in "Q" or "L" and the related problem of the reasons for the divergent account in Matthew lie beyond the scope of this study. We would only affirm in conclusion that the Lucan version as it now stands is authentically Palestinian linguistically, culturally, and stylistically. It can be understood as originating at the earliest point in the tradition, and most probably stemming from Jesus of Nazareth.

The Theological Cluster

This parable has a series of at least four themes that must be seen in relationship to each other. These themes together create the impact of this parable.[46] We would hesitate to give any one of these motifs priority over the others. Each is important and all four must be seen together, not in isolation from each other.

One clear emphasis is the *joy* of the shepherd.[47] Giblin sees that this is the main point of the twin parable. He writes, "The dynamic theme is the invitation to share in joy over the conversion of sinners."[48] Thus the joy is expressed in and shared with a community.

Closely related to this first theme is the *joy in the burden of restoration*. In this parable Jesus is defending his welcome of sinners. This welcome involves

---

[44]Jones writes, "It is absurd to state that Jesus did not 'clinch' his parables with an explanatory conclusion" (*Art*, 150). Linnemann, *Parables*, 67–70, presents no case to show that the elements in the conclusion are "allegory" and not "metaphor."

[45]Jones, *Art*, 135–166; Raymond Brown, "Parable and Allegory Reconsidered," *Novum Testamentum* 5 (1962), 36–45. The simplest solution may be that of Oesterley, who says, "We have here another instance of a parabolic theme being used for more than one purpose" (*Jewish Background*, 117).

[46]The allegorizers have their usual field day with this double parable. The lamp becomes the "Holy Spirit," the shepherd of course is the "Good Shepherd" (even though the parable specifically blames him for having lost his sheep), the wilderness is the Jewish nation, the house is the "Church," and no doubt someone has an identification for the broom. With Jülicher, this type of arbitrary introduction of foreign elements into the parable must be rejected.

[47]Cf. P. J. Bernadicou, "The Lucan Theology of Joy," *Science et Esprit* 25 (1973), 75–98.

[48]Giblin, "Luke 15," 22.

restoration to a community. The wandering sheep must be brought back to the fold now gathered in the village. This, for any shepherd, has a price. The search has its price but so does the act of restoration. In this theme of the burden of restoration there are clear Christological implications which point in the direction of the passion. The shepherd must carry on his shoulders the burden of the lost sheep, a detail that is specifically mentioned. Without the shouldering of this burden there is no restoration. This task the shepherd accepts with joy.

A third prominent theme is that of the *gracious love* which seeks the sinner. This theme is picked up by Manson as being primary for both the Lost Sheep and the Lost Coin. He writes,

> In both parables the point is the same: the endless trouble that men will take to recover lost property, and their deep satisfaction when they succeed. The inference is that the publicans and sinners really belong to God, despite all appearances to the contrary, and that God himself wants them back and will take trouble to win them back to Himself. . . . The characteristic feature of these two parables is not so much the joy over the repentant sinner as the Divine love that goes out to seek the sinner before he repents.[49]

One must be cautious in labeling this love "divine." The listening Pharisaic audience is encouraged to identify with the shepherd. Jesus seems to be saying, "The shepherd sought the lost. I seek the lost and so should you!" In the parable of the Lost Sons the Pharisaic audience is led to identify with the older son, not the father. Thus the father in that later parable more directly symbolizes divine love. Such divine love seems to be alluded to only indirectly in the parable of the Lost Sheep.

The last dominant theme is that of *repentance*. The parable raises two questions in relationship to repentance. The first is, "Who is expected to repent?" The second is, "What is the nature of this repentance?" The background to the first question is found in the rabbinic debate over the so-called "completely righteous." Some rabbis affirmed that there were indeed "completely righteous" persons whom God loved in a special way. Another opinion affirmed that God's greatest love was extended to repentant sinners. This debate is reflected in the Talmud, which reads,

> R. Hiyya b. Abba also said in R. Johanan's name: All the prophets prophesied only for repentant sinners; but as for the perfectly righteous (who had never sinned at all), "the eye hath not seen, O God, beside thee, what he hath prepared for him that waiteth for him."[50]

In this text Rabbi Abba is affirming that there are "the perfectly righteous." God loves them *more* than he does repentant sinners. The Talmud then offers the opinion of Rabbi Abbahu, who thinks "repentant sinners" are closer to God than these "perfectly righteous." He is in turn answered by an affirmation of the first

---

[49]Manson, *Sayings*, 283f.
[50]b. Tal. *Sanhedrin* 99a.

opinion, namely, that God prefers the "completely righteous."[51] The Talmud clearly gives Rabbis Abba and Joḥanan the last word.[52]

However, some centuries earlier, Ben Sirach wrote, "Do not revile a repentant sinner; remember that we all are guilty."[53] This text seems to deny the category of the "perfectly righteous." Such a denial is in keeping with Isaiah 53:6, where *all* sheep are reported to have gone astray. Jesus' view seems more in harmony with Isaiah and Ben Sirach than with the Talmud. In the synoptic Gospels the theme of "the perfectly righteous" is not apparent but the universal need for *all* to repent is affirmed.[54] Thus, in line with Ben Sirach and Isaiah 53:6, the reference in Luke 15:7 to "the ninety-nine righteous persons who need no repentance" is perhaps best understood as irony.[55] For Jesus all are lost sheep who need a shepherd to guide them. All men must repent. The literary structure obliges the listener to relate stanza I and stanza III. In stanza I the ninety-nine are left *in the wilderness*. The listener does not know if they are home or not. Jesus may be saying, "The angels cannot rejoice over the ninety-nine 'righteous' because they are not yet home." That is, the literary form reinforces the suggestion of irony. This brings us to the question of the nature and function of this repentance.

For first-century Judaism repentance was a way of bringing in the kingdom. In the preaching of Jesus repentance was a response to the kingdom already come. Bornkamm points out that for the rabbis repentance was a precondition for grace; it was a work by which a righteous man showed himself righteous. All this is clearly silenced in the parable of the Lost Sheep, where, as Bornkamm observes, "So little is repentance a human action preparing the way for grace, that it can be placed on the same level as being found."[56] The sheep does nothing to prompt the shepherd to begin his search except to become lost. In the parable the shepherd finds the sheep. Then, in the conclusion to the parable, there is reported joy over "one sinner who *repents*." Here "being found" is equated with "repentance."[57] Thus the parable of the Lost Sheep sets out a radically new understanding of the nature of repentance.

In summary, the parable of the Lost Sheep is a Palestinian parable constructed along the lines of a Form VI poem, with features that link it to other three-stanza poems in the synoptic Gospels. The cultural features are authentic and identify it as earlier than the Matthean version. Four theological themes interlock

---

[51]*Ibid.* "Repentant sinners" are בעלי תשובה. "Completely righteous" are צדיקי גמורה.
[52]Str.-B., II, 211f.
[53]Sir. 8:5.
[54]Cf. Luke 13:3.
[55]Miller, *Luke*, 120; Plummer, *St. Luke*, 369; Stuhlmueller, *Luke*, 148; Saʻīd, *Lūqā*, 403.
[56]Bornkamm, *Jesus*, 82.
[57]This new understanding of repentance is expanded in the parable of the Lost Sons, where an older son is also "found" but there is no repentance. Thus, there is more involved than just "being found." The one found must accept his lost condition and his need to be found and restored. One could argue that all this is implied in the parable of the Lost Sheep. In any case, it is clearly spelled out in the larger discussion in Luke 15:11–32.

in the parable. These are, joy in restoration to community, joy in the burden of that restoration, an unconditioned grace that seeks the lost, and a new understanding of repentance. Much of the same theology is reinforced by the second story, that of the Lost Coin, to which we now turn.

The Parable of the Lost Coin (15:8–10)

The Parable of the Lost Sheep and the Lost Coin may be viewed as a double parable. The Lost Coin has a literary structure that is simpler and less precise than that of the Lost Sheep. The cultural details are genuine. The theme of the burden of restoration is missing. This second half of the parable reinforces the themes indicated in the first half; yet there is some progression.

Once again we must analyze the structure of this part of the parable. The Lost Coin exhibits the following pattern:

Or what woman, having ten silver coins,[58]

    A   if she *loses* one coin

        B   does not light a lamp and sweep the house
            and seek diligently until she *finds* it, and *finding*

            C   she calls together her friends and neighbors
                saying, "*Rejoice with me*

        B' for I have *found* the coin

    A' which I had *lost*."

Even so, I tell you, there is *joy* before the angels of God over *one* sinner who repents.

The major semantic relationships are as follows:

Introduction—a woman[59] with ten coins

    A   one is *lost*

        B   search until she *finds*

            C   *joy* in community over restoration

        B' because she has *found*

    A' what was *lost*

Application—*joy* over *one* that repents.

---

[58]The parable of the Lost Coin is almost universally accepted as an original part of this twin parable. This rests on the similarity of the two images and on the ἤ which alone unites them. This ἤ represents the Aramaic *min*; cf. Jeremias, *Parables,* 141. He sees no reason to divide these even though the Lost Sheep was preserved independently (*ibid.,* 91). The Coptic Gospel of Thomas has another form of the Lost Sheep in Logion 107. For a good discussion of that Logion in relation to the synoptic accounts see J. B. Sheppard, "A Study of the Parables Common to the Synoptic Gospels and the Coptic Gospel of Thomas" (unpublished Ph.D. thesis, Emory University, Atlanta, 1965), 227–244.

[59]Jeremias calls her a "widow," but there is no evidence for this and the culture neither suggests nor demands it (*Parables,* 133).

The stylistic features in this parable show a number of similarities and some differences from the Lost Sheep. There is only one stanza. The entire structure is looser in construction, shorter and simpler. The introduction is shortened to "which woman," because to have said "which woman of you" to a group of Oriental men would have been an unpardonable insult. The basic inversion is the same in the two poems, but in this latter case the theme of joy is not doubled. The reason for this is obvious. In the case of the parable of the Lost Coin there is no burden of restoration. Once the coin is found it is automatically restored. Yet the theme of joy does appear in the center and the end and is thus again the climax of the poem/parable. The Aramaic play on words with "one" and "joy" (see above, p. 146) also occurs at the end.

Finally, in regard to the entire double parable, Luke 15:4–10 has a Form IV poetic outline. That is, it has two stanzas in which the second stanza is a repeat of the first, with the semantic units in the same order. This identification is not precise in that the parable of the Lost Sheep has three stanzas, as we have noted. Yet there is a general repetition of the structure, and the inversion at the center of each outline is identical to the other.

A number of cultural elements need to be noted. Rihbany makes the helpful observation that "the scarcity of money in the hands of the people makes the loss of a coin . . . a sad event."[60] Rihbany's point is that the peasant village is, to a large extent, self-supporting, making its own cloth and growing its own food. Cash is a rare commodity. Hence the lost coin is of far greater value in a peasant home than the day's labor it represents monetarily.

It has often been observed that the coin may be a part of the woman's jewelry or dowry.[61] However, a distinction must be made between the bedouin and the villager. Bedouin women wear their dowry in the form of coins hanging on their veils; village women do not. Sa'īd believes the coin is most likely part of a necklace. Village women do wear coins on necklaces. Obviously the beauty of the necklace as a whole is destroyed when one coin is lost. Again, the loss is more than the value of the single coin.[62]

The movement of peasant women in the village was and is extremely limited.[63] This woman clearly knew that the coin was in the house. She had not been out. Her diligence was prompted by the knowledge that it could be found if she would keep sweeping.[64]

---

[60]Rihbany, *Syrian,* 153.

[61]Bishop, *Jesus,* 191.

[62]Sa'īd, *Lūqā,* 394f.

[63]Jeremias, *Jerusalem,* "Appendix: The Social Position of Women," 359–376, esp. 359–363. Jeremias notes that village women could go to the well but that "it was considered preferable for a woman, and especially an unmarried girl, in general, not to go out at all" (p. 360).

[64]The floor is most likely packed earth, not stone (Rihbany, *Syrian,* 154; against Jeremias, *Parables,* 135). Contrasting the shepherd as relatively rich and the woman as poor is strained (Jeremias, *loc. cit.*). They are both relatively poor.

In the cultural world of first-century Palestine, the very use of a woman in an illustration required a moral decision. Jesus is again rejecting Pharisaic attitudes toward groups of people in society. First it was the proscribed shepherds, now the inferior woman.[65]

Two aspects of the imagery in the parable of the Lost Sheep are intensified in the parable of the Lost Coin. First, the relative value of the thing lost is intensified. It is now one in ten, not one in a hundred; and, as we have noted, the coin may have had value beyond its monetary worth. Then second, the place of search for the lost is more narrowly confined. It is now the confines of a house, not the wide wilderness. Thus the assurance is intensified that the lost one *can* be found if the searcher is willing to put out sufficient effort.

In summary, we have noted that the structure is not as complex or as precise as Luke 11:9–13 and 16:9–13. The two parables form a single literary unit in which the second half reinforces the first half. The cultural elements are authentic and striking. Theologically the theme of "the burden of restoration" is missing, but joy, grace, and repentance are all present.

THE FATHER AND THE TWO LOST SONS (LUKE 15:11–32)

This parable has for centuries been called "*Evangelium in Evangelio.*"[66] Nearly everyone who wrestles seriously with this pericope ends up with a sense of awe at its inexhaustible content. C. F. W. Smith writes,

> While Jesus was not a philosopher or a theologian (in the accepted sense), his parables alone provide material that neither the philosopher nor the theologian can exhaust. This is the mark of Jesus' supreme genius. We have a curious tendency, even in dealing with Jesus' humanity, to overlook his sheer intellectual stature.[67]

Here again structural and cultural elements may shed some new light on the nature of Jesus' creative genius.

This unit will be seen as a second double parable using the parabolic ballad type. The ballad form will be presented first; and then the different cultural aspects of the parable will be examined in the order in which they appear in the parable itself. Lastly, the parable will be seen to contain the themes of sin, repentance, grace, joy, and sonship.

Before proceeding to an examination of the ballad form of the parable, a word must be said about the imagery used. The parable is not an allegory. The

---

[65]The attitudes toward women in Ben Sirach and those described in Jeremias' "Appendix" noted above are roughly identical to what I have experienced among peasants today. In conservative areas, the speaker must apologize for using the word "woman" if the turn of conversation requires it.

[66]Arndt, *St. Luke,* 350.

[67]C. W. F. Smith, *Parables,* 19.

father is not God *incognito,* but an earthly father, as is conclusively demonstrated in verse 18. Yet he is a symbol of God. Jeremias writes, "The father is not God, but an earthly father; yet some of the expressions used are meant to reveal that in his love he is an image of God."[68] Jones says, "The parable about the prodigal son is not primarily about a spendthrift boy, but about the relations between God and the sinner and the self-righteous."[69] Giblin makes the useful distinction between strict identification and characterization.[70] His point is that to identify the older son as the Pharisee is to unduly narrow the intent of the parable. Jesus is describing a type of person; if we, or any part of his listening audience, fit the characterization, well and good.[71]

The Literary Structure of Luke 15:11–32

The previous verses (4–11) proved to be a double parable. Each half had a similar yet distinct structure. The same is true for verses 11–32. Here also we have a double parable and each half has its own structure. Again the two halves are similar yet different. As in all the parables, culture and literary structure must both be given due consideration for an adequate interpretation. The structure of the first half is as follows:

A   There was a man who had two sons

1   and the younger of them said to his father, "Father,   A SON IS LOST
     give me the share of property that falls to me."
     And he divided *his living* between them.

   2   Not many days later the younger son sold all he had,   GOODS WASTED IN
        journeyed into a far country   EXPENSIVE LIVING
        and wasted *his property* in extravagant living.

     3   And when he had spent everything   EVERYTHING LOST
           a great famine arose in that country
           and he began to be *in want.*

       4   So he went and joined himself   THE GREAT SIN
              to one of the citizens of that country   (FEEDING PIGS
              and he sent him to his fields *to feed* pigs.   FOR GENTILES)

         5   And he would gladly have eaten the pods   TOTAL
                 which the pigs ate   REJECTION
                 and no one gave him *anything.*

           6   But when he came to himself he said,   A CHANGE
                    "How many of my father's servants have bread to spare   OF MIND
                    but I perish here with *hunger.*

---

[68]Jeremias, *Parables,* 128.
[69]Jones, *Art,* 210.
[70]Giblin, "Luke 15," 18.
[71]Derrett understands the parable as another illustration of *kal va homer.* If an earthly father can act this way, then how much more God! (Derrett, "Prodigal Son," 72).

6' "I will arise and go to my father and say to him, Father, AN INITIAL
I have sinned against heaven and before you   REPENTANCE
and am no more worthy to be called your son; **make me a servant.**' "

5' And he arose and came to his father.   TOTAL
And while he was at a great distance his father saw him ACCEPTANCE
and **had compassion** and ran and embraced him and kissed him.

4' And the son said to the father, "Father,   THE GREAT
I have sinned against heaven and before you   REPENTANCE
and am **no more worthy** to be called your son."

3' And the father said to the servants,   EVERYTHING GAINED
"Bring the best **robe** and put it on him   RESTORED TO SONSHIP
and put a **ring** on his hands and **shoes** on his feet.

2' And bring the fatted calf and kill it   GOODS USED IN
and let us eat   JOYFUL CELEBRATION
and **make merry,**

1' for this my son was dead and is alive,   A SON IS FOUND
he was lost and is found."
And they **began to make merry.**

When filled out with a bit more detail the parallels of the inversion are as follows:

1   A son is lost—"Give me my share"
  2   Goods wasted in extravagant living
    3   Everything lost—"he spent everything—he began to want"
      4   The great sin—"feeding pigs for gentiles"
        5   Total rejection—"no one gave him anything"
          6   A change of mind—"he came to himself—I perish here"
          6'   An initial repentance—"make me a servant (I will pay it back)"
        5'   Total acceptance—"his father ran and kissed him"
      4'   The great repentance—"I am no more worthy to be called your son"
    3'   Everything gained—a robe, ring, and shoes (restoration to sonship)
  2'   Goods used in joyful celebration
1'   A son is found—"My son was dead and is alive, was lost and is found."

The structure is a type D (parabolic ballad), which in this case has twelve stanzas that match each other using inverted parallelism. The second six reverse the first six, as we have observed. The first speech to the father is at the beginning. The second reversing the first comes in the middle. The end of the structure reverses the beginning. The center is again the point of turning as is expected in the use of the inversion principle. At the same time a series of lesser correspondences appear once the basic structure is seen. The last line of each of the first six stanzas (note the italics) has to do with his physical desires, losses, and needs. The second six stanzas in their final lines (note boldface type) deal progressively with the restoration to sonship and its ensuing joy. Remarkably this matchless ballad also has a type of counterpoint that we have observed in a significant number of literary structures in the New Testament. The same twelve stanzas with their inversion seen above also relate to one another thematically using step parallelism. This can be seen as follows:

The first six stanzas
  speech I
  he leaves
  in need but unrepentant
  becomes a pig herder
  eats nothing
  is dying

The second six stanzas
  speech II
  he returns
  in need and truly repentant
  becomes an honored son
  feeds on fatted calf
  is alive

In addition to the overall parallelisms there are a number of lesser correspondences worthy of note. Both 5' and 6' end with joy. The second line of stanzas 2, 3, and 4 mentions the *country*. A comparison of the second and third lines of 5 and 6 brings out that the pigs eat, his father's servants eat, but he is given nothing and is starving. In terms of the flow of the story the third line of 5 is redundant and out of place, but it functions significantly when the structure is once seen. With these semantic correspondences in mind the cultural elements must now be examined, some of which in turn will illuminate other parallelisms.

The Opening Stanza (15:11–12)

The opening stanza sets the stage for all that will follow. The prodigal is shown as wishing for his father's death in his request for his portion. The father demonstrates almost unbelievable love by granting the request. The older son's silence indicates a rejection of his responsibility to reconcile his brother to his father.

After affirming the presence of a father with two sons, the parable begins with the request of the younger, "Father, give me the share of property that falls to me." [72] For over fifteen years I have been asking people of all walks of life from Morocco to India and from Turkey to the Sudan about the implications of a son's request for his inheritance while the father is still living. The answer has almost always been emphatically the same. As I have noted elsewhere, the conversation runs as follows:

---

[72]Derrett ("Prodigal Son," 68) makes the observation that in Jewish history "Younger brothers are traditionally rebels. The older is worldly, niggardly, orthodox and hypocritical." All the patriarchs after Abraham were younger brothers, as were Abel, Jacob, Joseph, Gideon, David, and Judas Maccabaeus. Thus the younger brother–older brother characterization in this parable is in line with traditional types (cf. *ibid.*).

"Has anyone ever made such a request in your village?"

"Never!"

"Could anyone ever make such a request?"

"Impossible!"

"If anyone ever did, what would happen?"

"His father would beat him, of course!"

"Why?"

"This request means—he wants his father to die!"[73]

Levison writes, "There is no law or custom among the Jews or Arabs which entitles the son to a share of the father's wealth while the father is still alive."[74] Can it be confirmed from ancient literature that this son's request is an extraordinary insult to the father? In the following section we will try to demonstrate that this can be confirmed and that this cultural aspect of the parable sets the stage in a crucial way for all that follows.

In the Old Testament there are two customs worthy of note. The first is the oral will. Isaiah said to Hezekiah, "Command with respect to thy house, for thou shalt die" (2 Kings 20:1).[75] The context is clearly that of approaching death. The oral will was common all through the Old and New Testament period. It was always enacted under the shadow of imminent death and is thus irrelevant to the parable of the Prodigal Son, because in Luke 15:12 the father is assumed to be in good health.[76] The Old Testament also mentions giving a specific gift to someone in order to eliminate him from any rights in the inheritance. This seems to be the case in Genesis 25:6, where Abraham's sons by Keturah are given "gifts" and sent away "from his son Isaac." In the next verse Abraham dies. This disposition then is also some kind of final settlement at the end of his life. Daube notes,

> The whole arrangement in this case was due to the initiative, not of the sons to be emancipated—they were not as adventurous as the prodigal of the parable—but of Abraham, who wished to secure Isaac from possible rivals.[77]

---

[73]In the literally hundreds of times I have asked the question, "Do you know of anyone who has made such a request?" only twice did I receive a positive answer. In the first case Pastor Viken Galoustian of Iran, with a convert church of Oriental Jews, reported to me that one of his leading parishioners, in great anguish, reported to him, "My son wants me to die!" The concerned pastor discovered that the son had broached the question of the inheritance. Three months later the father, a Hebrew Christian (a physician), in previously good health, died. The mother said, "He died that night!" meaning that the night the son dared to ask for his inheritance the father "died." The shock to him was so great that life was over that night. In the second case a Syrian farmer's *older* son asked for his inheritance. In great anger his father drove him from the house. Cf. K. E. Bailey, *The Cross and the Prodigal* (St. Louis: Concordia, 1973), 31.

[74]Levison, *Local Setting*, 156.

[75]Cf. Deut. 21:16; Gen. 49:28–31; 2 Sam. 17:22; 1 Kings 2:1–9.

[76]Horowitz has a full discussion of wills, *Jewish Law*, 402–421.

[77]Daube, "Inheritance," 331.

Daube observes that Keturah's sons do not initiate the process, but he misses the cultural implications. Isaac and Keturah's sons wait respectfully for Abraham to make his own decision. There is no breath of a suggestion that Abraham is under any pressure. In all the Old Testament the prodigal's action is unknown.

Turning to the intertestamental period, there is the significant section in Ben Sirach where the sage argues in forceful terms against giving one's property to son, wife, brother, or friend during one's lifetime.[78] The day "life draws to a close" is the right time for such distribution.

Manson argues that people must have been guilty of passing on their property while in good health, otherwise Ben Sirach would not caution against it.[79] That such is not necessarily the case can be shown by an illustration. One can read in literature coming out of the American South in the late nineteenth century the strong admonition to distrust the "Yankees." Using Manson's line of argumentation we would have to affirm, "The Southerners during that period must have been prone to trust Yankees and thus there is this admonition against doing so." It is more likely, however, that Southerners of that period both did *not* trust Yankees and specifically warned each other not to do so. In like manner Ben Sirach's statement most likely reflects the accepted notion that passing on one's inheritance while in good health was unthinkable.[80]

In the Mishna the key passage, to which we shall return again and again, is *Baba Bathra* viii.7, which reads,

> If one assign in writing his property to his children, he must write, "from today and after [my] death." . . . If one assign in writing his estate to his son [to become his] after his death, the father cannot sell it since it is conveyed to his son, and the son cannot sell it because it is under the father's control. . . . The father may pluck up [produce] and feed it to whomsoever he pleases, but whatever he left plucked up belongs to his heirs.[81]

To the phrase "after [my] death" the editor appends this note: "This refers to a healthy person who desires to retain the right to benefit from his possessions (usufruct) during his lifetime." Jeremias and others have accepted this passage as being the best explanation of the legal situation behind the parable.[82] The Babylonian Talmud has a note giving an illustration of the kind of situation in which a man in good health might sign his estate over to his sons. The note explains the Mishna quoted above and reads,

---

[78]Sir. 33:20–24.

[79]Manson, *Sayings*, 287.

[80]Even if we grant that such a disposition may on occasion have taken place, there is the further crucial question as to who initiates the process. Ben Sirach assumes the father's initiative and says he should not do it. In the parable the son pressures his father, a possibility not even mentioned by Ben Sirach.

[81]*Order Nezikin*, Vol. IV in *Mishnayoth*, trans. and ed. Philip Blackman (London: Mishna Press, 1954), 212.

[82]Jeremias, *Parables*, 128.

I.e., a person in good health who desired, for example, to marry a second time, and wished to protect the sons that were born from his first marriage from the possible seizure of his estate by his second wife, in payment of her *kethubah*. [83]

Thus for special circumstances the Mishna provides for the willing over of one's inheritance before death, but there is no hint of any father having done so under pressure from a younger son.

Baba Mezia of the same Talmud reads, "Our Rabbis taught: Three cry and are not answered. Viz., he who has money and lends it without witnesses; he who acquires a master . . . ." The text then explains that among those who "cry out and are not answered" is "He who transfers his property to his children in his lifetime. . . ." [84] This quotation demonstrates that Ben Sirach's attitude was maintained unchanged at least until the writing of the Talmud. Derrett confirms that the major reason for a father's dividing his estate and signing it over to his sons during his lifetime was for the purpose of "determining what they would have after him and obviating disputes." [85] Derrett never suggests that a father did this under pressure from his sons.

Thus it can be documented that often the father before his death did "divide his living between them." But the startling fact is that, to my knowledge, in all of Middle Eastern literature (aside from this parable) from ancient times to the present, there is no case of any son, older or younger, asking for his inheritance from a father who is still in good health.

The prodigal's actions are all the more remarkable because his request is twofold. He requests the division of the inheritance. His request is granted. But this gives him ownership without the right to dispose of his share. The property is his but he cannot sell it. He wants more, so he pressures his father into granting him full disposition immediately. The Mishna quoted above provides for the legal settlement, but not for disposition by the sons during the father's lifetime. After signing over his possessions to his sons the father still has the right to live off the proceeds (the usufruct) as long as he is alive. Here the younger son gets, and thus is assumed to have demanded, disposition to which, even more explicitly, he had no right until the death of his father. The implication of "Father, I cannot wait for you to die" underlies both requests. It is even stronger in the second.

The misunderstanding of this crucial drama at the opening of the parable is of long standing. Jülicher thinks the boy is not at all impertinent, and that the title

---

[83]*The Babylonian Talmud, Seder Nezikin, Baba Bathra* II, trans. and ed. I. Epstein (London: Soncino, 1935), 573, n. 1.

[84]b. *Baba Mezia*, 75b.

[85]Derrett, "Prodigal Son," 59. This remains true in the East. It is standard procedure for the village father in Syria to settle his inheritance when he is old or anxious to "retire." He always reserves for himself what is called "ḥaqq al-manfaʿah," literally "the right of the profits" (usufruct). The purpose is exactly what Derrett reports, to prevent a quarrel after his death. Rihbany writes, "As a rule neither the law nor custom gives legal standing to a will. . . . As a general rule the father who does not divide his property legally between his sons before his death leaves to them a situation fraught with danger" (*Syrian*, 155f.).

"Father" in his initial request is as affectionate as the τέκνον in the mouth of the father at the end.[86] Linnemann quotes some of the biblical and rabbinic material that we have examined above, but fails to note that none of it shows a son requesting his inheritance from a healthy father.[87] She notes that there was a steady flow of Jews into the diaspora and assumes that this would be a normal event. This is not true. We have a similar situation in Lebanon today with nearly two million Lebanese living and working all over the world in their own "diaspora." But the young man with a living healthy father who goes off to make his fame and fortune does not request, receive, and sell his portion of the family estate before he goes! The most he can expect is his ticket and a little pocket money.[88]

Linnemann makes the amazing statement, "A farm was by the law of the time a family possession, and together with all that belonged to it passed to the eldest son."[89] She has taken this from J. Schmid,[90] who drew this remarkable conclusion from Leviticus 25:23, which reads, "The land shall not be sold in perpetuity." This passage refers to the time of the Jubilee and has nothing to do with inheritance. The request in Luke 12:13, "Teacher, bid my brother divide the inheritance with me," quickly demonstrates that estates were divided among sons.[91]

Not all scholars have failed to notice that the younger brother's request amounts to wishing his father's death. Bornkamm says of the prodigal that he "demands his own portion of his goods, and treats the father as if he were already dead."[92] Miller has written that it was the normal custom "for the heirs to receive their share at the death of the father (Hebrews 9:16–17)."[93] Via catches this implication in the second request; he writes, "Thus the prodigal's demand for the right of disposal was to treat his father as if he were dead."[94] Ancient literature and modern customs converge, and the request is seen as a profound break of relationship between the father and his son. The boy is indeed lost.

In light of the implications of the request, it is all the more remarkable that the father concurs. In the Middle Eastern milieu the father is expected to explode and discipline the boy for the cruel implications of his demand. It is difficult to imagine a more dramatic illustration of the quality of love, which grants freedom even to reject the lover, than that given in this opening scene. Derrett senses the

---

[86]Jülicher, *Gleichnisreden,* II, 338.

[87]Linnemann, *Parables,* 74f.

[88]This is not uniquely Middle Eastern. Many a young American farm boy in story and in fact leaves the farm to make his "fame and fortune." How many of them request, receive, and sell their portion of the family farm before they go?

[89]Linnemann, *Parables,* 74f.

[90]J. Schmid, *Das Evangelium Nach Lukas* (Gütersloh: Bertelsmann, 1934), 252.

[91]Cf. also Horowitz, *Jewish Law,* 378.

[92]Bornkamm, *Jesus,* 126.

[93]Miller, *Luke,* 120. Derrett, "Prodigal Son," 60f., makes a great deal of the fact that the son was expected to stay home and obey, and that his adventurous spirit is not admired. But he fails to appreciate the real nature of the assumption inherent in the request.

[94]Via, *Parables,* 169.

radical nature of the father's action, and argues in the light of Ben Sirach (Sir. 33:20–44) that no father would have granted such a request without making a tacit but certain reservation in his own favor. The father, says Derrett, "will by no means have prejudiced his own position."[95] He explains that the father must have made the "dismission" with the reservation that the son was still responsible for the father financially, if and when the father in his old age might need support. Derrett appreciates the radical nature of the situation. If the father does grant this request, he is jeopardizing his own "living." This, Derrett feels, no father would have done. We can grant to Derrett that no father known to the listener/reader would have concurred with the request without the kind of reservation Derrett suggests. However, the father in this story does grant possession *and* disposition. The son has ownership and the right to sell. If the father had made a reservation on the inheritance, he would not have granted the right of disposition. When the boy is allowed to sell his inheritance and emigrate, all reservations are rendered meaningless.

We get the same insight more directly from Sa'īd, who writes,

> The shepherd in his search for the sheep, and the woman in her search for the coin, do not do anything out of the ordinary beyond what anyone in their place would do. But the actions the father takes in the third story are unique, marvelous, divine actions *which have not been done by any father in the past.*[96]

Sa'īd himself was an Oriental patriarch of the old school, and sensed rightly that the actions of the father in this story are unique. The father is still an earthly father and is believable. At the same time, he demonstrates qualities of love beyond what is experienced and expected from any earthly father.[97]

Daube, Derrett, and Yaron are convinced that the inheritance is not distributed at this point, but rather that the father makes a "dismission" (*Abschichtung*) of a portion of his property which he gives to the younger son, who then loses all further claims to the inheritance.[98] The difficulty with this alternative is that it does not deal adequately with the phrase "and he divided to *them* his living," nor with the words of the father at the end of the story, "*All* that I have is yours." With Jeremias and Manson, the provision of "gift," whereby the property is assigned to the sons during the life of the father, seems to fit the context of the story more adequately.[99]

---

[95]Derrett, "Prodigal Son," 62.

[96]Sa'īd, *Lūqā,* 395f. (emphasis mine).

[97]W. H. Simcox writes, "The affectionate father in the parable trusts his sons more than the son of Sirach thought safe or wise" ("The Prodigal and His Brother," *The Expositor,* Series 3, 10 1889, 126). The parable also shows the father's impartial love toward both sons. Both sons are assigned their portion. Luke 15:11 reads, "He divided to *them* his living." Giblin comments that v. 12 "reflects the father's impartial love for both sons as his sons" ("Luke 15," 29, n. 40).

[98]D. Daube, "Inheritance," 330; Derrett, "Prodigal Son," 60; Reuven Yaron, *Gifts in Contemplation of Death* (Oxford: Clarendon, 1960), 44.

[99]Jeremias, *Parables,* 128; Manson, *Sayings,* 287.

There is one final note in rabbinic legislation that is at times overlooked. In the case of a man in good health assigning his property to his sons as a "gift" with the reservation that they have the right of disposition only after his death, the "gift" was not valid unless it was a purely voluntary act free from all duress.[100] The father in this parable is specifically under duress. All he need do is admit this and the son gets nothing. Legally he must act as if he has decided on his own to give away his property and ignore that this is not the case. The remarkable nature of the love of this particular father becomes clearer and clearer the deeper one goes into the circumstances that may well have colored a first-century understanding of the story.

Daube makes another suggestion, which is picked up and turned into the major theme of a monograph by K. H. Rengstorf.[101] This suggestion has to do with the first-century Palestinian ceremony of the *qeṣaṣah*. The word literally means "a cutting off." The ceremony is described in *Ruth Rabba* vii.11 on 4:7, which reads,

> What is *keẓaẓah*? R. Jose b. Abin answered: If a man sold his field to a Gentile, his relatives used to bring barrels full of parched corn and nuts and break them open in the presence of children, and the children would gather them and proclaim, "So-and-so is cut off from his inheritance." If it was returned to him, they used to say, "So-and-so has returned to his inheritance." And likewise if a man married a woman who was not fitting for him, his relatives used to bring barrels full of parched corn and nuts and break them open in the presence of children, and the children would gather them and proclaim, "So-and-so is lost to his family." When he divorced her, they used to say, "So-and-so has returned to his family."[102]

Other rabbinic references to the same custom indicate that it was a jar or a pot that was broken.[103] Rengstorf asserts that the custom fell into disuse by the end of the first century, but that it was in force at the time of Jesus.[104] Rengstorf argues that this formal act of "cutting off" and then of restoration, which he calls "reinvestiture," is the specific background of the parable. His long argument is, however, unconvincing. The two acts that triggered the *qeṣaṣah* ceremony are given as selling land to a gentile and marrying an impure woman. Rengstorf himself states that the cause for this ceremony in the case of the prodigal son was that he took his property and wasted it in a foreign country.[105] However, the sale to gentiles, or more generally the loss of the property to gentiles, did not take place at the time of the son's leaving. When he left he had not violated either of the conditions that would have brought on the *qeṣaṣah*.[106] If the family had heard from

---

[100]Horowitz, *Jewish Law,* 374.

[101]Rengstorf, *Re-Investitur.*

[102]*Ruth,* trans. L. Rabinowitz, in *Midrash Rabbah,* ed. H. Freedman and M. Simon (London: Soncino, 1939), 87.

[103]Cf. p. *Kid.* i.5; p. *Ket.* 26d; p. *Kid.* 60c; p. *Ket.* ii.10.

[104]Rengstorf, *Re-Investitur,* 23.

[105]*Ibid.,* 71.

[106]That is, unless we assume he sold his share to gentiles when he left, which Rengstorf does not claim and the story does not suggest.

the prodigal while he was gone that he had lost everything to the gentiles and then carried out the qeṣaṣah, we would have to presuppose a great many details not given in the parable.[107] When the prodigal leaves he has had no dealings with the gentiles. Rengstorf's entire argument fails at this crucial point.

At the same time, the qeṣaṣah ceremony provides insight into the first-century Palestinian community important for an understanding of the culture of the parable. The fact of the qeṣaṣah ceremony is extremely significant as evidence of the solidarity of the extended family and the community. Family property lost to gentiles was a serious matter. An erring son who violated the community solidarity was dealt with in radical fashion. When the prodigal comes home, he has, in fact, lost his share of the family's property among gentiles. The village community will soon discover this. At that time, they may well break the jar in the street and cut him off. What he has done is a serious matter, not just toward his father but as regards the village and the entire extended family.[108] The son is breaking relationships not only with his father and brother but in a very radical way with the community at large.

The older son is mentioned twice in this opening scene. We are told in verse 11 that the father has two sons. In verse 12 we hear that the older son also receives his share of the inheritance. We expect him to respond in two ways. First he should loudly refuse to accept his share in protest against the implications of his brother's request. His silence strongly suggests that his relationship with his father is not what it should be. Then second, at this point the Oriental listener/reader also expects the older son to enter the story verbally and take up the traditional role of reconciler. Breaks in relationships are always healed through a third party among Middle Easterners.[109] The third party is selected on the basis of the closeness of the relationship to each side. In this case, the role of reconciler is thrust upon the older son by all the pressures of custom and community. His silence means refusal. The Talmud notes specifically that it was the sons who carried out the qeṣaṣah ceremony.[110] They were responsible for reconciliation as well as for the sign of its failure. If the older son hates his brother, he will still go through the motions of trying to reconcile for the sake of his father. This older son remains silent. Again his silence tells us of problems in his relationship to his father. Finally, as we have observed, the father "divided to *them* his living." Thus the older son also benefits from the transaction. He knows that the request is improper and is expected to refuse with loud assertions of unending loyalty to the father. Rather he accepts in silence. With the background in Old Testament literature which characterized

---

[107]Rengstorf's discussion of the shoes, the robe, and the ring, while presenting some good material and making a number of thoughtful observations, fails to assess adequately the culture of the Middle East. His arguments will be examined later.

[108]Daube notes, "Evidently, the younger son cut his personal ties with this kin as well as his proprietary ones" ("Inheritance," 329).

[109]U.S. Secretary of State Henry Kissinger in the winter of 1973/74 managed to achieve delicate disengagement settlements in the Middle East because he was willing to function in this classic Middle Eastern role.

[110]b. *Ket.* 28b.

older sons as "niggardly, orthodox and hypocritical"[111] it is easy to finish out the picture this parable sketches of this older son, a picture already visible in the opening verses.

In connection with this parable, Daube discusses the Old Testament technical term *yashabh yahadh* (to dwell together), which referred to the dwelling together of brothers on an estate after the death of the father. This state of affairs was considered the norm; as an institution it was idealized in Psalm 133:1.[112] (Thus Luke 12:13 is considered a deplorable request and indeed is so treated in the Lucan account.) Here the younger son, by selling his portion and leaving, refuses to attempt any future "dwelling together" with his brother. Yet, surely, both sons must be blamed for this failure. The ill will evidenced from the older brother's side at the end of the story is not "a root out of dry ground."

In the next stanza, after "not many days," the younger son turns his portion into cash.[113] The reason for the need for haste (not many days) is easy to reconstruct. It is not just his concern to "get on with it." Rather, as he goes from one prospective buyer to another, the intensity of the community hatred and disgust mounts. At every turn he is greeted with amazement, horror, and rejection. The Middle Eastern peasant's attachment to his land is as old as Naboth's relationship to his vineyard. The family estate is a significant part of the Middle Easterner's personal identity.[114] Although, as indicated above, the prodigal did nothing in the opening scene to call upon himself the *qeṣaṣah*, yet he certainly earned the intense displeasure of the entire community. Thus, even though in the Middle East the sale of property ordinarily drags on for months, the prodigal finished in a hurry and left.

To summarize this opening scene, the prodigal requests and receives possession and disposition of his portion of the inheritance. Both requests are unheard of in Eastern life and thought. Each means the son is in a hurry for his father to die. The father is expected to refuse and punish the prodigal. Instead, in an unprecedented act of love, the request is granted. The older son is expected to refuse his share and to fulfil the roll of reconciler. He fails on both counts. These failures indicate that his relationships to both his brother and his father are broken. Both sons fail even to try to live together in unity. The *qeṣaṣah* ceremony illustrates group attitudes toward members of the community who sell to gentiles.

Stanzas 2–6—In the Far Country (15:13b–17)

In this section the cultural aspects will be treated as they appear in the text. Here the prodigal gradually descends into his own hell. The six-stanza structure of the first half of the prodigal's story makes this clear.

---

[111]Derrett, "Prodigal Son," 68.

[112]Daube, "Inheritance," 327.

[113]Cf. Bauer-A., G., *Lexicon*, 789, *s.v.* συνάγω.

[114]The strongest evidence for this is that a million Palestinian refugees in the contemporary Middle Eastern scene do not want and will not accept resettlement elsewhere. The home village with its family inheritance is an integral part of their identity. The land does not belong to them; they belong to the land.

In the far country, the prodigal's money is soon gone. Foerster explains the phrase ζῶν ἀσώτως as follows:

> the dissipated life of the Prodigal without specifying the nature of this life . . . is simply depicted as carefree and spendthrift in contrast to the approaching dearth.[115]

This phrase does not tell us whether the money was wasted in moral or in immoral ways. By contrast, the Oriental versions are unambiguous. The Old Syriac decides the issue one way by an additional line which makes the text read, "He scattered his property in foods that are not fitting, because he was living wastefully with harlots." Starting with the Peshitta, this addition is removed and the text translated unambiguously in the other direction. A wide variety of words are used in the Arabic versions, but all of them (with one nineteenth-century exception) have terms meaning "expensive," "indolent," "luxurious," and "wasteful." These words all bring the Peshitta and the Arabic versions clearly in line with Foerster's definition. They do not label the prodigal as "immoral" but only as "wasteful." That the Greek text and the vast majority of the Oriental versions do not condemn the prodigal for immorality is significant, and provides a background for understanding properly the older son's remarks in verse 30, as we shall see.

Jeremias has traced a series of ten famines in and around Jerusalem, from 169 B.C. to A.D. 70 (excluding those resulting from war.)[116] Famine would have been a very powerful image for any first-century Palestinian audience. Furthermore, a lone Jew in a far country without money or friends would have been especially vulnerable in a great famine. The text seems to note this by adding an emphatic pronoun. Verse 14 reads, "*He* began to be in want."[117] He more than others was in need.[118]

The text then tells us graphically that he "glues" himself to a citizen of that country.[119] This lad is known in the community as having arrived with money and thus is expected to have some self-respect left. The polite way a Middle Easterner gets rid of unwanted "hangers-on" is to assign them a task he knows they will refuse. Anyone with food in a severe famine has a throng of petitioners at his door daily.[120] However, the pride of the prodigal is not yet completely broken and, to

---

[115]W. Foerster, *TDNT*, I, 507.

[116]Jeremias, *Jerusalem*, 140–44.

[117]The passage is full of Semitisms. Cf. Jack Sanders, "Tradition and Redaction in Luke XV, 11–32," *NTS* 15 (1969), 435. From the point of view of Semitic as well as Greek syntax, αὐτός is emphatic.

[118]The emphatic nature of the αὐτός in v. 14 is clear from v. 24, which has καὶ ἤρξαντο εὐφραίνεσθαι with no pronoun. In the Oriental versions the Syriac, the Peshitta, and the Harclean preserve the extra pronoun. Ibn al-'Assāl has "and *he also* began to be in want," thus making use of the emphatic nature of the pronoun but interpreting it to mean that the son as well as everybody else was in want. It can also mean he in particular, as an outsider, was in want. Cf. also Goebel, *Parables*, 202.

[119]Only someone who has lived in the East can fully appreciate this vocabulary. In the Middle East, the desperation of the indigent leads him to attach himself like glue to any potential benefactor. The Greek word is κολλάω.

[120]Arndt notes that "he forces himself on a citizen of the country. His services had not been requested" (*St. Luke*, 351).

the amazement of the listener/reader, the citizen's attempt to get rid of the younger son fails. He accepts the job of pig herder.

The "citizen" is most likely an "independent inhabitant with his own property."[121] The original Greek meaning of πολίτης as a political word, indicating a person of authority in the community, must be rejected.[122]

Linnemann feels that the "joining to a citizen" is a clear reference to the tax collectors and their going into the service of foreigners.[123] Jeremias reasons that the prodigal could not have observed the Sabbath, would be in association with unclean animals,[124] and thus was "practically forced to renounce the regular practice of his religion."[125]

The son is reported as "longing to fill his belly with the carob pods which the pigs ate." This sentence poses a number of problems. What were the pods? Did the prodigal eat them? If he did, why was he not filled? If he did not, why not? The carob pods are almost universally identified with the *ceratonia siliqua*.[126] The Harclean and the Old Syriac Sinaitic transliterate the Greek word, but the rest of the Oriental versions without exception use the word *kharnūb*. This same word in Aramaic rabbinic literature is an edible pod eaten by the poor. As a food it symbolized repentance. Rabbi Aha said, "Israel needs carob, (i.e. poverty) to be forced to repentance (i.e. only when Israel are reduced to such a state of poverty that they must eat carob do they repent of their evil ways)."[127] The difficulty is that *kharnūb* is eaten by and enjoyed by people of all ages all over the countryside of Palestine, Syria, and Lebanon. Rihbany writes regarding the carob pods,

> They are sold in almost every town in western Syria for food. Children are very fond of *kherrūb*. Some of the pods contain no small amount of sugar. In my boyhood days, a pocketful of *kherrūb*, which I procured for a penny, was to me rather a treat.[128]

Thus the *ceratonia siliqua* is edible and nourishing. There is a reference in rabbinic literature to a Rabbi Hanina ben Dosa who kept himself alive with carob pods.[129]

---

[121]H. Strathmann, *TDNT*, VI, 534.

[122]*Ibid*. The Oriental versions support this. The London-Paris Polyglots have "a man from the noblemen of the city," but the rest of the Arabic and Syriac versions read simply, "one of the sons of the city."

[123]Linnemann, *Parables*, 75f.

[124]M. *Ba. Kam.* viii.7, "no one may raise swine in any place"; "at the approach of the Messiah, pigs, the natural abode of devils, must hide themselves and pig keepers must fear for their safety" (Derrett, "Prodigal Son," 66). b. *Ba. Kam.* 82b tells of a pig sent up the walls of Jerusalem in a basket, which causes the earth to quake over a distance of four hundred pharasangs; and it is said, "Cursed be the man who would breed swine and cursed be the man who would teach his son Grecian wisdom."

[125]Jeremias, *Parables*, 129.

[126]Stuhlmueller, *Luke*, 148; Manson, *Sayings*, 288. It is also called "St. John's bread"; cf. Bauer-A., G., *Lexicon*, 430; *Str.-B.*, II, 241.

[127]Feldman, *Similes*, 124.

[128]Rihbany, *Syrian*, 158f. He admits there is a lot of pulp and little food value. *Kherrūb* is the colloquial word for *kharnūb*.

[129]*Str.-B.*, II, 214.

This renders unacceptable Jeremias' conclusion that the prodigal was too disgusted to eat the carob pods.[130] Linnemann's solution that he was *unable* to eat them implies that someone else was feeding the pigs and standing over the prodigal to see that he did not eat any of the pigs' feed. Her suggestion creates more problems than it solves.[131] Rihbany himself concludes that the text must mean simply that the prodigal was poor. But this solution is inadequate because of the verb ἐπ-εθύμει.

Jeremias has established linguistically that ἐπεθύμει with an infinitive in the Lucan source expresses an unfulfilled wish.[132] So the problem is that the text says the prodigal was unable to fill his stomach with κεράτιον. The word κεράτιον as we have noted is usually identified with *ceratonia siliqua*, which is commonly eaten every summer all across Lebanon and Syria. Everybody fills his stomach with *kharnūb*. Why was the prodigal not able to do so? The problem has not been recognized, because scholars have not realized that the *ceratonia siliqua* is eaten and enjoyed by all.

Clearly the identification of κεράτιον with *ceratonia siliqua* must be challenged. The latter contains enough sugar that molasses is made from it.[133] In a time of severe famine it is hard to imagine anything with significant human food value being fed to the pigs. The answer to this dilemma is found in that the Middle East has two kinds of *kharnūb*. This was observed nearly fifty years ago by Rendel Harris.[134] Harris translated from an Arabic dictionary entitled *al-Tāj* (the crown)[135] as follows:

> Carob: Abu Hanifa says: There is a wild and a Syrian variety of this shrub. The wild variety (called also thorny carob) has thorns and is used as firewood. It grows up to a cubit in height, has branches and bears berries light in weight and inflated, but these berries are harsh and are not eaten, *except in time of exigency.* The Syrian kind is sweet and eaten.[136]

Harris goes on to note an Old Syriac lexicon which also differentiates the two varieties. Lane, in his definitive Arabic dictionary, has this to say about the carob:

> There are two kinds, wild [*barrī*] and Syrian [*shāmī*]: . . . the former kind is thorny, . . . used as fuel, rising to the height of a cubit, with a fruit . . . black . . . and . . . disagreeable in taste, . . . not eaten except in cases of difficulty or distress; . . . the Syrian kind [is that to which the name of *Kharrūb* is now

---

[130]Jeremias, *Parables*, 129.

[131]Linnemann, *Parables*, 151, n. 11.

[132]Jeremias, *Parables*, 129, n. 75.

[133]Thomson, *The Land*, I, 22. Thomson also gives a picture of the tree and of the pod. The tree itself is large. Anyone picking pods for the pigs could certainly eat all he wanted in the process.

[134]Rendel Harris, "The Charobs of the Sea," *The Expositor*, Series 9, 2 (Oct. 1924), 301–304. The article is primarily a discussion of the obscure reference to "carobs of the sea" which appears in the Old Syriac. But at the end of the essay Harris offers a solution that seems most adequate to the problem. His suggestion was ignored most likely because few realized the fact of the problem.

[135]I have not been able to locate this dictionary. Harris gives the reference as Vol. I, 231.

[136]Harris, *loc. cit.*, 304; emphasis his.

commonly applied, the carob, or locust-tree; *ceratonia siliqua*; the fruit of which] is sweet, and is eaten. . . .[137]

This wild carob, not the *ceratonia siliqua*, fits the picture of the parable. The wild carob is more of a shrub, and pigs could grub for its berries. It *can* be eaten by humans, but is bitter and without nourishment. The prodigal could not fill his stomach with them. Regardless of how much he ate, he was not filled. The wild carob does not have enough nourishment to keep a man alive.[138] In summary, the parable depicts a pig herder trying desperately to get enough nourishment to keep alive from black, bitter berries which the pigs root from low shrubs. This shrub is not the *ceratonia siliqua* but is a wild carob that grows in the pasturelands of the Middle East.

"And no one gave him anything," is the concluding comment that fills in the picture. The verb is in the imperfect tense and thus may better be translated, "No one was giving to him." This can possibly mean that he tried his hand at begging and failed even at that.[139] It is probably better understood to mean, "No one was feeding him regularly." Obviously, he received something for feeding pigs; but in a time of famine, with the availability of a cheap labor force of the starving, his subsistence dole would have been very little. He specifically says, "I perish here with hunger." He is clearly not getting enough to stay alive. Presumably the pigs were eaten by the citizen. If and when the owner butchered, the herders (following Middle Eastern practice) would naturally be given the less desirable portions of the pig. It is easy to imagine a Jew of a noble family quite unable to eat such food even if he were starving. All the Syriac versions have a past tense of the verb "to be" followed by a present participle, reading specifically, "No one was giving him." This reinforces the possibility of our suggestion.[140] In any case, he was starving and needed to find some solution. This brings us to a consideration of the nature of his repentance in the far country.

There is rabbinic evidence that the phrase "he came to himself" in some sense means "he repented." In this section we will argue that this contemplated "repentance" in the far country is significantly different from his actual repentance before his father. Strack and Billerbeck argue that the phrase "he came to himself" means "he repented."[141] This simple conclusion needs careful examination.

Strack and Billerbeck identify חזר בו and הדר ביה as lying behind εἰς ἑαυτὸν δὲ ἐλθὼν in Luke 15:17a. In defense of their proposal it can be said that

---

[137]E. W. Lane, *An Arabic-English Lexicon*, Book I, Part 2 (New York: 1955 [1865]), 717a; brackets in 1955 ed. Most of the ellipses replace letter-references to Arabic sources.

[138]At the same time, the rabbi mentioned above *could* just manage to stay alive eating the sweet "Syrian carob."

[139]Jeremias' suggestion that he was stealing is unnecessary. Vat. Borg. Ar. 71 reads, "No one gave him alms," which understands specifically that he was begging, unsuccessfully.

[140]The Arabic versions have the verb "to be" in the past followed by a present tense, indicating also continuous action in the past.

[141]*Str.-B.*, II, 215.

ἔρχομαι at times does carry the idea of "come back, return," and the Semitic ב is closely related to Greek εἰς. Thus the Aramaic *hozer bo* does look linguistically very much like the "to himself he came" of verse 17.[142]

At the same time, a number of important factors weigh heavily against their proposal. First of all, the phrases Strack and Billerbeck have selected as lying behind the Greek do not necessarily represent the Greek of Luke 15:17a; and, furthermore, these phrases are relatively weak if thought of as referring to repentance. Strack and Billerbeck translate both rabbinic phrases "in sich gehen." Both expressions appear in a single passage in the Talmud.[143] The first phrase occurs early in the passage, which reads, אמר הקדוש ברוך הוא אם חוזר בו, which Strack and Billerbeck translate, "Gott sagt; Wenn der Gottlose in sich geht."[144] Goldschmidt translates the same phrase, "der Heilige, gebenedeiet er, sprach nämlich: wenn er umkehrt."[145] Thus there is some disagreement as to whether *hozer bo* should be translated "in sich geht." The same is true of the second phrase.[146] This in turn means that we cannot be quick to identify these Aramaic phrases as lying behind the Greek of Luke 15:17a.

The Aramaic word with its preposition *hozer bo* means "to turn around, return, retract, repent." Jastrow translates the imperative *hazor beka* as "come back (repent)." The perfect verb form, again with the preposition, is used of a woman who "reconsiders" her consent to marriage. She *hozrah beh*.[147] The second phrase, *hadar beyh,* means "to go around, come back, return." Jastrow defines it as a man who "went back on himself, changed his opinion."[148] Thus, as Aramaic phrases, these words have the distinctive meaning of "turning back" and can mean "reconsider" or "change an opinion" as well as, occasionally, "repent."[149] They can mean "repent" but they are relatively weak when used for "repentance."

A second consideration is that Luke 15:17a does not have μετανοέω. If the prodigal's prepared confession is a full repentance, why is this theological word not used?

Third, the rabbinical term for repentance is *tob,* the Aramaic equivalent of the Hebrew *shub*. Behm writes,

---

[142]Bauer-A., G., *Lexicon,* 310. The majority of the Arabic versions use *raja'a,* which is specifically "he came back."

[143]b. *Schab.* 104a.

[144]*Str.-B.,* II, 215.

[145]Lazarus Goldschmidt, *Der Babylonische Talmud* (Haag: Martinus Nijhoff, 1933), I, 592.

[146]The second phrase, הדר ביה, which also appears in b. *Schab.* 104a, is also translated "in sich geht" by Strack and Billerbeck and "er umkehrt" by Goldschmidt, *loc. cit.*

[147]M. Jastrow, *A Dictionary of the Targumim, the Talmud Babli and Jerushalmi, and the Midrashic Literature* (New York: Pardes, 1950), I, 446.

[148]*Ibid.,* I, 334.

[149]Significantly, *Ta'an.* 23b has "she prayed that they might repent," where the Aramaic is דליהדרו בתובתא, lit. "that they might return with repentance." Thus "repentance" is added to "return" indicating that *hadar* alone is not enough to mean "repent."

What the religious language of the OT expressed by שׁוב and the theological terminology of the Rabbis by תשׁובה, עשׂה תשׁובה or תתובא, עבד תתובתא the NT, like the Jewish Hellenistic writings, expresses by μετανοέω and μετάνοια.[150]

Thus the phrases suggested by Strack and Billerbeck are *not* used by the rabbis in their major discussions of repentance. In the key passages on repentance in the Mishna, the Talmud, the Midrashim, and the Shemone Esre, the words used are those listed above.[151]

Fourth, Syriac has the same theological term for repentance as the Aramaic (*tob*). This word is not used in the Syriac translations of Luke 15:17. They read, instead, "he came to his *nefesh*."[152] The word *nefesh* is an important term in Oriental thought. Its introduction in this text shifts the emphasis to a frame of reference distinctively different from that of "repentance." It is clear that the Oriental churches through the centuries have not understood this phrase as simply meaning "he repented."[153]

Fifth, in Luke 18:4 Codex Bezae has the identical words ἦλθεν εἰς ἑαυτὸν, which in that context clearly means something less than repentance. The judge feels no remorse—he merely wants to get rid of the woman who is giving him a headache, so he changes his mind.

In conclusion, we can admit that Strack and Billerbeck may have the right phrase underlying the Greek text. But even if this is the case, it is much weaker as a theological phrase than any expression using *shūb* or *tūb*. Some type of "return" or "repentance" is most probably indicated by verse 17, but only in a qualified sense.

The exact content of this repentance must now be examined in detail. Like the unjust steward in Luke 16, the prodigal does not offer excuses. He repents, but for what? Bornkamm has rightly identified the son's motive in the far country. He says, "For it is not his remorse for the sins he has committed, but to begin with, quite simply the realization that he has come to the end of his tether, which makes the son turn back."[154] Derrett, writing from a Jewish point of view, asks the significant question, "Many wonder how repentance preceded that return. Repen-

---

[150]J. Behm, *TDNT*, IV, 999.

[151]*Ibid.*, *s.v.* "μετανοέω," *passim*; Montefiore, *Rabbinic*, 390–422, "Appendix III on Repentance."

[152]The majority of the Arabic versions also include the word *nefesh* in their translation. The Polyglot reads, "he understood," and Ibn al-ʿAssāl has the very attractive "when his heart returned to him."

[153]Modern village colloquial speech in the Middle East has a very striking phrase that may be significant. When someone is so flustered as not to know where he is or what is happening around him, like a small child on hearing an unexpected automobile horn, they say, "He doesn't know where his *nefesh* has gone." The implication is that one's *nefesh* is something that can be separated from one and when this happens, confusion results. The Greek ἐξίστημι etymologically implies something of the same background.

[154]Bornkamm, *Jesus*, 126f. Jones also notes the shallow nature of the prodigal's motivation in the far country (*Art*, 182). Bruce writes, "his repentance has its source in hunger, and its motive is to get a bit of bread" (*Parabolic*, 285).

tance of what? Was he sincere? Was the father as foolish to readmit him as he was to give him the share initially?" Derrett tacitly answers his own question with the further statement, "This might well be the fundamental weakness of the parable."[155] Derrett also observes that when the boy says, "I have sinned against heaven and in your sight," he is confessing having failed to hold himself in readiness to take care of his father in his old age. The sin prompting his confession is a loss of money that had a moral responsibility attached to it, which, so far, he has refused to acknowledge.[156] The implication of this understanding of his sin is crucial. He thinks that if he had not lost the money, he would not have sinned. Thus the prodigal is motivated by hunger and he repents for having lost the money.

The further question of his relationships in the home community must be examined. His primary relationships are to his father, his brother, and to the village community.

The first and most important of these three is his relationship to his father. The key to understanding the prodigal's intentions in regard to his father is found in his face-saving plan. He will work as a hired servant (stanza 6'). The exact nature of the hired servant is generally overlooked in the literature. Oesterley identifies the three levels of servants on a first-century Jewish estate as follows:

1. *Bondsmen* (δοῦλοι), who as slaves were a part of the estate and indeed almost a part of the family.

2. *Slaves of a lower class* (παῖδες), who were subordinates of the bondsmen.

3. *Hired servants* (μίσθιοι).

Regarding this last class Oesterley writes,

> The "hired servant" was an outsider, he did not belong to the estate, he had no personal interests in the affairs of his temporary master; he was merely a casual laborer to be employed when required. . . . His position was, therefore, precarious, . . . though, *unlike them, he was a free man.* . . .[157]

Oesterley states, however, that the "hired servant" though free was lower than the other two types of servants. This evaluation of his social status is contradicted by Jewish scholarship. Heinemann writes,

> Work and the worker were held in high esteem in Tannaitic times. . . . It is a well-known fact, that most Tannaim were themselves artisans; a good many were even day labourers. No difference in social status appears to have existed between the dependent wage-earner and the more independent artisan (their

---

[155]Derrett, "Prodigal Son," 58. Derrett is right. From a Jewish understanding of repentance, as we shall note, the prodigal's motivation in the far country is suspect and needs some clear verification. The motivation is hunger. If he had been financially successful, he would not have considered returning home.

[156]*Ibid.*, 65. Derrett's point is that the prodigal has broken the fifth commandment. Bruce adds, "He will go home and he will make confession of his sin in well-premeditated form, suited at once to propitiate an injured father" (*Parabolic,* 287).

[157]Oesterley, *Jewish Background,* 186; emphasis mine.

legal status, too, was identical; both were called "hired workers"), nor was the worker considered socially inferior to his employer.[158]

Heinemann's work is well documented and can be considered authoritative. What he says is crucial to a proper understanding of what the prodigal is proposing as a solution to the problem of his future relationship to his father's house. As a "hired servant" he will be a free man with his own income living independently in the local village.[159] His social status will not be inferior to that of his father and his brother. He can maintain his pride and his independence. But there is more.

If the prodigal becomes a hired servant, he may be able to pay back what he has lost. In this connection Derrett writes,

> Working as a hired servant (sleeping off the premises) he could see to it that eventually with his wages, if not in other ways, he could give his father what, so long as the father lived, was only his due.[160]

With Derrett we can agree that the prodigal perhaps intended to work and thereby fulfil his moral responsibilities to the father. In losing the money he failed in these responsibilities. Now he will make up for what he has lost. In short, he will save himself. He wants no grace.[161]

There is possibly another aspect to what the prodigal plans to say to his father, which sheds light on the prodigal's understanding of their hoped-for future relationship. This dimension is clearly a part of the translation in the manuscript Vatican Borgianus Arabic 95, copied in 885. In that version, the word "make me" in the phrase "make me one of your hired servants" is translated *iṣna'nī*.[162] This can be translated, "Fashion out of me." The background of ποιέω clearly carries

---

[158]Joseph H. Heinemann, "The Status of the Labourers in Jewish Law and Society in the Tannaitic Period," *HUCA* 25 (1954), 265f. The period of the Tanna' im is reckoned from R. Hillel, which puts us clearly back into the first century. Cf. Horowitz, *Jewish Law,* xxxvii. Hillel himself, at least while a student, was a day laborer; cf. Jeremias, *Jerusalem,* 112f., 116.

[159]In the modern village the "hired servant" likewise lives in the village, not on the estate. A wealthy man may hire an artisan and bring him from some distant place with his helpers. In such an exceptional case the artisan and his assistants are housed temporarily on the estate. For example, a team of plasterers, famous in a given area, will be housed on the estate until the contractual work is finished.

[160]Derrett, "Prodigal Son," 65; Jülicher also identified the "hired servant" as a day laborer, a *Tagelöhner* (*Gleichnisreden,* II, 347). Cf. also Arndt, *St. Luke,* 351.

[161]The Palestinian Talmud has an interesting reference to the making of amends for misdeeds. It speaks of חזרת גמורה, a "true restoration" which involved חזירת ממון לא חזרת דברים. When mammon is involved then mammon must be returned, not just *debarim.* p. Tal. *Rosh Hash-Shaneh,* i.57c; quoted in Jastrow, *op. cit.,* I, 446f.

[162]Vat. Bor. Ar. 95 is an exceptionally important ms. It is translated from a Greek ms. of high quality and is carefully done. Luke has never been transcribed, to my knowledge. Matthew and Mark were published (cf. B. Levin, *Die griechish-arabische Evangelien-Übersetzung* [Uppsala: n.p., 1938]). The translator is faithful to his Greek original and at times even a bit too literal. Yet he leaves himself enough freedom to make his own exegetical understanding of the text felt. Having spent some time with this ms. I have the impression of a very perceptive exegetical insight appearing time and again in the selection of a key word or a turn of phrase. In Luke 15 he makes at least four culturally or theologically oriented exegetical decisions. This is the first of them.

this freight. Braun traces the word from its Old Testament roots as a term referring all through biblical literature to the creative activity of God. In the New Testament it is used "with reference to His helping and redeeming activity."[163] This may be a part of what the prodigal intends to say to his father. The son is commanding his father, which in itself is significant. The prodigal has a plan he feels is worthy of execution. He intends to order his father to carry it out. He may be implying, "Disregard the past; I'm sorry for what I have done. But I am not useless to you. I am still good raw material. Fashion out of me a workman."[164] Thus, in regard to the father the prodigal fully intends to confess his failure. That failure seems to be understood in terms of money lost. He has a plan that will give him independence from his father and provide an opportunity to compensate for his errors. With pride intact he intends to order his father to make him a hired servant. Stanza 6' balances 6 precisely. This brings us to a consideration of the prodigal's relationship to his brother.

If the prodigal works as a hired servant, he will not be eating his brother's bread. He knows full well that everything left in the estate is legally signed over to his brother. From the profits of the farm, the father has the right to feed whom he likes. But, if the Mishna can be applied, whatever is not consumed by the father and his friends is then added to the capital which the older brother will in time inherit.[165] Thus the older brother will most likely resent the prodigal's presence. Living at home would entail reconciliation to his brother, and apparently this is rejected. In any case, he works out an alternative that makes this kind of reconciliation unnecessary.

The prodigal's final problem is his relationship to the village. Any status in the village will initially be very difficult to achieve. He has failed in the far-off country. It is always difficult for any emigrant to return to his home village unless he has succeeded.[166] In the case of the prodigal, his return to the home village is greatly complicated by the manner of his leaving. He left having offended the entire community by taking and selling his inheritance while his father was still living. Now he has lost the money to the gentiles. Thus he can fully expect the extended family to cut him off with an enactment of the qeṣaṣah. His entry into the village will be humiliating and ruthless as the pent-up hostilities of the village are vented on him for having insulted his father, sold the land, and now lost it. For this problem he apparently has no solution. The village will simply have to be faced.

The prodigal's three primary relationships, as he sees them from the far country, can now be summarized. He plans to live in the village as a hired servant.

---

[163]H. Braun, *TDNT*, VI, 464.

[164]The verb is an aorist imperative implying the beginning of a new action. Cf. A. T. Robertson, *A Grammar of the Greek New Testament in the Light of Historical Research* (Nashville: Broadman, 1934), 851.

[165]Cf. Mishna *Baba Bathra* viii.7, "The father may pluck up (produce) and feed it to whomsoever he pleases, but whatever is left plucked up belongs to his heirs."

[166]My Lebanese friends tell me that the Lebanese emigrant never goes back to his village for any reason if he has failed economically in the diaspora.

With such a position his status will be secure. He can perhaps fulfil his responsibility to his father, and the problem of any relationship to his brother is eliminated. The village with its mockery will have to be faced. He will have to pay this bitter price in order to get home. He must go home because he is starving.

Having seen what the prodigal's planned confession meant in terms of his primary relationships, we may now examine this same confession in the light of rabbinic teaching on repentance. We shall attempt to show in this section that the planned confession is in harmony with rabbinic attitudes.

The rabbinic doctrine of repentance made use of Lamentations 5:21 and Malachi 3:7.[167] Lamentations reads, "Turn thou us unto thee, O Lord, and we shall be turned"; and the Malachi text gives, "Return unto me, and I will return unto you, saith the Lord." The confusion in the above Lamentations and Malachi texts over who must turn first, Israel or God, was resolved by the rabbis, who wrote, "A Bible verse says, 'Turn thou us and we shall be turned'; therefore God should begin. But another verse says, 'Turn unto me, and I will turn unto you.' So let us turn together simultaneously."[168] The Eighteen Benedictions also mention repentance where they read, "Cause us to return, O our Father, unto thy Law; draw us near, O our King, unto thy service, and bring us back in perfect repentance unto thy presence. Blessed art thou, O Lord, who delightest in repentance" (number five, *Teshubah*). This statement seems to indicate that man needs help from God for true repentance. At the same time, the worshiper who prays this benediction is already penitent and concerned to do what must be done to be sure of God's favor. He is afraid lest he not be able to do the work of repentance; and so God's help is invoked. The idea that repentance is a "work" which man does prior to God's acceptance of him is found all through rabbinic literature. Another midrash reads, "Three things can cancel evil decrees; namely, prayer, almsgiving and repentance."[169] And again,

> If Israel says, "We are poor, we have no offering to make," God replies, "I need only words." If they say, "We know nothing" [for by words the Midrash means the words of the Law], God says, "Then weep and pray before me, and I will accept your prayer."[170]

Thus for the rabbis repentance was primarily a work of man which assured him of God's favor.

Furthermore, the idea of reparations and of atonement became a part of the doctrine of repentance. A man was expected to make reparations before he could repent. This was why a shepherd could not fully repent; he did not know how many fields he had trespassed, therefore he could not make adequate reparations.[171] The

---

[167]Montefiore, *Rabbinic*, 390–422.

[168]Lam. R. on v. 21; Midrash Ps. 85:4.

[169]Midr. Ps. 18:3.

[170]Montefiore, *Rabbinic*, 404.

[171]*Ibid.*, 402. Montefiore feels that this injunction against the shepherds has to be taken with a grain of salt.

act of repentance was itself an atoning work. Reparations and atonement were made by the act of repentance. After the destruction of the temple the atoning aspect of repentance became dominant. According to Maimonides repentance replaced the sacrificial system. He wrote, "There is nothing left us but repentance which, however, atones for all transgressions."[172] In this connection, Montefiore writes,

> Fasting and prayer, repentance, and "good works," ritualism independent of sacrifice, and high doctrine transcending it, enable the people and their teachers to overcome the shock of the Temple's loss, and to fashion a religion superior to that of the priests.[173]

In this statement Montefiore lists repentance as one of the theological elements used by the rabbis to replace the entire sacrificial system, which ended with the destruction of Jerusalem.

In summary, it can be said that for the rabbis, repentance was a work that man did to earn God's favor. At times man needed God's help. God had to come part of the way as man came the rest of the way. The work of repentance had to be sincere and accompanied by reparations for the sin along with a determination to avoid all further sin. Repentance atoned for sin.

Applying this to the prodigal, we see him preparing to make the reparations that will demonstrate his sincerity. The confession itself can be understood as a partial work of atonement by which he begins to make up for what he has done. It is clear that Derrett, from his Jewish point of view, feels that, if this kind of plan had been carried out, the parable would have been more believable and would have avoided its "fundamental weakness."[174]

The Oriental farmer and landowner lives in his village, not in isolation out on his land. This has always been the case. The background of Isaiah 5:8 makes this clear. It reads,

> Woe to those who join house to house
>   and add field to field,
> until there is no more room,
>   and you are made to dwell alone
>   in the midst of the land.

Clearly the picture is that of buying field after field of the agricultural land and of joining house to house in the village where the homes are in tight proximity to each other. The threat is that if the wealthy continue their practice, they will finally buy out all the surrounding families, forcing them out of the village and off the land. The result will be that the wealthy will end up dwelling alone in the midst of the land, which is the worst possible fate for the gregarious Middle Eastern villager. Even into modern times, the larger houses of the older Oriental estates usually do

---

[172]*Ibid.*, 396.
[173]*Ibid.*, 394.
[174]Derrett, "Prodigal Son," 58.

not stand in grand isolation at the center of the cropland.[175] Thus we can confidently assume that the father lives in a village as part of the community.

Most likely the father expects his son to fail. He is assumed dead. If he makes it back, it will be as a beggar. The father also knows how the village (which certainly has told him he should not have granted the inheritance in the first place) will treat the boy on his arrival. The prodigal will be mocked by a crowd that will gather spontaneously as word flashes across the village telling of his return. Ben Sirach mentions four things that terrify him. Two of them are "slander by a whole town, the gathering of a mob."[176] The prodigal son returns to face both of Ben Sirach's terrors, the slander of a whole town and certainly the gathering of a mob. As soon as the prodigal reaches the edge of the village and is identified, a crowd will begin to gather. He will be subject to taunt songs and many other types of verbal and perhaps even physical abuse.

The father is fully aware of how his son will be treated, if and when he returns in humiliation to the village community he has rejected. What the father does in this homecoming scene can best be understood as a series of dramatic actions calculated to protect the boy from the hostility of the village and to restore him to fellowship within the community. These actions begin with the father running down the road.

An Oriental nobleman with flowing robes never runs anywhere. To do so is humiliating.[177] Ben Sirach confirms this attitude. He says, "A man's manner of walking tells you what he is."[178] Weatherhead writes, "It is so very undignified in Eastern eyes for an elderly man to run. Aristotle says, 'Great men never run in public.' "[179] The text says, "He had compassion." We would suggest that this "compassion" specifically includes awareness of the gauntlet the boy will have to

---

[175]Thomson gives a population listing for all the principal cities of Syria, Lebanon, and Palestine for the nineteenth century and adds, "I need scarcely remind you that the entire population is gathered into towns and villages" (The Land, I, 247). This is so universally evident from archeology as to need no documentation.

[176]Sir. 26:5f. The pressures of the community in the tightly knit Oriental village must be felt to be believed. Custom demands that a mother or sister or wife caught in any type of extramarital sex be killed by the men of the family. The execution is unfailing and immediate. Conversation in depth with the people involved is revealing. Question: "How can you do this? Do you not love your mother?" Answer: "O yes, very, very deeply." Question: "Then how can you bring yourself to do this?" Answer: "The talk of the people! You cannot bear the talk of the people! You must do it!"

[177]A pastor of my acquaintance was not accepted as the pastor of a particular church because, in the judgment of the elders, he walked down the street too fast. This custom is preserved even in a modern Middle Eastern metropolis by the Orthodox priest who, of course, still wears the long robes and is careful to walk at a slow, dignified pace.

[178]Sir. 19:30. It is not fully clear what Ben Sirach is referring to, but the most natural assumption is that he is discussing the slow, stately walk expected of men of position, age, and rank in that society.

[179]L. P. Weatherhead, In Quest of a Kingdom (London: Hodder and Stoughton, 1943), 90. Weatherhead does not document his quotation from Aristotle. Cf. also Jeremias, Parables, 130. Bengel wrote in the eighteenth century, "Parents ordinarily are not disposed to run and meet their children" (Gnomon, I, 474); cf. E. C. B. MacLaurin, "The Semitic Background of the use of 'En Splachnois'," Palestinian Exploration Quarterly 103 (1971), 42–45.

face as he makes his way through the village. The father then runs this gauntlet for him, assuming a humiliating posture in the process! Bruce has noted that such an action would "soon draw a crowd to the spot."[180]

The father makes the reconciliation public at the edge of the village. Thus his son enters the village under the protective care of the father's acceptance. The boy, having steeled his nerves for this gauntlet, now, to his utter amazement, sees his father run it for him. Rather than experiencing the ruthless hostility he deserves and anticipates, the son witnesses an unexpected, visible demonstration of love in humiliation. The father's acts replace speech. There are no words of acceptance and welcome. The love expressed is too profound for words. Only acts will do. Sa'īd writes,

> Christ reports for us the words of the son to his father, but does not give anything about a speech of the father to his son. For in reality,
>> the father substitutes kisses for words
>> and replaces assertion with expression
>> and eyes speak for the tongue.[181]

Stanza 5 is a picture of total rejection. Here in stanza 5' is *total* acceptance. In this public visible demonstration of unexpected love the father is just as earnestly searching for his son as the shepherd and the woman searched for what they had lost.[182]

Quoting Bornhäuser, Linnemann asserts that the kiss on the cheek is a sign of equality and that the father's kiss prevents the son from kissing the hand or the feet of his father.[183] This latter part of the assertion is quite likely correct. The boy would have kissed his father's hand or perhaps even his feet but is prevented from doing so.[184]

The first part of Bornhäuser's assertion is in error. The father's kiss is not a sign of equality. An Oriental father is never his son's equal. Rather it is a sign of reconciliation and forgiveness. When a serious quarrel has taken place in the village and reconciliation is achieved, a part of the ceremony enacted as a sacrament of reconciliation is a public kiss by the leading men involved.[185] There is no assumption of "equality." One party may be of higher status and the other of

---

[180]Bruce, *Synoptic Gospels,* 582. Bruce is the only author I have found who has noted the inevitable presence of a quickly gathered crowd. Derrett thinks "small boys" would have brought word from a previous village. This is unlikely, but he notes correctly that an ever present crowd of young boys is an inevitable part of anything that happens in the village. Cf. Derrett, "Prodigal Son," 65.

[181]Sa'īd, *Lūqā,* 401. With his matchless command of the Arabic language Sa'īd here breaks into rhymed prose. Sa'īd then observes that the father is pouring out kisses on a dirty son, and says, "The father is not kissing the son's cleanliness, but his person (*nafsahu*)" (*ibid.*).

[182]Miller, *Luke,* 120f.

[183]Linnemann, *Parables,* 77. She is quoting K. Bornhäuser, *Studien zum Sondergut des Lukas* (Gütersloh: n.p., 1934), 114.

[184]Rihbany writes, "Upon coming home from a journey I always saluted my parents by kissing their hands, as a mark of loving submission" (*Syrian,* 337).

[185]Cf. Gen. 33:4. Esau is not saying, "You are my equal," but rather, "I forgive you."

lower. It would be unthinkable for any father publicly to assert that his son was his equal!

The word καταφιλέω can mean either "kiss tenderly" or "kiss again and again." The first meaning would be feminine and quite inappropriate. The second is in Middle Eastern custom fully masculine and culturally accurate.[186]

The son responds with only a *part* of his prepared speech. The listener/reader has already been told the entire speech and so knows what to expect. The offer of a solution, "Make me as one of your hired servants," is missing.[187] Commentators too numerous to note assume that the father interrupted him.[188] It is our understanding that this misses the crucial nature of what is happening here at a very critical part of the story. If the boy is interrupted, he can finish his speech later, after the father completes giving his orders to the servants. We *could* assume that his failure to do so indicates a self-interest which says, "This is better than I expected. Why not take all I can get? I'll keep silent and accept. If he will give me sonship, who cares about being a workman?"

Certainly this is not what the omission signifies. Given the prodigal's previous mind-set, sonship has certain distinct disadvantages. If he accepts sonship, he will have to live with his brother and be fed from his brother's property. He will again be under the total authority of his father. He will be denied the self-satisfaction of having "earned his own way." Accepting sonship requires a deliberate decision with broad ramifications. Clearly he has changed his mind. Via has understood the significance of this change. He writes, "Repentance finally turns out to be the capacity to forego pride and accept graciousness."[189]

Following this line of argument, we must ask, "Why did he change his mind?" and, more precisely, "What are the ramifications of his decision?" As we have seen, the prodigal comes home with a rabbinic understanding of repentance. He is shattered by his father's demonstration of love in humiliation. In his state of apprehension and fear he would naturally experience this unexpected deliverance as an utterly overwhelming event. Now he knows that he cannot offer any solution to their ongoing relationship. He sees that the point is not the lost money, but rather the broken relationship which he cannot heal. Now he understands that any new relationship must be a pure gift from his father. He can offer no solution. To

---

[186]Against Manson, *Sayings,* 288.

[187]Harmonizers tried to "improve" on the story by adding "make me as one of your hired servants" to this verse. The best textual evidence omits it. All our Oriental versions except the Harclean also omit the phrase. Ibn al-'Assāl does not even list the phrase in his apparatus.

[188]There is a strong exegetical tradition from at least the Reformation that translates the εἶπεν δέ of the beginning of v. 21 with "*but* he said," indicating a contrast. (Luther, King James, American Standard Version, Revised Standard Version, New English Bible, Jerusalem Bible.) The one modern exception is the New American Bible. The Oriental versions, however (with the exception of the Peshitta and the Harclean), imply continuity rather than contrast. With the Oriental versions, the father's actions are understood to be in continuity with the radically new attitude seen suddenly in the speech of the son.

[189]Via, *Parables,* 171.

assume that he can compensate his father with his labor is an insult. "I am unworthy" is now the only appropriate response.[190]

In his famous eleventh-century Arabic commentary on the Gospels, Ibn al-Ṭayyib gives some astute Oriental insights into this text. He writes,

> The text says, "Make me as one of your hired servants." This means those who have repented but who are not yet worthy of the position of sons because their repentance is not complete. The text says, "And he arose and came to his father." This means he was inclined toward God with repentance. . . . The text says, "He (the father) hurried and fell upon his bosom and kissed him," as a sign of the greatness of his mercy and compassion and that he does not hold his son's monstrous sins against him but welcomes him with joy. The text says, "He said to him, 'Father, I have sinned against heaven and before you and I am no longer worthy to be called your son,' " because you are good and I am evil. It says that he was determined, if he met his father, to say to him, "Make me one of your hired servants." But he did not say this. We say that he did not say it because of what he saw of his father's love.[191]

In this comment Ibn al-Ṭayyib affirms that the hired servant plan had something to do with an incomplete or partial repentance. The father's welcome is clearly an outpouring of grace. But of special note for our discussion is Ibn al-Ṭayyib's comment on the reason for the omission of the offer to become a hired servant. He says that the prodigal changed his mind "because of what he saw of his father's love." Love was demonstrated and became visible. This worked a change of mind. The son decided against offering to become a servant. The willingness to become a hired servant itself signified for Ibn al-Ṭayyib a partial repentance. Full repentance came as a result of a demonstration of love.

After the prodigal's repentance and confession (stanza 4') the father turns to address the servants (stanza 3'). The servants are there on the road with the crowd.[192] They are specifically told to *dress* the son as servants do a king. He is not told to go and bathe and change his clothes. This order to dress the prodigal assures

---

[190]Via has noted that the boy undergoes a very significant change at the edge of the village. He writes, "Only when the event of forgiveness occurred and shattered his own view of things did his understanding change. . . . Natural man's legalistic understanding of the divine-human relationship is shattered only by the unexpected event of forgiveness which comes to him from beyond himself (*Parables,* 174).

In the nineteenth century, Godet wrote, "There is a wide difference between the confession uttered by the prodigal son, ver. 21, and that which had been extracted from him by the extremity of his misery (ver. 18, 19). The latter was a cry of despair; but now this distress is over. It is therefore the cry of repentant love. The terms are the same: *I have sinned*; but how different is the accent. Luther felt it profoundly; the discovery of the difference between the repentance of fear and that of love was the true principle of the Reformation. He cannot come to the end; the very assurance of pardon prevents him from finishing and saying, *make me as* . . . according to his first purpose" (*St. Luke,* 378). With the exception of Via, Godet's point has been neglected. It is our contention that the cultural scene presents strong evidence that his insight is correct.

[191]*Sharḥ al-Injīl li-Ibn al-Ṭayyib,* Paris Arabic 86, folio 131; my translation.

[192]Arndt correctly observes, "The father calls out an order to the slaves, who may be imagined to have followed him as he went out to meet the beggarlike person approaching in the distance" (*St. Luke,* 352; against Plummer, *St. Luke,* 375).

proper respect from the servants, who naturally are eagerly awaiting some clue from the father to tell them how they should treat the son. If the father had indicated displeasure with so much as an indifferent shrug of the shoulder, the servants would have done nothing for him.

The best robe is most certainly the father's.[193] The Oriental listener/reader would immediately assume this. The "first" (i.e., best) robe would be the robe the father wore on feast days and other grand occasions.[194] The point is that, as the guests arrive at the banquet, and as people stream in to see him, to hear his story, and to congratulate him on his return, the father's robe will assure acceptance by the community. With this command the father assures reconciliation between his son and his servants. At the same time, the father assures the completion of the son's reconciliation to the community.[195]

Does the robe carry any eschatological significance? Quite likely. Jeremias argues at some length that it does. Isaiah 61 is given special attention in the teachings of Jesus. Verse 10 of that chapter reads, "For he has clothed me with the garments of salvation, he has covered me with the robe of righteousness."[196] Jeremias writes,

> It may be remembered that Jesus spoke of the Messianic Age as a new garment (Mark 2.21 par. . . .), and that he compared forgiveness with the best robe with which the father clothed the prodigal son (Luke 15.22); hence we cannot doubt that it is this comparison that underlies Matt. 22.11–13. God offers you the clean garment of forgiveness and imputed righteousness.[197]

The ring is quite likely a signet ring, which means that he is trusted in a remarkable way.[198] The shoes are the sign of his being a free man in the house, not a servant.[199] Derrett writes regarding the servants, "They put his sandals on as a sign that they accept him as their master—indeed no order could have expressed this more conclusively."[200]

---

[193]Plummer has rightly observed that it cannot be the son's robe without an αὐτοῦ (St. Luke, 376). Rengstorf argues at great length that his robe is an official ceremonial robe that was publicly stripped from the boy when he was cut off in a qeṣaṣah ceremony (Re-Investitur, 39). I find his discussion unconvincing. The story specifically states that the son "gathered together" (realized) all that he had. The fact of such a ceremonial robe is undemonstrated. The qeṣaṣah was most likely not invoked. Furthermore, the rabbinic references to the qeṣaṣah make no mention of any ceremonial robe.

[194]Cf. Esther 6:9, where wearing the king's robe is described as a special honor.

[195]This latter is already accomplished to a large degree by making the welcome public. Dressing him in the father's best robe confirms and seals what he has already done at the edge of the village.

[196]Cf. Matt. 5:3; 11:5; Luke 4:18; 7:33. Cf. L. C. Crockett, "The Old Testament in the Gospel of Luke with Emphasis on the Interpretation of Isaiah 61:1–2" (unpublished Ph.D. thesis, Brown University, Providence, R.I., 1966).

[197]Jeremias, Parables, 189.

[198]Cf. Derrett, "Prodigal Son," 66; 1 Macc. 6:15; Gen. 41:42; Esther 3:10; 8:2; Jeremias, Parables, 130; Rengstorf, Re-Investitur, 30.

[199]Jeremias, Parables, 130.

[200]Derrett, "Prodigal Son," 66. Rengstorf argues that putting on shoes is a sign of asserting ownership. In the Middle East, shoes and feet in any reference are degrading and insulting. Shoes are unclean. They are combined in common speech in all kinds of insults. Rengstorf interprets the removal of shoes at the

Lastly the father orders the killing of the fatted calf. The selection of a calf rather than a goat or a sheep means that most, if not all, the village will be present that evening. The entire animal will spoil in a few hours if not eaten. Jeremias thinks the banquet is only for the family and the servants.[201] This is certainly in error. To kill a calf and not invite the community would be an insult to the community and a waste for the family. Indeed, the main point of killing such a large animal is to be able to invite the entire community. As with the woman and the shepherd, the joy must be shared on all sides.

Rihbany discusses the covenantal nature of killing an animal for the sake of a guest. He writes,

> The ancient custom, whose echoes have not yet died out in the East, was that the host honored his guest most highly by killing a sheep at the threshold of the house, upon the guest's arrival, and inviting him to step over the blood into the house. This act formed the "blood covenant" between the guest and his host. It made them one. To us one of the most cordial and dignified expressions in inviting a guest, especially from a distant town, was, "If God ever favors us with a visit from you, we will kill a *zebihat!*"
>
> In his great rejoicing in the return of his son, the father of the prodigal is made to receive him as he would a most highly honored guest. "The fatted calf"—and not only a sheep—is killed as the *zebihat* of a new covenant between a loving father and his son, who "was dead and is alive again"; was lost, and is found.[202]

Middle Eastern peasants have preserved customs of this kind from antiquity. When a new house is built, a sheep is killed and its blood spread on "the lintel and the two doorposts" in a manner that sounds very much like Exodus 12:21–27. Without other evidence, however, I am uneasy about accepting Rihbany's conclusion. I have not found Rihbany's proposal to reflect a deep and widespread attitude. Yet, on the positive side, he does point up the extraordinary honor that is extended to the

---

burning bush as meaning, "I take off my shoes as a sign that God owns this ground." It is better understood as, "I take off my shoes because I do not want to defile *holy* ground with my unclean shoes." Rengstorf argues that a man takes off his shoes when going into a house rather than putting them on. This also is not quite true. He takes off his shoes to have his feet washed. But he does not then go around barefoot. If the floor is packed earth, it is too dirty; if it is stone it is too cold. A man takes off his shoes when he reclines on a couch, or sits cross-legged on it. In a number of the foot-washing scenes in the New Testament the people involved were reclining. Rengstorf also uses Ps. 60:8, "Upon Edom I cast my shoe," as evidence of asserting ownership. Rather it is a very strong insult. At Assiut College in Egypt in the early sixties a young American teacher, inexperienced in Oriental attitudes toward shoes, woke a sleeping student one morning by throwing a shoe across the room at him. A thousand students rioted that day in protest over the "insult." In a public speech the speaker apologizes before using the word "shoes" in deference to its being nearly a four-letter word. The only place in biblical literature where there is some relationship between shoes and ownership is Ruth 4:7. However, there the author has to explain the custom to the reader because already by his time it had died out. This section of Rengstorf's discussion is very weak. Cf. Rengstorf, *Re-Investitur*, 39.

[201]Jeremias, *Parables*, 130.

[202]Rihbany, *Syrian*, 160.

son by the slaughter of such a large animal. This size feast requires over a hundred people in attendance to eat the animal. A calf is slaughtered for the marriage of the eldest son, or the visit of the governor of the province, or some such occasion. The calf means at least a joy so great that it must be celebrated with the grandest banquet imaginable. The purpose of such a banquet includes a desire to reconcile the boy to the *whole* community.

The father's speech ends in stanza 1'. The prodigal still has the option of preferring the freedom of an independent status in the village, far from the complications of living with his brother. Perverted pride would lead him to insist that he is "too humble" for sonship. Rather, he accepts pure grace. Grace wins. His abbreviated confession is his last word. Via describes this acceptance as a move from irresponsibility to a new contextual freedom.[203] Now the father and his younger son can begin to make merry. Indeed a son is found.

The first half of the parable ends with the beginning of the celebration of the return. The story has now come full circle. The literary structure presented above can now be more fully understood. In the light of the underlying culture it is of particular interest to compare the son's first speech at the beginning and his second in the center. Each line has its match. This can be seen as follows:

> *Speech I*
> a. Father
> b. give me my share of property
> c. (he divided his living.)
>
> *Speech II*
> a'. Father
> b'. I have sinned against heaven and you
> c'. I am no more worthy to be called your son.

Line a is an address. Line b means he wants his father to die. Line b' reflects this as he confesses the enormity of his sin. Line c tells us that he receives all that is his due and thereby cuts his relations with the family. Line c' admits this. In stanza 6 he admits he needs help—he is starving. His proposed self-help solution matches this in 6'. As is usual in such structures, the real point of turning occurs just past the center. In stanza 5' is the unbelievable visible demonstration of unexpected love in humiliation. A genuine repentance flows from that in 4' and the rest of the stanzas flow in sequence. Thus the literary structure reinforces the cultural elements in determining the movement of the story.

This homecoming scene presents the picture of a servant who plans to confess and compensate. The father then demonstrates unexpected love in humiliation. The servant is overwhelmed by grace and becomes a son. The scene provides a new understanding of repentance as acceptance of grace and the confession of unworthiness. The two rejoice together.

---

[203] Via, *Parables*, 166.

The Christological Implications of the Homecoming Scene

The apparent absence of any reference in this parable to the work of Christ is a problem that has been given four basic types of answers in modern times. These must be considered.

First, there were the nineteenth-century liberals who rejoiced that the true gospel has no atonement. The gospel in Harnack's view has to do "with the Father only and not with the Son."[204] This view fails to take into account the cultural background we have outlined above. It solves the problem by saying, "There is no problem."

A second approach is to claim that, after all, this parable is not a "complete compendium of theology." Those who take this approach say in effect, "The parable teaches that God loves sinners *while* they are still sinners. This is enough. We should not expect a full theological statement. The atonement is missing, never mind."[205] This answer dismisses the problem. Granted, the parable should not be thought of as a "complete compendium of theology." At the same time, the parable does depict how God reconciles men to himself.

A third position affirms that there are indirect, yet clear Christological references in the parable; never mind the atonement. Jeremias writes,

> Jesus . . . claims that in his actions the love of God to the repentant sinner is made effectual. Thus the parable, without making any kind of christological statement, reveals itself as a veiled assertion of authority: Jesus makes the claim for himself that he is acting in God's stead, that he is God's representative.[206]

Giblin says,

> Jesus's activity as man is the way in which God's mercy is seen and realized. Thus, in Lk 15 we seem to have a theologically analogous statement of the words in Jn 14.9, . . . "He who has observed me has observed the Father. . . ." . . . It is He [Jesus] to whom the character portrayal of the Father most immediately applies.[207]

This view offers thoughtful answers to the question of Christology generally but leaves unanswered this same question as it relates specifically to the atonement.

---

[204]Adolf von Harnack, *What Is Christianity?* trans. Thomas B. Saunders (New York: Harper, 1957 [1900), 144. Harnack uses as his primary evidence the publican in the temple, the widow and her mite, and the lost son (*ibid.*, 143). For centuries Islam has used the parable of the Prodigal Son in anti-Christian polemic attempting to prove that Christian theology is at odds with the message of Jesus. They claim the parable of the Prodigal Son to be in perfect harmony with Muslim theology. Jülicher asked the question, "Kann denn ein Sünder sich von selber bekehren, und wird ihm vergeben ohne Christe Mittlerschaft, ohne seinen Opfertod?" He answers his question with a clear "Yes." Cf. *Gleichnisreden,* II, 364f. For Jülicher the atonement was merely "die Lieblingsdogmen der 'Biblizisten' " (*ibid.*, II, 334).

[205]Manson, *Sayings,* 286.

[206]Jeremias, *Parables,* 132; his emphasis. Cf. Via, *Parables,* 171f.

[207]Giblin, "Luke 15," 25. Giblin affirms that the point of the parable is "to explain the plan of salvation which goes beyond strict justice" (*ibid.*, 24).

A fourth view finds Christology and hints of the atonement in certain elements of the parable. Karl Barth attempts what he calls a "not allegorical but typological or *in concreto* Christological exposition. . . ."[208] He sees no simple identification of Jesus with the lost son. Instead, as he puts it,

> . . . We do not do justice to the story if we do not see and say that in the going out and coming in of the lost son in his relationship with the father we have a most illuminating parallel to the way trodden by Jesus Christ in the work of atonement, to His humiliation and exaltation.[209]

Giblin sees the same symbolism in Luke 15.[210] These identifications of Christological elements in the prodigal himself by Barth and Giblin seem strained. The prodigal is a symbol of the publicans and sinners.[211] It is a long jump from them to Jesus. Can Jesus and the publican be symbolized by the same prodigal?

Gollwitzer has seen Christological overtones in other aspects of the parable. He writes, "Jesus ist das Entgegenlaufen des Vaters heraus aus dem Hause. Jesus ist aber auch die Kraft der Erinnerung an die Vaterschaft Gottes."[212] Gollwitzer then concentrates on the second statement.[213] Of all those in this fourth category, Giblin is the most satisfying. He neither introduces some new type of allegorizing nor does he violate the cultural influences that inform the text. He writes,

> . . . His [Christ's] redemptive love is reflected in the activity of His public life, too, not just on Calvary (where Christ's sacrificial love was perfectly achieved and also where His act of satisfaction was completed). Redemptive love is the *creative* love which truly makes us God's people in spite of ourselves. . . . In the subtle portrayal of redemptive love in Luke 15, Jesus is the one in and through whom the heavenly joy is shown to men: the Father is thus seen in and through Jesus's contact ("mediation") with men. Jesus Himself is the efficacious sign of the reconciliation and new life (cf. Lk 15, 32 *ezēsen*) . . . .[214]

---

[208]Karl Barth, *Church Dogmatics*, trans. G. W. Bromiley (Edinburgh: T. & T. Clark, 1958), IV/2, 25.

[209]*Ibid.*, 23. This view is endorsed by Stuhlmueller, *Luke*, 148f.

[210]Giblin, "Luke 15," 30.

[211]The prodigal son himself, at least since Augustine and likely before, was identified with the gentiles. It is highly unlikely that this identification was intended by Jesus. The prodigal begins *at home*. He is not a stranger brought in from the outside. Ibn al-Ṭayyib mentions this identification of the prodigal with the gentiles and argues against it (Paris Arabic Ms. 86, folio 129).

[212]Helmut Gollwitzer, *Die Freude Gottes, Einführung in das Lukasevangelium* (Berlin-Dahlem: Burckhardthaus-Verlag, 1952), 176.

[213]However, regarding the prodigal's *Erinnerung* of his father, if we would look for some theological identification here, the Holy Spirit might be more appropriate. The "spirit" of the father stirs the boy to remember a better life in a better fellowship. Yet this also must be rejected. To move in this direction would be to try indeed to make the parable a complete compendium of theology. This temptation must be resisted. If we would look for theology that is perhaps more "overheard" than "heard," it must be clearly a part of the cultural setting in which the parable was first told. To fail to adopt this as a methodological principle is to surrender the parable again to some new form of irresponsible allegorization.

[214]Giblin, "Luke 15," 30.

In harmony with the cultural setting we have outlined above, we would propose an expansion of this fourth position.

For Palestinian listeners, initially the father would naturally be a symbol of God.[215] Then, as the story progresses, the father comes down out of the house and, in a dramatic act, demonstrates unexpected love publicly in humiliation.[216] The literary structure and the cultural milieu of the story identify this dramatic act as the turning point of the first half of the parable. Surely Jesus intended his listeners to see in this act a dramatic representation of his welcome of sinners. When the father leaves the house to come out to his son in love and humility, he demonstrates at least a part of the meaning of the incarnation and the atonement.[217]

It is instructive to reflect on what would have happened in the story if the father had not presented a visible demonstration of unexpected love. The result would obviously have been one more hired servant, but no son. As we shall see, the father already had a servant-type son in the house. He wanted something more; and this was the only way to get a son, given the fact of estrangement and the mind-set of the boy. The father's love was always deep and abiding. But the son did not understand it. If the father had waited in the house, he would have had another servant. If he goes out in a shattering, humiliating demonstration of that love, the boy will see and may understand. If he does, then the father will have a son. In conclusion, then, the atonement is at least "overheard" in the parable.

The Older Son (15:24–32)[218]

In this section the literary structure will be examined and then the cultural aspects of the story will be discussed. Finally the theological cluster will be analyzed. The burden of the argument will be to show that this second half of the parable is culturally and stylistically a repetition of the first half. The externals are different, but the essential nature of each of the two halves is the same. Furthermore, the father's response to each of his sons is essentially identical.

The older son appears on the scene in the fields. He is outside the house. His path to the banquet hall is step by step presented as parallel to the road just traveled by the prodigal. This path is illuminated by the literary structure, which will now be examined.

B   Now the elder son was in the fields

---

[215]Cf. Isa. 63:16, "Thou, O Lord, art our Father."

[216]We shall see that the father is obliged to do the same thing for the older son (Via, *Parables,* 171).

[217]This is an expansion of Gollwitzer's first statement, above, p. 189.

[218]The unity of 15:11–32 has been accepted by the majority of scholars in the past sixty years. In historical order these include: Jülicher, Manson, C. W. F. Smith, Daube, Jeremias, Bultmann, and Linnemann. The most recent challenge to the parable's unity is from Jack T. Sanders, "Tradition and Redaction in Luke XV, 11–32," *NTS* 15 (1969), 433–38. Sanders has been fully answered by Jeremias, "Tradition und Redaktion in Lukas 15," *ZNW* 42 (1971), 172–189. Cf. also Jeremias, *Parables,* 131. Thus Manson's judgment still stands: "There is, in fact, no good reason for supposing that the story is anything but a perfect unity" (*Sayings,* 285).

1   and as he came and drew near to the house
        he heard music and dancing
        and he called one of the boys and asked what this meant.
	HE COMES

2   And he said to him, "Your brother has come
        and your father has killed the fatted calf
        because he received him with peace."
	YOUR BROTHER—SAFE
	A FEAST

3   But he was angry and refused to go in
        so his father came out
        and was entreating him.
	A FATHER COMES
	TO RECONCILE

But he answered his father, "Lo these many years *I have served you* *and I have never disobeyed* your commandments yet *you never gave me a kid* to make merry with my friends.	COMPLAINT I (HOW YOU TREAT ME)

4'   "But when *this son of yours* came
        who has *devoured your living with harlots*
        you killed for him the fatted calf."
	COMPLAINT II
	(HOW YOU TREAT HIM)

3'   And he said to him, "Beloved son,
        you are always with me
        and all that is mine is yours.
	A FATHER TRIES
	TO RECONCILE

2'   "It was fitting to make merry and be glad
        for this your brother was dead and is alive,
        he was lost and is found."
	YOUR BROTHER—SAFE
	A FEAST

[And he came and entered the house and joined in the music and dancing and he began to make merry.	????????[MISSING]
And the two sons were reconciled to their father.]	

Again we are dealing with a parabolic ballad (Type D), which forms three-line stanzas. The inversion principle is again used. The correspondences between the matching stanzas are clear and strong. In the climactic center the two complaints match line for line in step parallelism. In stanza 3 the father comes to reconcile while in 3' we hear his reconciling speech. Stanza 2 is a report of the feast and the banquet by a young boy; in 2' the father defends his inauguration of these same events. The ending is missing—there is no stanza 1'. The significance of this will become evident as we proceed. Here we can note that the structure of the parabolic ballad makes clear that something is unfinished. In brackets we have tried to reconstruct what might have been there if the second half of the parable had ended joyfully like the first half. With the structure in mind we turn to the details of the text.

The older son draws near and hears συμφωνίας and dancing. The word συμφωνία perhaps refers to a double pipe.[219] The ancient Oriental versions

---

[219]George F. Moore, "συμφωνία—Not a Bagpipe," *JBL* 24 (1905), 166–175. Moore is answering Barry, who in a previous issue tried to argue that it was a bagpipe. Moore is agreed that the word refers to a musical instrument. He is uncertain exactly what instrument is implied but writes, "The name

universally include singing. In most cases this seems to have come from under-standing συμφωνία as meaning "voices together." This verse has more variety in translation in the Oriental versions than any verse examined for this study. The following are all represented:

1. "The voice of singing and symphonia" (Old Syriac)

2. "The voice of much singing" (Peshitta, Diatessaron, Ibn al-Ṭayyib)

3. "The voice of singing and dancing" (Harclean)

4. "Voices singing together and boisterous clapping" (Vat. Borg. Ar. 71)

5. "Voices singing together" (Ibn al-'Assāl)

6. "Voices and dancing" (Vat. Borg. Ar. 95, Polyglots)

7. "Joining of voices and singing" (Propagandist)

8. "Singing and dancing" (Shidiac, Jesuit–1, Jesuit–2)

9. "The voice of musical instruments and dancing" (Van Dyke, 'Abd al-Malik)[220]

It is clear that there is a loud, boisterous, joyous celebration in progress when the older son approaches the house.

The question of why the older son was not notified immediately is handled most adequately by Linnemann, who calls it a "stage-managed" effect. She writes,

> The listener to a parable is quite content with such "stage-productions" as long as it passes only the bounds of probability and not of possibility. If the story as a whole seems credible, he will not be worried by small divergences from what is customary in real life.[221]

At the same time, there are good reasons for not notifying him. Doubtless the father knows that the older brother will be upset and, if notified, may even try to prevent the banquet. In any case, the parable has him appear when he does in order to heighten the comparison between the two sons.

συμφωνία, in its etymological sense, would apply more properly to the double pipe" (*ibid.*, 172). Cf. Phillips Barry, "On Luke xv. 25, συμφωνία: Bagpipe," *JBL* 23 (1904), 180–190.

[220]The very curious feature of all these is that in spite of the variety they all include "singing" (except the two modern Protestant versions). Even the critically translated, scholarly "Jesuit-2" finished in 1970 includes singing. It is beyond the range of this study to try to sort out the textual maze that lies behind these versions. It can be said that the heavy emphasis on "singing" means the Oriental churches have understood the assembled guests to be boisterously involved in the celebration. The musical instruments would be played by a select few (not necessarily professional). The dancing would be done by men individually and again would be the activity of a few known to be skilled. The singing (accompanied with loud rhythmic clapping, cf. Vat. Borg. Ar. 71) would engage a much wider circle. The scene is not that of sedate guests entertained quietly by professionals, but of a loud party with everyone involved. This, at least, is the picture the Oriental churches have seen. The guests are "rejoicing together" (cf. 15:4, 7).

[221]Linnemann, *Parables*, 10.

The timing of the feast is significant. Jeremias writes, "After the feast comes music (loud singing and hand clapping) and dancing by the men."[222] However, this presupposes more order than is customary in the unstructured life of the Oriental village.[223] As soon as the father decides to butcher a calf and thus decides to invite most, if not all, of the village, all attention in the village is focused on the father's house. The calf is not roasted on a spit but cut into sections and baked in bread ovens. Obviously, most of it will have to be timed to be ready for the early evening, when the men return from the fields. When some of it is cooked, the music starts. This may be the pipes and/or a drum. The music signals to the village that there is something to eat. There is no formal, official "beginning." People come, sing, dance, drink wine (which will naturally flow on such an occasion), talk, eat, go out, come back, and so forth. Everything is in motion. The music does not start after the meal but before it. The meal cannot be over at the time when most of the men come in from the fields, which is naturally the time when the older brother also appears. The eating and drinking will last half the night. In summary, the sound of music means things are in progress, food is being served, guests have arrived. We can assume that many are in process of arrival at the hour of return from the fields.

True to his character, the older son is initially suspicious. A son with a normal relationship to his family would enter immediately, eager to join the joy, whatever its source. On hearing the beat of the music he knows immediately that it is a joyous occasion. Village rhythms are specific and known. The older son does not rush in as expected. He is unnaturally suspicious.

An explanation is demanded from a "young boy." The word can mean "son" or "servant" or "young boy." The traditional translation is "servant." Evidence from a number of directions points to "young boy" as preferable. The Syriac versions all have *talyo*, which is primarily "young boy." Burkitt translates this phrase in the Old Syriac "He called one of the lads."[224] Ibn al-Ṭayyib, the Polyglots, and Vat. Borg. Ar. 71 translate with *al-fityān*, which clearly means "young boy."[225]

---

[222]Jeremias, *Parables*, 130.

[223]This is an important aspect of nearly everything that happens in the Oriental village. The Arabic proverb says, "Movement is blessing," which turns out to mean "confusion is blessing." The point is that life is dull in the village. When any event takes place it causes movement and results in confusion. The more confusion the more enthusiasm, the more enthusiasm the more *barakah* (blessing).

[224]Burkitt, *Evangelion da-Mepharreshe*, I, 353. The Peshitta is unambiguous, reading "young boys." This Syriac word has two plurals. The consonants are identical; the change is in the vowels. The word written *ṭulye'* means "young boys," but written *ṭalyo'* means "servants." The Peshitta uses the former and thus specifically reads "young boys." Cf. T. H. Robinson, *Paradigms and Exercises in Syriac Grammar* (Oxford: Clarendon, 1962), 48; R. P. Smith, *A Compendious Syriac Dictionary*, ed. J. P. Smith (Oxford: Clarendon, 1903), 174; C. Brockelmann, *Lexicon Syriacum* (2nd ed., Halle: Max Niemeyer, 1928), 276.

[225]ʿAbd Allah al-Bustānī defines this word clearly as "young boy." He admits only tentatively that it may carry the connotation of "servant." Cf. ʿAbd Allah al-Bustānī, *Fākihat al-Bustān* (Beirut: American Press, 1930), 1055. With both the Syriac word and the early Arabic we are dealing with a

In addition to this evidence from the Oriental versions, two specific elements in the story dictate that it is a young boy and not a servant. First, the older son in the text calls to ἕνα τῶν παίδων. He calls to one out of a group. We are not dealing with an American farm. The entrance to the house is not through the kitchen. In the Oriental home the door from the street opens into a courtyard which provides access to the front part of the house. The older son meets the παῖς before he reaches the house.[226] In the Oriental village, when a large banquet is held, the adults attend but not the children. The young boys in particular congregate in great numbers outside the house, stir up great clouds of dust, sing and dance in tune to the music, join in the excitement of the feast. Although not officially present, they are an inevitable part of any village celebration. They are the first group the son would meet.

The second detail is more conclusive. The young boy calls the father "your father." No servant would talk this way. If he were a servant he would have to say, "My master has done thus and so." His vocabulary indicates rather conclusively that he is a young boy and not a servant.[227]

Arndt notes the imperfect in verse 26. That is, "he kept asking him," implying a series of questions.[228] The past continuous is significant because the older son must find out if his brother came back wealthy or poor. Later in the story, the older son in fact knows his brother lost everything. The listener/reader is left to assume he found out from this boy.

The older son reflects on the state of affairs and quickly decides not to enter the house. Custom requires his presence. At such a banquet the older son has a special semi-official responsibility. He is expected to move among the guests, offering compliments, making sure everyone has enough to eat, ordering the servants around and, in general, becoming a sort of major-domo of the feast. The custom is widespread all across the Arab world and on into Iran, where in the village the older son stands at the door barefoot to greet the guests. Part of the meaning of the custom is the symbolic nature of the gesture, by which the father says, "My older son is your servant."

To reinforce this symbolic meaning, many times the older son does not eat with the guests. This custom or attitude is significant for the parable. Even if we attribute this to a later development in village attitudes in the Middle East, clearly

---

word like "boy" in English. In certain specific contexts the word "boy" can mean a servant. When a British colonial official at dinner called "Boy," this is what he meant. Such a word ordinarily, however, does not in English, Syriac, or Arabic carry this meaning. The rest of the Arabic versions have *ghilmān,* which is also primarily a "young boy" but in certain contexts can mean "servant."

[226]The servants are all busy with the banquet *in* the house.

[227]In addition to this evidence, both δοῦλος and μίσθιος have already been used in the story. If the παῖς is a servant, why is not one of these words used? Moreover, the most important thing the servants have done in connection with the events of the day is to dress the prodigal. This the παῖς talking to the older son does not mention. For a "young boy" in the street the most important event is the feast, which the lad does mention in his response.

[228]Arndt, *St. Luke,* 352. Only three of our Oriental versions use a past continuous.

the sons of the host are a part of the family that is giving the banquet and honoring the special guest. If the older son enters the house, he is at least seen to join the family in honoring the prodigal. He himself affirms that a circle of guests is present when he says, "You never gave me a kid that I might make merry with my friends." The obvious implication is, "You are making merry with your friends and you have denied me the privilege of making merry with my friends." If he wants to fight with his father over the way his brother was received, he should first enter the house and fulfil his role as joint host. He is expected publicly to embrace and congratulate his brother, and to accept the compliments that will be showered on him from the guests who assume his joy at having his brother back. He is expected to show special honor to his brother as the honored guest. When all are gone, *then* he can complain that the boy should not be trusted and should not have been welcomed in this public fashion. Rather, the older son chooses to humiliate his father publicly by quarreling while the guests are present.

Middle Eastern customs and the Oriental high regard for the authority of the father make the older son's actions extremely insulting. Yet it is certainly an insult in any culture publicly to refuse to participate in a banquet hosted by the father and so to exhibit a serious quarrel in the family to public gaze.[229]

There is now a break in relationship between the older son and his father that is nearly as radical as the break between the father and the younger son at the beginning of the parable.[230] The story of Esther has a similar scene. King Ahasuerus summoned Queen Vashti to appear at a banquet. She refused. The king "was enraged and his anger burned within him."[231] Her refusal was a very serious matter. She was deposed.

Arab literature provides a very interesting illustration of the same theme of a son insulting his father at a banquet. The story is told of 'Āmir ibn 'Āmir Mā al-Samā surnamed Muzayqiyah, who sat on the throne of Ma'rib (the Yemen) in the third century. The agriculture of the kingdom of Ma'rib was sustained during this period by a great diversion dam called the Ma'rib dam. The king, so the story goes, discovered that the dam would break before the general public had any suspicions about its condition. Knowing that a general announcement would destroy all property values and anxious to sell his lands at a good price, he set up a clever ruse. He invited the chief men of the city to a splendid banquet and arranged for his older son to insult him with the guests present. When this charade was enacted the king vowed that he would have to kill his boy. The guests remonstrated, whereupon the king insisted that if he could not kill his son, then at least he would not stay in a city where he had been insulted publicly by his son

---

[229]The tenses of the verbs should not be given too much weight. The verse reads, "He was angry (aorist) and was not willing (imperfect) to go in." His refusal to enter the house was clearly a continuous action, but so was his anger, as evidenced by his speech to his father.

[230]Derrett identifies the older son's actions as a clear violation of the Fifth Commandment ("Prodigal Son," 68).

[231]Esther 1:12.

before his guests. He proceeded to sell all his property at a good price and then announced the imminent break of the dam and led a pilgrimage of people away from the doomed valley.[232]

For our purposes this story is a magnificent illustration of how serious a matter it is when a son in the Middle East insults his father at a banquet. In the case of this story, such an insult is serious enough to provide a convincing reason for the king's sale of his property. Luke 15:28 must be seen in the light of such attitudes. The father butchers a calf. All the important people of the village will naturally attend. The anger and refusal to participate on the part of the older son are profoundly deep public insults against the father.

The listener/reader expects anger similar to that of King Ahasuerus to burn within the heart of the father. He is expected to ignore the boy and proceed with the banquet, or in some way punish him for public insolence, or at least demonstrate extreme displeasure. However, for the second time in one day, the father goes down and out of the house offering in public humiliation a demonstration of unexpected love. Bornkamm writes, "Here, too, the father comes out, no less anxious for the older one, and entreating him, just as he had the younger one."[233] The father comes out to entreat,[234] not to scold or to rebuke, as is expected. What will be the response? We are now at the climax of this second half of the parable (stanzas 4 and 4').

It is surely hard to find in the history of literature any man who so completely condemns himself with his own words as this older son. The younger son was stunned by the awareness of the price paid by the father to demonstrate unexpected love publicly. A significant shift in his total attitude resulted. The older son has invited harsh punishment for insolence. The father comes entreating. It is only reasonable to expect this demonstration of unexpected love to have a similar telling effect on the older son. Unfortunately this does not happen.

What, then, will his response be? Instead of a confession, there is a double complaint.[235] What specifically does the son say and what do his words imply? At the least the following can be noted:

1. The older son addresses his father with no title. Titles are used all through the story in direct speech up to this point. The sudden absence of any title is significant.[236]

2. The older son demonstrates the attitude and spirit of a slave, not a son. Literally he says, "I have *slaved* for you. . . ."

---

[232]Reynold A. Nicholson, *A Literary History of the Arabs* (Cambridge: University Press, 1962), 15f.

[233]Bornkamm, *Jesus,* 127f. As Plummer notes, ἐξελθών here is parallel to δραμών in v. 20 (*St. Luke,* 378). Linnemann says, "The same gesture of love is again repeated" (*Parables,* 79); cf. Manson, *Sayings,* 289; Jones, *Art,* 202. These sources all see love offered, but fail to appreciate its price.

[234]The imperfect is again used—παρεκάλει. The entreating was a process.

[235]If the older son's problem is the killing of the calf, as Derrett points out, the father is fully in his right in using the *usufruct* of the estate as he sees fit; cf. Mishna *Baba Bathra* viii.7.

[236]In the Johannine story of the woman at the well, the title dramatically disappears when the woman is surprised and irritated; cf. John 4:17. The steward in Luke 16 also fails in his haste to use any titles.

Sa'īd lists the principal characteristics of the older son. First on his list is "His failure to offer the esteem of a son to his father. . . . He has been living in the house with the spirit of a slave, not with the familiarity of a son."[237] The older son's entire perception is warped by this attitude. Giblin writes,

> The older son's complaint thus reflects his judgment that the feast was meant to show what the younger son was worth (as the kid he felt he himself should have received would have been given in payment of what his long-standing services were worth). In reality, the feast was an expression of the father's heartfelt joy.[238]

His attitude is clearly, "I have worked, where is mine?" He reflects the atmosphere of a labor dispute over wages.

3.   He has just insulted his father publicly and yet is able to say, "I have never disobeyed your commandment."[239] Sa'īd again writes,

> This is the spirit of the Pharisees by which he (the older son) enters into the ranks of the "ninety-nine who need no repentance"; thus even if he has never disobeyed his father's commandments, yet he has with this action broken the commandment of love.[240]

Sa'īd elaborates on the meaning of the older son's action in a comparison between the two sons. He writes,

> The difference between him and his younger brother was that the younger brother was estranged and rebellious while absent from the house, but the older son was estranged and rebellious in his heart while he was in the house. The estrangement and rebellion of the younger son were evident in his surrender to his passions and in his request to leave his father's house. *The estrangement and rebellion of the older son were evident in his anger and his refusal to enter the house.*[241]

---

[237]Sa'īd, *Lūqā,* 403. Derrett writes, "The ex-prodigal was willing to be a servant, as the elder brother was content to be thought (v. 29)" ("Prodigal Son," 66).

[238]Giblin, "Luke 15," 28. Jones comments, "The older son's obedience has always been based on a misunderstanding" (*Art,* 171).

[239]There is definitely a crowd listening. The Oriental listener/reader gets the distinct feeling that the older son is playing to the gallery. The young boys in the street are all there. The music and dancing will automatically stop the moment the crowd is stunned by the father's act of unexpected love. All the guests wait and listen initially expecting the boy to be punished. What is said will be remembered and retold in the village for literally years.

[240]Sa'īd, *Lūqā,* 402.

[241]*Ibid.,* 403; emphasis mine. Sa'īd is, of course, writing for an Arab reader. There is thus naturally no explanation or elaboration or defense of these points. They are self-evident in Oriental culture. The key word *murtaddan* I have translated "estrangement and rebellion." This forceful word is the Islamic term for a Muslim who has apostatized and left the religion of Islam, and thus on Islamic terms betrayed his family, his country, and his religion. It is the most powerful word Sa'īd could have used in this context. Caird writes, "The elder contrived, without leaving home, to be as far away from his father as ever his brother was in the heathen pigsty" (*St. Luke,* 182).

4.   The older son accuses his father of favoritism with the words, ''To me you never gave a kid.'' This sentence is very egocentric. The preposition ''to me'' stands first in the word order.[242] The older son's complaint includes the contrast, ''He gets a calf, I don't even get a goat.'' This can be read a number of different ways. Derrett thinks it is a false humility. The difficulty with this is that the mood of false humility does not fit the emotion of anger.[243] Assumptions of sarcasm must be rejected.[244] The phrase is better seen as an accusation of favoritism. The older son is saying, ''You obviously love this worthless fellow more than you love me. You have given him a calf. I have yet to receive even a goat.''[245] Sa'īd writes, ''He (the older son) denies all the unmerited favor his father has extended to him. 'You never gave me a kid'; for whom then was the fatted calf?''[246] The accusation of favoritism is unfair.

5.   The older son declares that he is not a part of the family. Again Sa'īd is helpful with his Oriental perspective on family relationships and his understanding of the meanings of the phrases used. He writes,

> He [the older son] shows disgust with his father's house. [He says] "that I might make merry with my friends." Thus he is no better than the prodigal son who took his portion and traveled into a far country. The difference between them is that the prodigal son was an "honorable sinner" in that he was perfectly open to his father. He told his father all that was in his heart. But the older brother was a "hypocritical saint" because he hid his feelings in his heart. He re-

---

[242]Goebel, *Parables,* 208. In the Oriental versions only the literal Harclean places the preposition first in the sentence. These versions demonstrate that placing the preposition first is unusual for a Semitic sentence. Goebel, reading it as a Greek sentence, also affirms it to be emphatic. Ibn al-'Assāl, the great medieval Coptic exegete, caught this emphasis in his translation, which reads, *lam tu'ṭini ana.* (The pronoun is suffixed to the verb and then repeated a second time for emphasis.)

[243]Derrett, ''Prodigal Son,'' 70. Derrett writes, ''This implies his own abstemiousness in comparison with the younger generally'' (*ibid.*). The Mishna characterized the stubborn and rebellious son as one who gorges himself on beef (M. *San.* viii.2; b. *San.* 68–70). If this line of reasoning is followed we would see the older son asserting moral superiority over his brother and implicating his father in having provided the opportunity for the younger ''rebellious'' son to gorge himself on beef. This is perhaps a bit too complicated.

[244]Sarcasm is a non-Middle Eastern form of speech. There is no equivalent in Arabic; I have tried in vain to explain this particular form of speech to my Arab friends and have failed. Irony is known, but not sarcasm.

[245]This interpretation is supported by the Old Syriac, which adds the word *ḥadd* (you did not give me *one single* kid, etc.). The recent Jesuit translation includes this phrase, as well as the medieval text used for the printing of the Propagandist version. The nineteenth-century Jesuit and the modern Bulusiyya translations add, ''And you, you never gave me,'' which again emphasizes the accusation of favoritism, although in a slightly different way.

[246]Sa'īd, *Lūqā,* 403. The older son is living off his father's usufruct. Every meal is a gift out of the father's bounty. In the last phrase Sa'īd means to say that the calf is killed for the entire family and the entire family gives the feast. The older son is full partner in the feast. He is expected to participate fully. He should be able to ''make merry'' fully at *this* feast. Linnemann concludes in error that there has been no feasting since the prodigal left. There is no hint of this in the story. The older son is complaining that he has not had a chance for a *special* party alone with his cronies. Linnemann, again in error, calls the ''kid'' a ''lamb'' (*Parables,* 79).

mained in the house all the while hating his father. He denies any relationship to his brother, and thereby denies any relationship to his father. He says, "This is your son" rather than saying "my brother." . . . With this statement the older son removed himself from the sacred family and passed judgment of "outcast" upon himself.[247]

Sa'īd states the case in strong yet appropriate language. The older son has removed himself from the fellowship of his family. This is all the more evident when we note that the older brother's friends do not include his brother nor his father nor the family's guests. Emotionally the older brother's community is somewhere else, and he says so.

6.   The older son announces his concept of "joy." For the older son, a good meal with his cronies is an appropriate occasion for joy. The recovery of a brother as from the dead is not.[248] He is not willing to rejoice at this banquet. Give him a goat and, apart from his family, he will rejoice. For the father the calf is a public symbol of the joy that is already present. The older son wants some good meat to create a different kind of "joy." The clear emphasis on joy all through Luke 15 makes these contrasting concepts all the more striking.

7.   The older brother attacks his younger brother. Derrett argues convincingly that the phrase "your living" (when we expect "his living") is really an attempt to say, "He doesn't love you. If he did, he would have preserved his portion to take care of you in your old age. See, he has devoured *your* living with *harlots*."[249] The more obvious insult is the reference to harlots. Sa'īd comments,

The word "harlots" is not heard in the story itself. He [the older son] volunteers this exaggeration in order to label his brother with this polluted accusation.[250]

There is also the distinct possibility that the older son is attempting to demonstrate that his brother is a rebellious son. If the prodigal can be made to fit this category, then he must be killed, according to the law in Deuteronomy 21:18–21.[251] Thus in summary, the older son's speech is a brilliant picture drawn by contrasting two

---

[247]Sa'īd, *Lūqā*, 403f. Plummer observes that the older son "wants to have his father's property in order that he may enjoy himself *apart from him*" (*St. Luke*, 378; his emphasis).

[248]All through the exegetical tradition of the Oriental churches reflected in their versions there is a very interesting emphasis made in this verse. From Vat. Borg. Ar. 95 and some mss. of the Diatessaron (cf. A. S. Marmardji, *Diatessaron de Tatien* [Beyrouth: Imprimerie Catholique, 1935], 253, n. 291) through to the modern Jesuit version there is the addition of *bihi*, which makes the verse read, "That I might make merry *with it* with my friends." The point is emphasized that the older son's idea of joy is a full stomach.

[249]Derrett, "Prodigal Son," 65. Vat. Borg. Ar. 95 adds another interpretive touch emphasizing the same point. It reads, "Who has eaten your living, *all of it* with harlots," thus stressing the enormity of the younger son's disregard for his continuing moral responsibility to take care of his father in his old age.

[250]Sa'īd, *Lūqā*, 404.

[251]Suggested by Derrett, "Prodigal Son," 56, n. 2. Jeremias thinks αὐτός is here used contemptuously, "This son of yours" (*Parables*, 131). This must be rejected because the same word is used by the father in both v. 24 and v. 32, where obviously no contempt is implied.

stanzas (4 and 4'). We see a son whose attitudes and relationships are sadly perverted and whose only redeeming feature is that he carries out orders.[252]

How will the father respond after this attack on his integrity? As observed in the first half of this parable, when a literary structure inverts there is usually a crucial new feature just past the center, a point of turning, a place of special emphasis. We are not disappointed in this ballad. The father is expected to be furious. Rather there is an outpouring of love. If he orders the son to enter the house and fulfil his duty as a member of the family, the son will certainly obey. But what would be gained? He already has a servant in the person of this young man. He wants a "son." The father bypasses the omission of a title, the bitterness, the arrogance, the insult, the distortion of fact, and the unjust accusations. There is no judgment, no criticism, no rejection, but only an outpouring of love. In striking contrast to the older son, he begins with a title and an affectionate one at that. Rather than υἱός he now uses τέκνον.

This conciliatory word τέκνον is all the more remarkable in light of the agony of rejected love which the father must endure. The offer of unexpected love in a public humiliating act has not produced a humble confession as in the case of the prodigal but rather a calloused arrogance. Sa'īd says of the father's final speech,

> These words come out of a wounded, suffering heart, because the father longed to have his joy complete in that he would be greatly pleased to see his two sons together in his house. But the love that knows no weariness makes a most gracious announcement.[253]

The father's final speech (stanza 3') is a verbal expression of the "entreating" mentioned in stanza 3.[254] The speech contains at least four major points.

1.   The father's words are an appeal for the son to rejoice in his brother's

---

[252]Amazingly, a small group of modern scholars find the older son's attitudes perfectly natural and reasonable, e.g., Linnemann, *Parables,* 79. Leaney writes, "The elder son's indignation is natural; it is false to the whole spirit of the story to represent him as a monster of hidden selfishness. His father does not rebuke him but reminds them that he is 'always with' him; the relation between them never needed mending (*St. Luke,* 219). Leaney's line of argumentation is clear. He assumes that if the older son had committed gross error he would have been sharply rebuked. But this is specifically not what happened to the prodigal. He did commit gross error. He was not rebuked. The second half of the story is a repeat performance of the first half. Linnemann and Leaney have missed the Oriental culture that is the background of Sa'īd's remarks above. Giblin observes Leaney's comment and affirms that "the elder son's reaction is 'natural'—at least in the sense that it places him with the majority of mankind under similar circumstances" ("Luke 15," 17f.). With Giblin we can agree; the natural man does not understand grace and the gospel any more than the older son did.

[253]Sa'īd is referring in this last sentence to the father's final speech (*Lūqā,* 404). Jer. 3:19b has no connection with the parable but echoes the same sentiment.

[254]The tenses of v. 28 may be significant. It reads, "He came out (aorist) and was entreating him (imperfect)." Manson understands from this that the father was entreating the son and his pleading was interrupted with the son's harsh complaint (*Sayings,* 298). This shift in tenses fits what is happening. However, we have noted places where similar changes of past tenses have not been significant or such an understanding of them appropriate; thus we must be cautious here also.

return. The Greek text is ambiguous. We are not told specifically who is supposed to rejoice. Is the intent "we" should rejoice, or "you" should rejoice? The text simply says, εὐφρανθῆναι δὲ καὶ χαρῆναι ἔδει. Most modern English translations inject their own exegetical understanding into the translation with the addition of "we," thus resolving the ambiguity.[255] The Arabic versions of the last six hundred years agree. However, the earlier versions either leave the text neutral like the Greek or render it "you."[256] The manuscript Vat. Borg. Ar. 95 is especially noteworthy. We observed above that this particular text identified the older son's joy as focused in a full stomach. In this version the debate over the nature of authentic joy is continued in its reading of verse 32, "It is necessary for you that you should rejoice and sing hallelujah (tahallal)." This tells the older son what the focus of his joy should be in contrast to what it is.

It is impossible to be dogmatic regarding the intent of the text. However, with Luther and most of the older Oriental versions, the texts seem to suggest "you" rather than "we." The proximity of "yours" in the preceding phrase and "your" in the following verse supports this translation. In any case, the issue is clear. Is the welcoming of a brother who has not made reparations and has not demonstrated his sincerity an appropriate occasion for great joy or not? Or is joy better found in a good meal with like-minded friends? Giblin writes,

> He should have spontaneously joined in the rejoicing as one who understood how his own father's heart went out (esplagchnisthē, v. 20) to the other son who was, after all, his own brother.[257]

The stories of the Sheep, the Coin, and the Prodigal all have the theme of joy as a climax in or near the center of the story and at the end. Here joy is dramatically missing in both places. We can hardly imagine the father seeking this son in joy. The end is missing. We are not told if the father experiences the joy of finding him. There is no stanza 1'. The story only speaks of a pleading for the joy that is absent.[258]

2.   The father assures the older son that his rights are fully protected even though pure grace has been extended to the prodigal. Manson writes, "The assurance 'all that is mine is thine' is no doubt meant to tell the elder brother that the return of the prodigal does not affect his rights in any degree."[259]

3.   The father subtly points out to his older son that a servant category is inappropriate for their relationship. The son has said, "I have served all these years and have not even received a kid." The father answers, "You are the heir. You own everything already. All that is mine is yours. How can I possibly give you more?" The older son's request is based on a misunderstanding. Giblin writes,

---

[255]So King James, New American Bible, New English Bible, Jerusalem Bible, and the J. B. Phillips translation. The Revised Standard Version maintains the ambiguity.

[256]Outstanding among those which translate the text "you must rejoice" are the Curetonian Old Syriac, the Diatessaron, Vat. Borg. Ar. 95, and Ibn al-'Assāl. Luther has "Du solltest aber fröhlich."

[257]Giblin, "Luke 15," 29.

[258]Giblin finds in this an illustration of inclusio (ibid., 22, n. 23).

[259]Manson, Sayings, 290.

He is told that all the father has is his—that is, he is advised that he is simply not in a position to be paid as though he were a hired man (*misthios*); much less is he expected to work as a slave (*doulos*).[260]

This should have been evident from the father's offer of love in coming out to the older son. No master humiliates himself publicly and leaves a banquet to go out to extend love to an insolent servant. Yet, his I-am-a-servant-where-is-my-pay speech comes *after* the demonstration of love.

At the same time, there is another unhappy aspect to the dialog. On the basis of the Mishnaic legislation discussed above[261] it is instructive to reflect on the direction the conversation is taking.

Older son: "You never gave me a kid."

Father: "All that I have is yours."

Older son: "Yes, but I don't have the right of disposition. I own everything but I still can't slaughter a goat and have a feast with my friends."

Father: "Oh, I see, you also want me gone."

The conversation does not reach this point, but the older son's mind is moving in this direction. He has owned everything since his brother left. He is irritated that he cannot dispose of it at will and host a banquet for his friends. This much he admits openly. From his perspective, starting with the problem he has posed, the obvious solution is *disposition,* which will be his right only after the father dies. His younger brother was granted disposition and had all the banquets he wanted. Why cannot the older son have the same privilege? So the story seems to have come full circle.

4.   The father's speech is neither an apology for the banquet nor a reproach directed against the older brother, but primarily a cry from the heart for an understanding of grace.[262] Very gently, the father reminds the older brother that this is *your* brother—but this hardly categorizes the speech as an attack.[263] On the other hand, I am uneasy with any connotations of the father's "apologizing," which an Oriental father never does to his sons, or even defending what he has done, as if it needed any defense. Rather his speech must be seen as an articulation of the compassionate appeal that has already been extended to the older son in the father's act of going out to him in the presence of the village.

As in the case of the younger son, again the father has no choice. If he punishes the son the answer will be, "Why are you punishing me? I have done nothing!" If he ignores him, the "servant" goes on demanding his own. The visible and verbal appeal of love offers the only hope to the father, who wants not

---

[260]Giblin, "Luke 15," 29.

[261]See pp. 163f.

[262]If the exegete translates "you should rejoice" he usually interprets the text as a reproach, "you ought to be glad; cease your anger." If he translates "we must rejoice" he sees the speech as a defense of joy, "We had to rejoice, don't blame us." Linnemann thinks both are really the same (*Parables,* 79).

[263]Against Sanders, *NTS* 15 (1969), 438.

servants but sons. The younger son was dead and is alive. The older son is likewise dead. Can he come to life?

It is certainly right not to make a one-to-one identification of the Pharisees with the older son and publicans with the younger son. Instead, Jesus is discussing two basic types of men. One is lawless without the law, and the other lawless within the law. Both rebel. Both break the father's heart. Both end up in a far country, one physically, the other spiritually. The same unexpected love is demonstrated in humiliation to each. For both this love is crucial if servants are to become sons.

This last half of the parable clarifies a potential misunderstanding of repentance that could be deduced from the first double parable. Repentance does not quite equal being found. The father goes out and finds both sons. One understands and accepts the status of being found. The other, so far as we know, does not, and remains lost.

The conclusion is missing. There is no stanza 1', as we have observed. Jones feels that this is one of the signs that the parable is truly great art.[264] The chapter begins with the question of eating. It ends with an open invitation for the complainers to join the banquet. Sa'īd writes,

> and it is to be regretted that "the curtain" dropped on this drama with the older son still outside!!! Did the father succeed in convincing him? Or did the older son remain outside to the end? The Pharisees had to give their answer to this question.[265]

The parable engrosses the sensitive listener/reader. Not only the scribes and Pharisees, but each man must decide what his response will be.

The Christological implications of this second section are the same as those of the first section. The father leaves the house in a visible demonstration of unexpected love offered in humiliation. The same implicit Christology "over-heard" in the first half of the parable can be found here as well.

Recent scholarship has questioned the unity of the chapter as a whole.[266] Some elements unite the chapter. Both double parables discuss the lost and found, the joy that must be shared, and the subject of repentance. Other elements divide 15:4–10 from 11–32. Each half of the parable of the Lost Sheep and the Lost Coin has an introduction and a conclusion. Luke 15:11–32 lacks both. Furthermore, Luke 15:11–32 is not linked with what precedes by $\check{\eta}$, as in the case of the parable of the Lost Coin. The parable of the Prodigal Son begins with $\epsilon\hat{\iota}\pi\epsilon\nu$ $\delta\acute{\epsilon}$, which parallels verse 3.[267]

---

[264]Jones, *Art,* 168.

[265]Sa'īd, *Lūqā,* 404.

[266]Giblin, "Luke 15," 20; Bultmann, *Tradition,* 328.

[267]Giblin argues that the father does not search for his son ("Luke 15," 20). He sees in this a further divergence between the two units. However, the father does go out in search, not only once but twice. The father does not go into the far country. The reason for this is now clear. Jesus wants to heighten the comparison between the two sons and point up the necessity of the father's going out to each of them in

In addition to these minor linguistic features, the most compelling reason to see these two units of material as redactionally combined is the shift of reference. In the first double parable, Jesus clearly wants the audience to identify with the shepherd and the woman. This is indicated by the question, "Which one of you?"[268] Then in the second double parable the audience is led to identify with the elder son, not the father. The missing conclusion is strong evidence for this. The audience is encouraged to see itself standing there in the person of the older son murmuring against the "sinner" seated at the banquet. The material is perhaps best understood as two units appropriately combined by the Lucan source,[269] or by Luke himself.[270] Each unit is a double parable. Jesus no doubt on many occasions faced Pharisaical complaints against his eating with sinners. Here parables spoken on two such occasions are combined.

Fuchs identifies the banquet at the end of the chapter as "the proleptic celebration of the kingdom of God."[271] To study the relationship between the banquet reported here and the messianic banquet of the end-time would be a study in itself and is beyond the scope of this work.[272] The suggestion is a good one and worthy of much reflection. If this could be substantiated there is little wonder the Pharisees were upset, because Judaism also identified the kingdom of God with a banquet, but for them no "sinners" would be honored guests at such a banquet.

A comparison between the literary structure of the first and the second half of this parable is noteworthy. The climactic center of each is a speech by a son. The first son (in stanzas 6 and 6') knows he is lost and in need. He knows where help can be found. The second son also gives a speech in the center of the literary form (stanzas 4 and 4') but it is a complaint. Unexpected love is demonstrated in response to these central stanzas in each case. The first son descends in stanzas 1–6 and then starts back up in 6'–1'. The older son also descends. In stanzas 1 and 2 he suspiciously inquires about the meaning of this joyous occasion. In 3 he is angry and insults his father. In 4 and 4' we hear two bitter complaints. There is then no return, no response to extended grace, no reversal of the chilling climax of the

---

turn. He achieves this with a unity of place (both meetings between father and son take place in the same approximate vicinity). There is a unity of time (both take place on the same day) and a unity of action (for both, the father must personally leave the house in a humiliating public demonstration of love).
[268]He cannot say, "Which woman of you," because even if there were some women in the audience, such a phrase would be an insult. He is content with "What woman. . . ."
[269]Manson, *Sayings,* 283.
[270]Bultmann, *Tradition,* 328.
[271]E. Fuchs, *Das Urchristliche Sakramentsverständnis* (Schriftenreihe der Kirchlich-Theologische Sozietät in Württemberg, 8 Bad Cannstatt, 1958), 24, 38, as quoted in Linnemann, *Parables,* 80; Jeremias, *Theology,* 115f. In reference to v. 2, Giblin writes, "The word *prosdechomai* is consistently associated in the N. T. with themes like the coming kingdom, redemption, parousia, envoys of and sharers in the 'good news' " ("Luke 15," 16).
[272]Another theme of significance that is beyond the scope of this study is the relationship of the theology of this chapter to the Pauline doctrine of Justification. Godet writes, "How from this parable St. Paul might have extracted the doctrine of Justification by Faith is easy to understand" (*St. Luke,* 381; cf. also Rengstorf, *Re-Investitur,* 69).

structure. The first structure is complete and resolves in joy. The second only reaches the father's speech, which is almost identical to each son (cf. A–1′ and B–2′). Finally the last note of the parable offers a hint of *inclusio*. At the beginning a living father is wished dead. At the end, a "dead" son is found alive. The similarity of speeches, the similarity of the father's actions, the similarity of insults against the father all make clear that the two sons are presented in the story as being essentially the same. They differ only in their responses to unexpected love.

The Pharisee listening to the telling of the parable is pressed to see himself in the figure of the older son and make the judgment, "I am the man." The ground and content of such a judgment are found in a theological cluster that contains at least five primary themes. These are as follows:

1. Sin.

    The parable portrays two basic types of sinful man and illustrates the nature of their sin and its results.

2. Repentance.

    Two types of repentance are demonstrated. One is the repentance of a man who thinks he can save himself. The other is the repentance of a man who knows he cannot.

3. Grace.

    The parable illustrates the nature of God's freely offered love and tells of its cost. It is a love that seeks and suffers in order to save.

4. Joy.

    Joy is known in finding and in celebrating communally the restoration of the one lost.

5. Sonship.

    One son is restored from death and from servanthood. A second insists on remaining a servant.

None of these can be dealt with in isolation. Each is seen in dynamic tension with the others. Each theme can be reflected upon separately, but to deal with one is to touch on all.

Finally, let us try to summarize all of Luke 15:11–32. A father's younger son requests and receives possession and the right of disposal of his portion of the inheritance. Both the request and the granting of it are exceptional in Eastern life and thought. The prodigal is in a hurry for his father to die. The father is expected to refuse and punish the prodigal. Rather than punish his son, the father grants the request in an unprecedented act of love. The older son refuses to be a reconciler. Both sons fail to try to live together in unity.

The prodigal sells, and leaves, and loses all. He sees his sin as primarily the loss of the money and his ensuing inability to care for his father. Reduced to herding pigs for a gentile and eating bitter wild carob beans, he decides to go back to his village but not to his home. Planning to work as a servant and live in the village, he intends to save himself. He presumably—and with reason—is intensely apprehensive of his initial reception in the village.

On his return, the prodigal is overwhelmed by an unexpected visible demonstration of love in humiliation. He is shattered by the offer of grace, confesses unworthiness, and accepts restoration to sonship in genuine humility. Sin is now a broken relationship which he cannot restore. Repentance is now understood as acceptance of grace and confession of unworthiness. The community rejoices together. The visible demonstration of love in humiliation is seen to have clear overtones of the atoning work of Christ.

The older son then insults his father publicly and demonstrates himself to be as "lost" as his brother was in the far country. The father extends the same love in humiliation, but no confession and repentance result. Rather, the older son launches a bitter tirade against the father. The parable closes with a final appeal for reconciliation. Both sons are seen as rebels needing a visible demonstration of love to win them from servanthood to sonship. Cultural and stylistic considerations make this similarity between the two sons clear. The listening Pharisee is pressed to see himself in the older son and to respond by accepting reconciliation. The major themes of the parable are sin, repentance, grace, joy, and sonship. When studied in the light of the Oriental culture that informs the text, this parable is indeed the *Evangelium in Evangelio*.[273]

---

[273]Arndt, *St. Luke,* 350.

CONCLUSIONS

In summary, it can be said that a new methodology has helped to delineate more precisely the cultural elements that inform the parables. The awareness of these elements has uncovered a new set of questions which have led to a new dimension of perception in parabolic understanding. The discovery of literary types and poetic forms has led to a more accurate division of traditional material into pericopes and a new understanding of the original meaning of the material itself. The parabolic ballad form used in the parables has helped to clarify key elements in the parables studied. The concept of the theological cluster has been discerned, providing a method of perceiving the multiplicity in unity that is the theology of parables. Pericopes previously identified as secondary comments on parables are seen to have their own distinct form, integrity, and subject. A "spilling" phenomenon has been identified where meaning from one pericope has spilled into a second pericope placed beside it by an editor. The spilling has blurred translation and interpretation in both pericopes as the interpreter tries to understand them together. A literary outline has been discovered for Luke 9:51–19:48 which seems to identify the material as a pre-Lucan document.

It is the earnest desire of the present author that this study may provide a stimulus for further research into both culture and literary structure, that more of the dust of the ages might be wiped from the parables of Jesus, and that we might hear, ponder, and respond as did the first audience.

APPENDIX A

A BRIEF DESCRIPTION OF THE ORIENTAL VERSIONS USED IN THIS STUDY

The major Middle Eastern versions are in Syriac, Coptic, and Arabic. Due to my own linguistic limitations, the only Coptic versions used have been those translated into Arabic.

Aside from language, three principles have guided the selection of the texts, namely, time, geography, and type. In regard to time, texts have been selected that stretch from the second or third to the twentieth century. As much geographic spread as possible has been represented. In the matter of type, the texts fall into three categories. Some texts are "church translations." Their translators are unknown. These versions had wide circulation in known Oriental churches and thus reflect the exegetical understanding of those churches as a community. A second category we have called "individual versions." These are the work of known exegetes of some fame in the Oriental Christian world. The third category has been named "Eastern-Western versions." These translations are the work of Oriental churchmen laboring with Western scholars who were resident in the Middle East.

The Church Translations

THE OLD SYRIAC (C. 200)

The Old Syriac is preserved in two mss., the Sinaitic and the Curetonian. Each of these was printed in the nineteenth century.[1]

---

[1]For a full description of all the old Syriac manuscripts, cf. Arthur Vööbus, "The Syriac Versions," in *Early Versions of the New Testament. Papers of the Estonian Theological Society in Exile* (Stockholm: n.p., 1954), VI, 67–132. For a more recent discussion, cf. H. S. Pelser, "The Origin of the Ancient Syriac New Testament Texts— A Historical Study," in *De Fructu Oris Sui. Essays in Honour of Adrianus van Selms,* ed. I. H. Eybers *et al. Pretoria Oriental Series* 9 (Leiden: Brill, 1971), 152–163. Pelser is convinced that the Old Syriac and the Diatessaron both stem from an earlier text tradition. The texts used for this study were R. L. Bensly, J. Rendel Harris, and F. C. Burkitt, *The Four Gospels in*

THE PESHITTA (C. FIFTH CENTURY)

The origin of the Peshitta is shrouded in mystery. Burkitt's long-accepted theory that Rabulla was its author has been exploded by Vööbus.[2] The version became the Syriac vulgate. The antiquity of the version, its popularity, and its gradual emergence from many hands give it unique significance for our exegetical purposes as a church translation. We have used the American Bible Society edition[3] along with Vatican Syriac 269.

VATICAN BORGIANUS ARABIC 71

Vööbus argues convincingly that this version, made in the twelfth century, is translated from the Old Syriac, not the Greek.[4] It enjoyed wide circulation in the Melkite churches of the East,[5] and for this reason we have selected it as one of our "church versions."

THE COPTIC VULGATE (10TH CENTURY)

The oldest copy of this version is at the University of Beirut and is dated 1048. The translation itself was made in the tenth century.[6] This remarkable version was the dominant text for the Coptic Christians for nearly a thousand years. We have used Vatican Coptic 9.

THE PARIS AND LONDON POLYGLOTS (17TH CENTURY)

The Paris Polyglot New Testament was printed in two volumes in Paris in 1630 and 1633. The London Polyglot appeared in 1654–1658. These versions were the first printed Arabic Bibles, and are the Arabic versions quoted in the critical notes of the Kittel Old Testament and the Nestle-Aland New Testament. This Arabic text was reprinted separately in England in 1811. It is this edition that we have used for our study.[7]

Syriac Transcribed from the Sinaitic Palimpsest (Cambridge: University Press, 1894); F. Crawford Burkitt, *Evangelion da-Mepharreshe* (Cambridge: University Press, 1904), 2 vols.; Agnes S. Lewis, *The Old Syriac Gospels* (London: Williams and Norgate, 1910).

[2]Vööbus, *loc. cit.*, 90.

[3]*The New Testament in Syriac* (London: British and Foreign Bible Society, 1905–1920). The Gospels are a reprint of a critical edition of the Peshitta published in 1901 by G. H. Gwilliam (Oxford: Clarendon, 1901). Pelser argues that the Peshitta stems from the third century. Cf. Pelser, *loc. cit.*, 162.

[4]Vööbus, *loc. cit.*, 290; against Ignazio Guidi, "Le Traduzione degli Evangelii in Arabo e in Etiopico," *Reale Accademia dei Lincei* 275 (1888), 6.

[5]Vööbus, *loc. cit.*, 289.

[6]John A. Thompson, "The Origin and Nature of the Chief Printed Arabic Bibles," *The Bible Translator* 6 (January 1955), 10.

[7]*The Holy Bible Containing the Old and New Testaments, in the Arabic Language* (Newcastle-upon-Tyne: Printed by Sarah Hodgson, 1811).

PROPAGANDIST VERSION (17TH CENTURY)

This version was produced by the Roman Catholic Congregatio de Propaganda Fide in Rome. Work began in 1622 and was not completed for fifty years. Competent Syrian church fathers labored over the text, drawing from a wide range of current Eastern manuscripts.[8]

The Individual Versions

THE ARABIC DIATESSARON

The question just how much of the Arabic *Diatessaron* reflects the text of Tatian is not our concern here. The translation to Arabic was most likely done in the early eleventh century by the famous Abu al-Faraj 'Abd Allah Ibn al-Ṭayyib, in Baghdad. This prince of Arab exegetes Graf calls "Philosoph, Arzt, Mönch und Priester in einer Person."[9] Thus we have a version made by an able eleventh-century Arab Christian scholar. For this study we have used the critical edition of Marmardji.[10]

ABU AL-FARAJ 'ABD ALLAH IBN AL-ṬAYYIB (11TH CENTURY)

This same Iraqi scholar is one of the known translators of the Peshitta into Arabic.[11] We have used Vat. Syr. 269 copied in 1368. In a number of cases the Arabic provides an insight into how the Syriac sounded to the ear of the author.[12]

THE HARCLEAN SYRIAC (7TH CENTURY)

This version was probably translated by Thomas Harclean; it is preserved in a magnificent manuscript (Vat. Syr. 268) which may be the autograph.[13]

VATICAN BORGIANUS ARABIC 95 (8TH–9TH CENTURY)

This famous codex is at the head of a group of codices translated from the Greek. It has been argued that the translation is prior to the rise of Islam.[14] Matthew and Mark were described and transcribed by Levin.[15] To my knowledge,

---

[8]For a full description of this version, cf. Thompson, *loc. cit.,* 51–55. This version was reprinted as *Kitāb al-'Ahd al-Jadīd* (London: Charles Watson, 1833).

[9]Georg Graf, *Geschichte der Christlichen Arabischen Literatur. Studi e Testi* 133 (Rome: Citta del Vaticano Biblioteca Apostolica Vaticana, 1947), II, 160.

[10]A. S. Marmardji, *Diatessaron de Tatien* (Beirut: Catholic Press, 1935).

[11]Cf. Graf, *op. cit.,* I, 150.

[12]For further information on this version cf. Louis Cheikho, "Nusakh 'Arabiyah Qadīmah fi al-Sharq min al-Injīl al-Tāhir," *Al Machriq* 4 (1901), 97–109, reprinted in Jūsif Qūshaqjī, *Ta'rīb al-Anajīl wa-A'māl al-Rusul* (Beirut: Catholic Press, 1964), 148–155.

[13]Vööbus, *loc. cit.,* 376. For further information cf. *ibid.,* 118–121. With Vat. Syr. 268 we have used J. White, *Sacrorum evangeliorum versio syriaca philoxeniana* (Oxford: Clarendon, 1778).

[14]Vööbus, *loc. cit.,* 293. Vööbus notes that this position was put forward by Baumstark but rejected by Graf.

[15]Bernhard Levin, *Die Griechisch-Arabische Evangelien-Übersetzung Vat. Borg. ar. 95 und Ber. orient. oct. 1108* (Uppsala: Almquist & Wiksells, 1938).

Luke has never previously been studied. The manuscript of Luke is badly water stained, yet the archaic script is beautiful when clear. The date of the copy used is from the ninth century. Evidently the Mount Sinai monastery is its place of origin. My own judgment is that it is the work of a very perceptive exegetical mind.[16]

HIBAT ALLAH IBN AL-'ASSĀL (13TH CENTURY)

Hibat Allah was one of three famous brothers who lived and wrote in Cairo in the thirteenth century. He produced a *critical* version of the four Gospels with an elaborate system of symbols so that he could record the variants between the Coptic, Greek, and Syriac versions available to him.[17]

The Eastern-Western Versions

THE SHIDIAC VERSION (1851)

This minor version was done by Faris al-Shidiac with the help of Thomas Jerrett of Cambridge.[18]

VAN DYKE–BUSTĀNĪ (1860)[19]

This Protestant version is notable for its simplicity, accuracy, and beauty. It soon became the major Arabic Bible for the masses in the Middle East among Protestants and Orthodox. The story of its translation has been fully told by Thompson.[20]

JESUIT–1 (1878)[21]

Jesuits working in Lebanon produced this version in 1878. Again Eastern and Western scholars labored together. The style is more classical than other versions.[22]

BŪLUSIYAH–FAKHŪRĪ (1954)[23]

This version was the first new Arabic translation effort in the twentieth century. Father George Fakhūrī, a Lebanese monk of the Paulist order, is the sole source of this thoughtful version.

---

[16]For a full introduction cf. Levin, 1–69.

[17]For a full description of this critical system, cf. Duncan B. Macdonald, "The Gospels in Arabic," *The Hartford Seminary Record* 3 (April 1893), 163–176; note esp. pp. 169f.; for a brief review of the three brothers and their works, cf. A. J. B. Higgins, "Ibn al-'Assal," *JTS* 44 (1943), 73–75; D. B. Macdonald, "Ibn al-'Assal," *Encyclopedia of Islam* (Leiden: Brill, 1927), II, 364. Macdonald by his own admission had only a brief span of time to look at the manuscript. He failed to discover the extent to which Ibn al-'Assāl gives *variant readings* in terms of the text and not just *variant translations* from versions of his time. Cf. British Museum Oriental Ms. 3382.

[18]*Kitāb al-'Ahd al-Jadīd Lerabbinā Jasū' al-Masīh* (London: SPCK, 1851).

[19]*Kitāb al-'Ahd al-Jadīd* (Beirut: American Press, 1860).

[20]Thompson, *loc. cit.,* 98–105.

[21]*Al-Kitāb al-Muqaddas al-'Ahd al-Jadīd* (Beirut: Jesuit Press, 1878).

[22]Cf. Thompson, *loc. cit.,* 146–49.

[23]*Al-Kitāb al-Muqaddas al-'Ahd al-Jadīd* (Harisa, Lebanon: Paulist Press, 1954).

JESUIT–2 (1969)

The second modern Jesuit version is the work of a French Jesuit, Father Hamawie of the Catholic Press in Beirut,[24] Ustaz Bustānī, a renowned Christian Arabic scholar, and Father Jūsif Qūshaqjī, a trained Syrian exegete of the Jesuit order.

'ABD AL-MALIK–THOMPSON (1973)

John A. Thompson and Butrus 'Abd al-Malik, under the sponsorship of the American Bible Society, have recently finished a new Protestant updating of the Van Dyke–Bustānī version.[25]

Dr. Thompson, a published Old Testament scholar, was for over twenty years professor of Old Testament in the Cairo Evangelical Seminary, Cairo, Egypt. Dr. 'Abd al-Malik was a professor of Oriental languages at the American University in Cairo.

---

[24] *Al-Kitāb al-Muqaddis al-'Ahd al-Jadīd* (Beirut: Catholic Press, 1969).
[25] *Kitāb al-'Ahd al-Jadīd* (Beirut: The Bible Societies in the Near East, 1973).

APPENDIX B

RESOURCE PERSONS

This is a selected, representative list of primary resource people who have, over a twenty-year period, helped the author understand the Middle Eastern culture that informs the parables of Jesus. A full list of resource people would run into the hundreds. My thanks go as well to all my Middle Eastern friends whose names do not appear here.

SUDAN

Wesley Stāsī

> Rev. Stāsī is director of the literature program of the Sudan Evangelical Church, Kartoum.

Nathaniel Kur

> Mr. Kur is a teacher of English and Religion. He is a member of the Dinka tribe from the South Sudan and a former student at the Near East School of Theology in Beirut, Lebanon. I am indebted to Mr. Kur and other African students who have helped me gain an insight into oral tradition from a people who have preserved centuries of the wisdom of their people exclusively in oral form. Mr. Kur's insights have provided points of contact with and contrast to Middle Eastern cultural points of view.

EGYPT

Adīb Qaldas

> Rev. Qaldas is a pastor in the village of Dayr abu Hinnis. Pastor Qaldas' people live in isolation across the Nile River in a community at least 1600 years old. For over a year I was privileged to listen to Pastor Qaldas preach to his own people. Many points of cultural significance assumed by both preacher and congregation were a new point of departure for me.

Fahīm 'Azīz, Ph.D.

> Dr. Fahīm was pastor of a small congregation in the south of Egypt for nearly twenty years. He now teaches New Testament at the Cairo Ev-

213

angelical Seminary in Cairo. He combines a genuine Oriental background
with exposure in depth to Western critical studies.

Ḥannā al-Khuḍārī, Ph.D.

Dr. Khuḍārī grew up in the simple village of al-Bayāḍīyyah in the south of
Egypt. I was privileged to work with him in the villages of Dayr al-Barshā
and al-'Izzīyah. Although his field is Systematic Theology, his own
upbringing in simple peasant surroundings has equipped him admirably to
help me ask the right questions of the parabolic text.

Ḥāris Quriṣah

For twenty-five years Rev. Ḥāris was pastor of village congregations in the
south of Egypt. He is a master at exposition in the peasant home in the
context of the traditional pastoral call. Listening to him teach and interact
with village people has been a significant source of new insights.

Ibrāhīm Sa'īd, D.D.

Dr. Sa'īd's book on Luke is quoted all through the exegetical section of this
study. I have benefited from his commentaries on Luke, John, Ephesians,
and Revelation. Because of Dr. Sa'īd's Oriental perspective and keen
mind, his books are a rare contribution to our subject.

Rifqī Matūshāliḥ

Rev. Rifqī is a pastor in the village of Dayr al-Barshā where my wife and I
were resident for nearly two years. While we were living in the same house
with pastor Rifqī, unnumbered conversations became opportunities for
him to interpret to us what was happening around us. We could witness a
given event in village life and understand the language spoken. Pastor Rifqī
told us what both meant.

Ṣamū'īl Ḥabīb

Rev. Ḥabīb is director of the Coptic Evangelical Society for Social Services. With his keen research-oriented mind, Pastor Ṣamū'īl has been a
crucial source of authentic and reliable information.

Shaykh Mus'ad

Elder Mus'ad is a patriarch of the village of Dayr al-Barshā. He is an
Oriental patriarch with the stature, dignity, and wisdom of the classical
sage, and is one of the most eminent Oriental wise men I have been
privileged to know. His indirect contribution to this study is immeasurable.

The People of Dayr al-Barshā

In their midst I saw an isolated Oriental village live and move and have its
being. After two years residence, contacts were maintained, and our
perception and awareness of Oriental life were significantly deepened by
this living community.

LEBANON, SYRIA, PALESTINE[1]

The People of 'Almā al-sha'b

This village lies on the southern border of Lebanon, and its people have

---

[1]The unity of culture across these three areas makes it appropriate to treat key resource people from
these three countries as a group.

extended to me a warm welcome. Conversations with shepherds, farmers, merchants, and teachers have answered many questions.

Ibrāhīm Dāghir

Rev. Dāghir served as a pastor in churches in southern Lebanon for thirty-five years. Now in his seventies, he has taught me more of Lebanese-Syrian culture than any other single person. His own boyhood in an isolated village above Sidon, his long service on the slopes of Mount Hermon, and his lifetime reflection on the Scriptures have made him a mine of information on Oriental life and how it influences the meaning of the text.

Samū'īl Ḥannā

Mr. Ḥannā is a theological student from the village of 'Ayn al-Sha'rah. This village is situated on the eastern slopes of Mount Hermon, not far from the villages where Aramaic is still spoken. Since there are no roads to the village, life there has kept its ancient flavor. Samū'īl's opinions have been given due consideration.

Jabrā Ḥelū

As a guest in Pastor Ḥelū's home in the village of Minyāra, Lebanon, I was privileged to spend many long and pleasant evenings listening to the retelling of the oral tradition of the Helu family and the Syrian people.

Riyāḍ Jarjūr

Mr. Jarjūr of Syria is a student at the Near East School of Theology. Nuhād (below), Riyāḍ, and Samū'īl are only examples of the Syrian and Lebanese students from whom I have learned so much.

Nabīl Jabbūr

Mr. Jabbūr, of Syria, has taken it upon himself to ask the Oriental question and see what it means for the text.

Qayṣar Ma'lūf

Mr. Ma'lūf is a farmer and pastor in villages on the slopes of Mount Lebanon. As a guest in Mr. Ma'lūf's pulpit and home in Khirbit Qanafār, I was able to learn far more than I could teach.

Nuhād Ibrāhīm

Nuhād, a student at the Near East School of Theology, has carried his own research questions back to his village and family and has contributed significantly to the gradual growth of this study.

Butruṣ Talyā

Mr. Talyā, a former resident of al-Jazīrah, Syria, wandered for two years as a shepherd while living with his family in an all-Christian village in upper Syria. Thus, in his youth he was in contact with ancient cultural forms of community life. Himself a trained biblical scholar, Mr. Talyā's help has been significant.

IRAQ

As in the case of textual criticism, it is not the weight of numbers but other factors that determine the significance of a given witness. My only resource person in Iraq has been Mr. *Jūsif Mattā* of Mosul and Baghdad. Mr. Mattā is from a village of northern Iraq. He spent nine years in a Syriac Orthodox monastery in preparation for the priesthood, but then became a Protestant. His knowledge of Syriac and his long-term exposure to village and ecclesiastical life in northern Iraq make him a vital resource person for this study.

IRAN

Because of its distance and the fact that a cultural and linguistic line is crossed once one moves from Iraq to Iran, resource people have not been sought in Iran. However, the unique background and ministry of *Viken Galoustian* has made it imperative that his insights be allowed to contribute to our search for cultural factors in biblical literature. Rev. Galoustian was for many years the pastor of a unique congregation in Teheran composed of roughly half Muslim converts and half Jewish converts. The questions that arose out of his ministry and some of the answers he found to those questions have proven significant as one more piece in a cultural puzzle.

SELECT BIBLIOGRAPHY

A. GENERAL

Beare, F. W., "Concerning Jesus of Nazareth," *JBL* 87 (1968), 125–135.

———. *The Earliest Records of Jesus*. New York: Abingdon, 1962.

Bornkamm, Gunther. *Jesus of Nazareth*. Translated by Irene and Fraser McLuskey with James M. Robinson from the 3rd German edition. New York: Harper, 1960.

Bultmann, Rudolf. *The History of the Synoptic Tradition*. Translated from the German by John Marsh. Revised Edition. New York: Harper, 1963.

———. *Theology of the New Testament*. 2 vols. Translated from the German by Kendrick Grobel. London: SCM, 1955.

Conzelmann, Hans. *An Outline of the Theology of the New Testament*. Translated from the German by John Bowden. New York: Harper, 1969.

Daube, David. *The New Testament and Rabbinic Judaism*. London: University of London, 1956.

———. *Studies in Biblical Law*. Cambridge: University Press, 1947.

Derrett, J. Duncan M. *Law in the New Testament*. London: Darton, Longman and Todd,1970.

Fuchs, Ernst, "Studies of the Historical Jesus," *Studies in Biblical Theology*, No. 42. Translated from the German by Andrew Scobie. London: SCM, 1964.

Jeremias, Joachim. *New Testament Theology*. New York: Scribner, 1971.

———. *The Problem of the Historical Jesus*. Translated from the German by Norman Perrin. Philadelphia: Fortress, 1964.

Jülicher, Adolf. *Itala Das Neue Testament in Altlateinischer überlieferung*, III. *Lucas Evangelium*. Berlin: de Gruyter, 1954.

Nicholson, R. A. *A Literary History of the Arabs*. Cambridge: University Press, 1962.

O'Leary, de Lacy E. *Comparative Grammar of the Semitic Languages*. London: Kegan Paul, Trench, Trubner, 1923.

Taylor, Vincent, *The Formation of the Gospel Tradition*. London: Macmillan, 1935.

Wright, William. *Lectures on the Comparative Grammar of the Semitic Languages*. 2nd edition. Amsterdam: Philo, 1966.

B. THE ORIENTAL VERSIONS

Bensly, Robert L., J. Rendel Harris, and F. Crawford Burkitt, editors. *The Four Gospels in Syriac Transcribed from the Sinaitic Palimpsest*. Cambridge: University Press, 1894.

Burkitt, F. C. *Evangelion da-Mepharreshe*. 2 vols. Cambridge: University Press, 1904.

Cureton, W. C. *Remains of a Very Ancient Recension of the Four Gospels in Syriac*. London: J. Murray, 1858.

Darlow, T. H., and H. F. Moule. *Polyglots and Languages Other Than English*. Vol. II in *Historical Catalogue of the Printed Editions of Holy Scripture in the Library of the British and Foreign Bible Society*. New York: Kraus Reprint, 1964.

Graf, Georg. *Geschichte der Christlichen Arabischen Literatur*. Vol. I. Vatican City: Biblioteca Apostolica Vaticana, 1944.

————. *Verzeichnis arabischer kirchlicher Termini*. Louvain: L. Durbecq, 1954.

Guidi, Ignazio, "Le traduzioni degli Evangelii in Arabo e in Etiopico," *Atti della Reale Accademia dei Lincei*, anno cclxxv [1888]. Pp. 5–37.

Guillaume, Alfred, "The Version of the Gospels Used in Medina circa A.D. 700," *Al-Andalus* 15 (1950), 289–296.

Higgins, A. J. B., "The Arabic Version of Tatian's Diatessaron," *JTS* 45 (1944), 187–199.

————, "Ibn al-'Assal," *JTS* 44 (1943), 73–75.

————, "The Persian and Arabic Gospel Harmonies," *Studia Evangelica*, I. Edited by Kurt Aland *et al.* Berlin: Akademie-Verlag, 1959. Pp. 793–810.

Hill, J. H. *The Earliest Life of Christ*. 2nd edition. Edinburgh: T. & T. Clark, 1910.

The Holy Bible containing the Old and New Testaments in the Arabic Language. Newcastle-upon-Tyne: Sarah Hodgson, 1811.

Hyatt, J. P., "Recent Contributions to the Study of the Ancient Versions of the New Testament," *The Bible in Modern Scholarship*. Edited by J. P. Hyatt, Nashville: Abingdon, 1965. Pp. 357–369.

de Lagarde, Paul, editor. *Die Vier Evangelien arabisch*. Leipzig: F. A. Brockhaus, 1864.

Levin, Bernhard. *Die Griechisch-Arabische Evangelien-Übersetzung Vat. Borg. ar. 95 und Ber. orient oct. 1108*. Uppsala: Almquist & Wiksells, 1938.

Lewis, Agnes S., and Margaret D. Gibson. *The Palestinian Syriac Lectionary of the Gospels*. London: n.p., 1899.

Macdonald, Duncan B., "The Gospels in Arabic," *Hartford Seminary Record* 3 (April 1893), 163–176.

Metzger, Bruce M., ''A Survey of Recent Research on the Ancient Versions of the New Testament,'' *NTS* 2 (1955/56), 1–16.

The New Testament in Syriac. London: British and Foreign Bible Society, 1905–1920, 1950.

Pelser, H. S., ''The Origin of the Ancient Syriac New Testament Texts— A Historical Study,'' *De Fructu Oris Sui. Essays in Honour of Adrianus van Selms.* Edited by I. H. Eybers *et al. Pretoria Oriental Series* 9. Leiden: Brill, 1971. Pp. 152–163.

Pusey, P. E., and G. H. Gwilliam. *Teraevangelium Sanctum Iuxta Simplicem Syrorum Versionem ad fidem Codicum.* Oxford, Clarendon, 1901.

Qūshaqjī, Jūsif. *Ta'rīb al-Anajīl wa-A'māl al-Rusul.* Beirut: Catholic Press, 1964.

Vööbus, Arthur. *Early Versions of the New Testament. Papers of the Estonian Theological Society in Exile,* VI. Stockholm: n.p., 1954.

———. *Studies in the History of the Gospel Text in Syriac. Corpus Christianorum Orientalium Subsidia Tome III,* CXXVIII. Louvain: L. Durbecq, 1951.

White, J. *Sacrorum Evangeliorum Versio Syriaca Philoxeniana.* Oxford: n.p., 1778.

Wright, William. *A Short History of Syriac Literature.* Amsterdam: Philo, 1966 [1894].

C. THE MODERN MIDDLE EASTERN PEASANT CULTURE AND THE PARABLES

Bishop, E. F. F. *Apostles of Palestine.* London: Lutterworth, 1958.

———. *Jesus of Palestine.* London: Lutterworth, 1955.

———, ''Local-Colour in Proto-Luke,'' *ExpT* 45 (1933/34), 151–56.

———. *Prophets of Palestine.* London: Lutterworth, 1962.

Dalman, G. H. *Arbeit und Sitte in Palästina.* 7 vols. Gütersloh: Bertelsmann, 1928–1942.

———. *Sacred Sites and Ways.* Translated from the German by Paul P. Levertoff. London: SPCK, 1935.

Grant, Elihu. *The Peasantry of Palestine: The Life, Manners and Customs of the Village.* Boston: Pilgrim Press, 1907.

Hanauer, James. *The Folklore of the Holy Land.* London: Duckworth, 1907.

Jeremias, Joachim. *Jerusalem in the Time of Jesus.* 3rd edition. Translated from the German by F. H. and C. H. Cave. Philadelphia: Fortress, 1969.

Levison, N. *The Parables: Their Background and Local Setting.* Edinburgh: T. & T. Clark, 1926.

Masterman, Ernest William Garney. *Studies in Galilee.* Chicago: University of Chicago Press, 1909.

Neil, James. *Everyday Life in the Holy Land.* London: SPCK, 1924.

Newton, F. E. *Fifty Years in Palestine.* London: Coldharbour Press, 1948.

Rihbany, A. M. *The Syrian Christ.* Boston: Houghton Mifflin, 1916.

Scherer, George H. *The Eastern Colour of the Bible*. London: National Sunday School Union, 1929.

Thomson, W. M. *The Land and the Book*. 2 vols. New York: Harper, 1871.

Wilson, Charles Thomas. *Peasant Life in the Holy Land*. London: John Murray, 1906.

D. THE ANCIENT JEWISH AND ARAMAIC BACKGROUND TO THE PARABLES

Billerbeck, P., and H. Strack. *Kommentar zum Neuen Testament aus Talmud und Midrasch*. 6 vols. 2nd edition. Munich: C. H. Beck, 1924.

Black, Matthew. *An Aramaic Approach to the Gospels and Acts*. 3rd edition. Oxford: Clarendon, 1967.

————, "The Recovery of the Language of Jesus," *NTS* 3 (1957), 305–313.

Crockett, L. C., "The Old Testament in the Gospel of Luke with Emphasis on the Interpretation of Isaiah 61:1–2." Unpublished Ph.D. Thesis, Brown University, Providence, R.I., 1966.

Dalman, Gustaf. *The Words of Jesus*. Translated from the German by D. M. Kay. Edinburgh: T. & T. Clark, 1902.

Dalman, G. H. *Jesus-Joshua; Studies in the Gospels*. Translated from the German by Paul P. Levertoff. New York: Macmillan, 1929.

Edersheim, Alfred. *The Life and Times of Jesus the Messiah*. 2 vols. 2nd edition. London: Longmans, Green, 1883.

————. *Sketches of Jewish Social Life in the Days of Christ*. New York: Hodder and Stoughton, n.d.

Epstein, I., editor. *The Babylonian Talmud*. 35 vols. London: Soncino, 1935–1960.

Falk, Z. W. *Hebrew Law in Biblical Times*. Jerusalem: Wahrmann Books, 1964.

Feldman, Asher. *The Parables and Similes of the Rabbis*. Cambridge: University Press, 1924, 2nd ed. 1927.

Fiebig, Paul W. J. *Altjüdische Gleichnisse und die Gleichnisse Jesu*. Tübingen: J. C. B. Mohr, 1904.

————. *Die Gleichnisreden Jesu im Lichte der rabbinischen Gleichnisse des neutestamentlichen Zeitalters*. Tübingen: J. C. B. Mohr, 1912.

Goldschmidt, Lazarus, editor. *Der Babylonische Talmud*. 11 vols. Haag: Martinus Nijhoff, 1933.

Heinemann, Joseph H., "The Status of the Laborer in Jewish Law and Society in the Tannaitic Period," *HUCA* 25 (1954), 263–325.

Horowitz, George. *The Spirit of Jewish Law*. New York: Central Book, 1953.

The Mishnah. Translated from the Hebrew by Herbert Danby with Introduction and Brief Explanatory Notes. 7 vols. London: Oxford, 1950.

Mishnayoth. 7 vols. Translated and edited by Philip Blackman. London: Mishna Press, 1954.

Montefiore, C. J. G. *Rabbinic Literature and Gospel Teaching*. London: Macmillan, 1930.

————. *The Synoptic Gospels*. 3 vols. 2nd edition. London: Macmillan, 1927.

Moore, George F. *Judaism in the First Centuries of the Christian Era, the Age of the Tannaim*. 2 vols. Cambridge: Harvard, 1927.

Oesterley, W. O. E. *The Gospel Parables in the Light of Their Jewish Background*. London: SPCK, 1936.

Seale, Morris S. *The Desert Bible. Nomadic Tribal Culture and Old Testament Interpretation*. London: Weidenfeld and Nicolson, 1974.

Smith, Morton, *Tannaitic Parallels to the Gospels*. Vol. VI of *JBL Monograph Series*. Philadelphia: Society of Biblical Literature, 1951.

Stewart, Roy A., "The Parable Form in the Old Testament and the Rabbinic Literature," *Evangelical Quarterly* 36 (1964), 133–147.

Torrey, Charles C. *Our Translated Gospels*. New York: Harper, 1936.

Yaron, R. *Gifts in Contemplation of Death in Jewish and Roman Law*. Oxford: Clarendon, 1960.

E. GENERAL STUDIES ON LUKE

Arndt, William F. *The Gospel According to St. Luke*. St. Louis: Concordia, 1956.

Bengel, Johann A. *Gnomon of the New Testament*. Translated from the Latin by C. T. Lewis and M. R. Vincent. 2 vols. New York: Sheldon, 1862 (1742).

Cadbury, Henry J. *The Making of Luke-Acts*. London: SPCK, 1958.

Caird, G. B. *The Gospel of St. Luke*. Baltimore: Penguin, 1963.

Conzelmann, Hans. *The Theology of St. Luke*. Translated from the German by Geoffrey Buswell. New York: Harper, 1961.

Creed, John Martin. *The Gospel According to St. Luke*. London: St. Martin, 1930; Macmillan, 1965.

Davies, J. H., "The Purpose of the Central Section of Luke's Gospel," *Studia Evangelica,* II. Edited by F. L. Cross. Berlin: Akademie-Verlag, 1963. Pp. 164–69.

Dillersberger, Josef. *The Gospel of Saint Luke*. Translated from the German. Westminster, Md.: Newman, 1958.

Ellis, E. Earle. *The Gospel of Luke*. London: Thomas Nelson, 1966.

Evans, C. F., "The Central Section of St. Luke's Gospel," *Studies in the Gospels. Essays in Memory of R. H. Lightfoot*. Edited by D. E. Nineham. Oxford: Blackwell, 1957. Pp. 37–53.

Farmer, W. R., "Notes on a Literary and Form-Critical Analysis of Some of the Synoptic Materials Peculiar to Luke," *NTS* 8 (1962), 301–316.

Geldenhuys, Norval. *Commentary on the Gospel of Luke*. Grand Rapids: Eerdmans, 1951.

Gollwitzer, Helmut. *Die Freude Gottes, Einführung in das Lukasevangelium*. Berlin-Dahlem: Burckhardthaus-Verlag, 1952.

Goulder, M. D., "The Chiastic Structure of the Lucan Journey," *Studia Evangelica*, II. Edited by F. L. Cross. Berlin: Akademie-Verlag, 1963. Pp. 195–202.

Hull, William E., "A Structural Analysis of the Gospel of Luke," *Review and Expositor* 64 (1967), 421–25.

Lampe, G. W. H., "The Lucan Portrait of Christ," *NTS* 2 (1956), 160–195.

Leaney, Alfred R. C. *A Commentary on the Gospel According to St. Luke*. 2nd edition. Black's New Testament Commentaries. London: A. & C. Black, 1958.

Manson, William. *The Gospel of Luke. The Moffatt New Testament Commentary*, III. New York: Harper, n.d.

Miller, Donald G. *The Gospel According to Luke*. Richmond: John Knox, 1959.

Ogg, G., "The Central Section of the Gospel According to St. Luke," *NTS* 18 (1971), 39–53.

Plummer, Alfred. *The Gospel According to St. Luke. International Critical Commentary*, XXVII. Edited by C. A. Briggs *et al*. New York: Scribner, 1906.

Reicke, Bo, "Instruction and Discussion in the Travel Narrative," *Studia Evangelica*, I. Edited by Kurt Aland *et al*. Berlin: Akademie-Verlag, 1959. Pp. 206–216.

Rengstorf, Karl Heinrich. *Das Evangelium nach Lukas. Das Neue Testament Deutsch*, V. Edited by Paul Althaus and Johannes Behm. Neubearbeitete Auflage. Göttingen: Vandenhoeck & Ruprecht, 1949.

Robinson, W. C., Jr., "The Theological Context for Interpreting Luke's Travel Narrative (9.51 ff.)," *JBL* 79 (1960), 20–31.

Sa'īd, Ibrāhīm. *Sharḥ Bishārat Lūqā*. Beirut: Near East Council of Churches, 1970.

Schlatter, Adolf von. *Das Evangelium des Lukas. Aus seinen Quellen erklärt*. Stuttgart: Calwer Verlag, 1960.

Schneider, J., "Zur Analyse des Lukanischen Reiseberichtes," *Synoptische Studien. Alfred Wikenhauser zum siebzigsten Geburtstag*. Munich: K. Zink, 1953. Pp. 207–229.

Stagg, Frank, "The Journey Toward Jerusalem in Luke's Gospel," *Review and Expositor* 64 (1967), 499–512.

Talbert, Charles H., "The Redactional Critical Quest for Luke the Theologian," *Pittsburgh Perspective* 11 (1970), 171–222.

F. POETICAL AND LITERARY ANALYSIS

Albright, William F., "A Catalogue of Early Hebrew Lyric Poems (Psalm 63)," *HUCA* 23 (1950/51), 1–19.

————, "The Earliest Forms of Hebrew Verse," *Journal of the Palestine Oriental Society* 2 (1922), 69–86.

Bertram, Stephen, "Symmetrical Design in the Book of Ruth," *JBL* 84 (1965), 165–68.

Bligh, John. *Galatians in Greek, A Structural Analysis of St. Paul's Epistle to the Galatians.* Detroit: University of Detroit Press, 1966.

Boling, Robert G., " 'Synonymous' Parallelism in the Psalms," *JSS* 5 (1960), 221–255.

Brown, Raymond. *The Gospel According to John.* 2 vols. *The Anchor Bible.* New York: Doubleday, 1966. Cf. cxxxv–cxxxvii, 267, 597, 667, 728, 859, 911.

Burney, C. F. *The Poetry of Our Lord.* Oxford: Clarendon, 1925.

Cross, F. M., and D. N. Freedman, "Studies in Ancient Yahwistic Poetry." Unpublished Ph.D. Thesis, Johns Hopkins University, Baltimore, 1950.

Curtis, William H., "His Form and Method of Teaching," *Jesus Christ the Teacher.* London: Oxford, 1943. Cf. pp. 66–82.

Dewey, J., "The Literary Structure of the Controversy Stories in Mark 2:1–3:6," *JBL* 92 (1973), 394–401.

Dupont, L., *et al.,* "Recherche sur la structure de Jean 20," *Biblica* 54 (1973), 482–498.

Ehlen, A. J., "The Poetic Structure of a Hodayat from Qumran." Unpublished Ph.D. Thesis, Harvard Divinity School, Harvard University, Cambridge, Mass., 1970.

Fenton, J. C., "Inclusio and Chiasmus in Matthew," *Studia Evangelica,* I. Edited by Kurt Aland *et al.* Berlin: Akademie-Verlag, 1959. Pp. 174–79.

Fitzgerald, A., "Hebrew Poetry," *The Jerome Biblical Commentary.* Edited by R. E. Brown *et al.* Englewood Cliffs, N.J.: Prentice-Hall, 1968. Pp. 238–244.

Forbes, John. *The Symmetrical Structure of Scripture.* Edinburgh: T. & T. Clark, 1854.

Freedman, D. N., "Prolegomenon" to G. B. Gray, *The Forms of Hebrew Poetry.* New York: Ktav, 1972. Pp. vii–liii.

————, "Archaic Forms in Early Hebrew Poetry," *Zeitschrift für die alttestamentliche Wissenschaft* 72 (1960), 101–107.

Goulder, M. D., "The Chiastic Structure of the Lucan Journey," *Studia Evangelica,* 11. Edited by F. L. Cross. Berlin: Akademie-Verlag, 1963. Pp. 195–202.

Gray, G. B. *The Forms of Hebrew Poetry.* New York: Ktav, 1972 (1915).

Grobel, Kendrick, "A Chiastic Retribution Formula in Romans 2," *Zeit und Geschichte.* Dankesgabe an Rudolf Bultmann zum 80. Geburtstag. Herausgegeben von Erich Dinkler. Tübingen: J. C. B. Mohr, 1964. Pp. 255–261.

Holladay, W. L., "Chiasmus, the Key to Hosea 12:3–6," *Vetus Testamentum* 16 (1966), 53–64.

————, "The Recovery of Poetic Passages of Jeremiah," *JBL* 85 (1966), 401–435.

Jebb, John. *Sacred Literature.* London: n.p., 1820.

Jeremias, J., "Chiasmus in den Paulusbriefen," *Abba.* Göttingen: Vandenhoeck & Ruprecht, 1966. Pp. 276–289.

Kosmala, Hans, "Form and Structure in Ancient Hebrew Poetry (a New Approach)," *Vetus Testamentum* 14 (1964), 423–445; 16 (1966), 152–160.

Kraft, Charles F., "Poetic Structure of the Qumran Thanksgiving Psalms," *Biblical Research* 2 (1957), 1–18.

————. *The Strophic Structure of Hebrew Poetry*. Chicago: University of Chicago Press, 1938.

Leon-Dufour, Xavier, "Trois Chiasmus Johanniques," *NTS* 7 (1961), 249–255.

Lohfink, Norbert. *Das Hauptgebot: Eine Untersuchung literarischer Einleitungstragen zu Dtn 5–11*. Rome: Pontifical Biblical Institute, 1963.

Lohr, C. H., "Oral Techniques in Matthew's Gospel," *CBQ* 23 (1961), 403–435.

Louw, J. P., "Discourse Analysis and the Greek New Testament," *The Bible Translator* 24 (1973), 101–118.

Lund, N. W. *Chiasmus in the New Testament*. Chapel Hill: University of North Carolina Press, 1942.

Malatesta, E., "The Literary Structure of John 17," *Biblica* 52 (1971), 67–78, 190–214.

Manson, T. W., "Poetic Form," *The Teaching of Jesus*. 2nd edition. Cambridge: University Press, 1935. Pp. 50–56.

Miesner, D. R., "Chiasm and the Composition and Message of Paul's Missionary Sermons." Unpublished Th.D. Thesis, Concordia Seminary in Exile, 306 North Grand, St. Louis, 1974.

Mowry, Lucetta M., "Poetry in the Synoptic Gospels and Revelation, a Study of Methods and Materials." Unpublished Ph.D. Thesis, Yale University, New Haven, 1946.

Robinson, D. W. B., "The Literary Structure of Hebrews 1:1–4," *Australian Journal of Biblical Archeology* 2 (1972), 178–186.

Robinson, T. H. *The Poetry of the Old Testament*. London: Oxford, 1947.

Schnackenburg, R., "Strukturanalyse von John 17," *Biblische Zeitschrift* N.F. 17 (1973), 196–202.

Schnider, F., and W. Stenger, "Beobachtungen zur Struktur der Emmausperikope (Lu 24:13–35)," *Biblische Zeitschrift* N.F. 16 (1972), 94–114.

Schubert, Paul, "The Structure and Significance of Luke 24," *Neutestamentliche Studien für Rudolf Bultmann*. Edited by Walter Eltester. Berlin: A. Töpelmann, 1954. Pp. 163–184.

Sider, R. D., "On Symmetrical Composition in Tertullian," *JTS* N.S. 24 (1973), 405–423.

Streeter, B. H., "Poems of Jesus," *The Hibbert Journal* 32 (1933/34), 9–16.

Talbert, C. H., "Artistry and Theology. An Analysis of the Architecture of Jn. 1,19–5,48," *CBQ* 32 (1970), 341–366.

Taylor, Vincent, "Sayings and Parables," *The Formation of the Gospel Tradition*. London: Macmillan, 1935. Pp. 88–118.

Thiering, Barbara, "The Poetic Forms of the Hodayoth," *JSS* 8 (1963), 189–209.

Torrey, C. C., "Metric Forms and Details," *The Second Isaiah*. Edinburgh: T. & T. Clark, 1928. Pp. 151–172.

Wilder, Amos, "The Poem," *Early Christian Rhetoric*. Cambridge: Harvard, 1971. Pp. 89–117.

Vanhoye, Albert. *A Structured Translation of the Epistle to the Hebrews*. Translated from the Greek and the French by James Swetnam. Rome: Pontifical Biblical Institute, 1964.

G. PARABOLIC HERMENEUTICS

Achtemeier, Paul J. *An Introduction to the New Hermeneutic*. Philadelphia: Westminster, 1969.

Barr, Allan, "The Interpretation of the Parables," *ExpT* 53 (1941/42), 20–25.

Black, Matthew, "The Parables as Allegory," *BJRL* 42 (1960), 273–287.

Brown, Raymond E., "Parable and Allegory Reconsidered," *Novum Testamentum* 5 (1962), 36–45.

Dodd, C. H., "The Gospel Parables," *BJRL* 16 (1932), 396–412.

Eaton, David, "Professor Jülicher on the Parables of Jesus," *ExpT* 10 (1898/99), 539–543.

Fuchs, Ernst, "Proclamation and Speech-Event," *Theology Today* 19 (1962), 341–354.

Hunter, Archibald M., "The Interpretation of the Parables," *Teaching and Preaching the New Testament*. Philadelphia: Westminster, 1963. Pp. 51–58.

———, "The Interpreter and the Parables," *Interpretation* 14 (1960), 70–84, 167–185, 315–332, 440–454.

———. *Interpreting the Parables*. London: SCM, 1964.

Marty, Martin E., "The Purpose of the Parables According to Mk. 4:10–12." Unpublished Bachelor's Thesis, Concordia Seminary, St. Louis, 1952.

Manson, W., "The Purpose of the Parables: A Re-examination of St. Mark 4:10–12," *ExpT* 68 (1957), 132–35.

Perrin, Norman, "The Modern Interpretation of the Parables of Jesus and the Problem of Hermeneutics," *Interpretation* 25 (1971), 131–148.

Piper, Otto A., "The Understanding of the Synoptic Parables," *Evangelical Quarterly* 14 (1942), 42–53.

Smart, James D., "A Redefinition of Jesus' Use of the Parables," *ExpT* 47 (1935/36), 551–55.

Vincent, J. J., "The Parables of Jesus as Self-Revelation," *Studia Evangelica*, II. Edited by F. L. Cross. Berlin: Akademie-Verlag, 1959. Pp. 74–99.

H. GENERAL STUDIES ON PARABLES

Barry, Colman, "The Literary and Artistic Beauty of Christ's Parables," *CBQ* 10 (1948), 376–383.

Beardslee, William A., "The Wisdom Tradition and the Synoptic Gospels," *Journal of the American Academy of Religion* 35 (1967), 232–240.

Brown, R. E. *The Parables of the Gospels*. New York: Paulist Press Doctrinal Pamphlet, 1963.

————, "Parables of Jesus," *The New Catholic Encyclopedia*, X. Edited by The Catholic University of America. New York: McGraw-Hill, 1967. Pp. 984–88.

Bruce, Alexander Balmain. *The Parabolic Teaching of Christ*. 3rd revised edition. New York: A. C. Armstrong, 1890.

Bugge, C. A. *Die Haupt-Parabeln Jesu*. Giessen: J. Ricker, 1903.

Cadoux, A. T. *The Parables of Jesus: Their Art and Use*. London: James Clarke, n.d.

Cantinat, Jean, "The Parables of Mercy," *Contemporary New Testament Studies*. Edited by M. Rosalie Ryan. Collegeville, Minn: Liturgical Press, 1965. Pp. 213–228.

Crossan, John D. *In Parables*. New York: Harper, 1973.

Dodd, C. H. *The Parables of the Kingdom*. Revised edition. London: Nisbet, 1961.

Findlay, J. A. *Jesus and His Parables*. London: Epworth, 1951.

Fonck, Leopold. *The Parables of the Gospel*. Translated from the 3rd German edition by E. Leahy. New York & Cincinnati: Frederick Pustet, 1914.

Funk, Robert W., "The Parables: A Fragmentary Agenda," *Jesus and Man's Hope*, II. Edited by Donald G. Miller and Dikran Y. Hadidian. Pittsburgh: A Perspective Book, Pittsburgh Theological Seminary, 1971. Pp. 287–304.

Goebel, Siegfried. *The Parables of Jesus: a Methodological Exposition*. Translated from the German by Professor Banks. Edinburgh: T. & T. Clark, 1883.

Jeremias, Joachim. *The Parables of Jesus*. Revised edition. Translated from the 6th German edition by S. H. Hooke. London: SCM, 1963.

Jones, Geraint Vaughan. *The Art and Truth of the Parables: A Study in Their Literary Form and Modern Interpretation*. London: SPCK, 1964.

Jülicher, Adolf. *Die Gleichnisreden Jesu*. 2 vols. Tübingen: J. C. B. Mohr, 1910.

Ladd, George Eldon, "The Life-Setting of the Parables of the Kingdom," *Journal of Bible and Religion* 31 (1963), 193–99.

Linnemann, E. *Jesus of the Parables*. Translated from the German by John Sturdy. New York: Harper, 1966.

Lithgow, R. M. *The Parabolic Gospel*. Edinburgh: T. & T. Clark, 1914.

Manson, T. W. *The Sayings of Jesus*. London: SCM, 1937, 1961.

————. *The Teaching of Jesus*. 2nd edition. Cambridge: University Press, 1935.

Martin, Hugh. *The Parables of the Gospels and their Meaning for Today*. London: SCM, 1937.

Michaelis, W. *Die Gleichnisse Jesu*. Vol. XXXII of *Die urchristliche Botschaft*. Dritte Auflage. Hamburg: Furche Verlag, 1956.

Mullins, Terence Y., "Parables as Literary Forms in the New Testament," *The Lutheran Quarterly* 12 (1960), 235–241.

Navone, John, "The Lucan Banquet Community," *The Bible Today* (December 1970), 155–161.

Robinson, Willard H. *The Parables of Jesus: In Their Relation to His Ministry*. Chicago: University of Chicago Press, 1928.

Scharlemann, Martin H. *Proclaiming the Parables*. St. Louis: Concordia, 1963.

Smith, B. T. D. *The Parables of the Synoptic Gospels*. Cambridge: University Press, 1937.

Smith, Charles W. F. *The Jesus of the Parables*. Philadephia: Westminster, 1948.

Stewart, R. A., "The Parable Form in the Old Testament and Rabbinic Literature," *Evangelical Quarterly* 36 (1964), 133–147.

Thielicke, Helmut. *The Waiting Father: Sermons on the Parables of Jesus*. Translated from the German by John W. Doberstein. New York: Harper, 1959.

Trench, Richard Chenevix. *Notes on the Parables of Our Lord*. New York: Harper/Revell, n.d.

Via, Dan Otto. *The Parables: Their Literary and Existential Dimension*. Philadelphia: Fortress, 1967.

Wilder, Amos. *Early Christian Rhetoric*. Cambridge: Harvard, 1971.

Wiles, M. F., "Early Exegesis of the Parables," *The Scottish Journal of Theology* 11 (1958), 287–301.

I. SPECIAL STUDIES RELATING TO SPECIFIC PARABLES

Arnott, William, "The Unjust Steward in a New Light," *ExpT* 24 (1913), 508–511.

Barry, Phillips, "On Luke xv. 25, συμφωνία: Bagpipe," *JBL* 23 (1904), 180–190.

Bishop, E. F. F., "The Parable of the Lost or Wandering Sheep," *ATR* 44 (1962), 44–57.

Bretscher, Paul G., "Brief Studies: The Parable of the Unjust Steward—a new approach to Luke 16:1–9," *Concordia Theological Monthly* 22 (October 1951), 756–762.

Bussby, F., "Did a Shepherd Leave Sheep Upon the Mountains or in the Desert?" *ATR* 45 (1963), 93f.

Danker, F. W., "Luke 16:16—An Opposition Logion," *JBL* 77 (1958), 231–243.

Davidson, J. A., "A 'Conjecture' About the Parable of the Unjust Steward (Luke xvi. 1–9)," *ExpT* 66 (1954/55), 31.

Daube, David, "Inheritance in Two Lukan Pericopes," *Zeitschrift der Savigny-Stiftung für Rechtsgeschichte, Romanistische Abteilung* 72 (1955), 326–344.

Derrett, J. D. M., "Fresh Light on St. Luke XVI. 1. The Parable of the Unjust Steward," *NTS* 7 (March 1961), 198–219.

———, "Law in the New Testament: The Parable of the Prodigal Son," *NTS* 14 (1967), 56–74.

Fitzmyer, J. A., "The Story of the Dishonest Manager (Lk. 16:1–13)," *Theological Studies* 25 (1964), 23–42.

Fletcher, D. R., "The Riddle of the Unjust Steward. Is Irony the Key?" *JBL* 82 (1963), 15–30.

Francis, F. J., "The Parable of the Unjust Steward," *ATR* 47 (1965), 103–105.

Fridrichsen, Anton, "Exegetisches zum Neuen Testament," *Symbolae Osloensis* 13 (1934), 38–41.

Friedel, Lawrence M., "The Parable of the Unjust Steward," *CBQ* 3 (1941), 337–348.

Gächter, P., "The Parable of the Dishonest Steward after Oriental Conceptions," *CBQ* 12 (1950), 121–131.

Giblin, Charles H., "Structural and Theological Considerations on Luke 15," *CBQ* 24 (1962), 15–31.

————, "Why Jesus Spoke in Parables— An Answer from Luke 15," *Chicago Studies* 7 (1968), 213–220.

Hiers, Richard H., "Friends by Unrighteous Mammon: The Eschatological Proletariat (Luke 16:9)," *Journal of the American Academy of Religion* 38 (1970), 30–36.

Kelley, Robert, "The Significance of the Parable of the Prodigal Son for Three Major Issues in Current Synoptic Study." Unpublished Ph.D. Thesis, Princeton University, Princeton, N.J., 1971.

Jeremias, Joachim, "Zum Gleichnis vom verlorenen Sohn," *Theologische Zeitschrift* 5 (1949), 228–231.

Kilpatrick, G. D., "φρόνιμος, σοφός and συνετός in Matthew and Luke," *JTS* 48 (1947), 63f.

Kosmala, Hans, "The Parable of the Unjust Steward in the Light of Qumran," *Annual of the Swedish Theological Institute* 3 (1964), 114–121.

Levison, N., "Importunity? A Study of Luke XI.8," *The Expositor*, Series 9, 3 (1925), 456–460.

Lunt, R. C., "Expounding the Parables: III. The Parable of the Unjust Steward (Luke 16:1–15)," *ExpT* 77 (1966), 132–36.

Marshall, I. H., "Luke xvi 8—Who Condemned the Unjust Steward?" *JTS* N.S. 19 (1968), 617–19.

Mitton, C. Leslie, "The Unjust Steward," *ExpT* 64 (1953), 307f.

Moore, F. J., "The Parable of the Unjust Steward," *ATR* 47 (1965), 103–105.

Moore, George F., "συμφωνία—Not a Bagpipe," *JBL* 24 (1905), 166–175.

Murphy, J. J., "Two Parables: The Prodigal Son (Luke xv. 11–32); The Labourers in the Vineyard (Matt. xix.27; xx.16)," *Expositor*, Series 3, 9 (1889), 290–303.

Paul, Geoffrey, "The Unjust Steward and the Interpretation of Luke 16:9," *Theology* 61 (1958), 189–193.

Preisker, Herbert, "Lukas 16:1–7," *Theologische Literaturzeitung* 74 (1949), 85–92.

Rengstorf, Karl H. *Die Re-Investitur des Verlorenen Sohnes in der Gleichniserzählung Jesu Luke 15:11–32*. Cologne: Westdeutscher Verlag, 1957.

Riggenbach, Eduard, "Zur Exegese und Textkritik zweier Gleichnisse Jesu," *Aus Schrift und Geschichte. Theologische Abhandlungen Adolf Schlatter zu seinem 70. Gebürtstage*. Stuttgart: Calwer, 1922. Pp. 17–34.

Sanders, Jack T., "Tradition and Redaction in Lk. XV, 11–32," *NTS* 15 (1969), 433–38.

Schniewind, Julius D., "Das Gleichnis vom verlorenen Sohn," *Die Freude der Busse*. Göttingen: Vandenhoeck & Ruprecht, 1960. Pp. 34–87.

Sheppard, J. B., "A Study of the Parables Common to the Synoptic Gospels and the Coptic Gospel of Thomas." Unpublished Ph.D. Thesis, Emory University, Atlanta, 1965.

Walls, A. F., "In the Presence of the Angels (Luke XV 10)," *Novum Testamentum* 3 (1959), 314–16.

Williams, F. E., "Is Almsgiving the point of the 'Unjust Steward'?" *JBL* 83 (1964), 293–97.

INDEX OF AUTHORS

INDEX OF REFERENCES